ASPECTS OF SOCIAL POLICY

GENERAL EDITOR: J. P. Martin
Professor of Sociology and Social Administration. University of Southampton

Planning for Welfare
edited by TIMOTHY A. BOOTH

The Social Context of
Health Care
PAUL BREARLEY, JANE GIBBONS,
AGNES MILES, EDA TOPLISS AND
GRAHAM WOODS

Social Policy
edited by MICHAEL H. COOPER

Images of Welfare
PETER GOLDING AND
SUE MIDDLETON

The Poverty Business
JOAN HIGGINS

State of Welfare
JOAN HIGGINS

Understanding Social Policy
MICHAEL HILL

Voluntary Social Services
NORMAN JOHNSON

The Family, the State and the
Labour Market
HILARY LAND

Health, Wealth and Housing
edited by R. A. B. LEAPER

The Child's Generation
Second edition
JEAN PACKMAN

The Sociology of Welfare
GRAHAM ROOM

The Organization of Soviet
Medical Care
MICHAEL RYAN

A Charter for the Disabled
EDA TOPLISS AND
BRYAN GOULD

Provision for the Disabled
Second edition
EDA TOPLISS

Alternative Strategies for
Coping with Crime
edited by NORMAN TUTT

Community Care
ALAN WALKER

Social Planning and
Social Policy
ALAN WALKER

Efficiency in the
Social Services
ALAN WILLIAMS AND
ROBERT ANDERSON

# Reserved For The Poor

*The Means Test in British Social Policy*

ALAN DEACON and
JONATHAN BRADSHAW

Basil Blackwell and Martin Robertson

First published in 1983 by Martin Robertson &
Company Ltd., 108 Cowley Road, Oxford OX4 1JF.

*British Library Cataloguing in Publication Data*

Deacon, Alan
    Reserved for the poor.
    1. Great Britain—Social policy
    I. Title      II. Bradshaw, Jonathan
    361.6'1'0941      HN390

    ISBN 0-85520-435-4
    ISBN 0-85520-436-2 Pbk

Typeset by Cambrian Typesetters, Aldershot, Hants.
Printed and bound in Great Britain by
Billing and Sons Ltd., Worcester

# Contents

|  |  | Page |
|---|---|---|
| *Acknowledgments* | | vii |
| 1 | Introduction | 1 |
| 2 | Bitter Legacy: The Means Test in the 1930s | 5 |
|  | The Poor Law | 5 |
|  | Other services | 9 |
|  | Transitional payments | 14 |
|  | The Unemployment Assistance Board | 22 |
|  | Conclusion | 26 |
| 3 | A Universal Welfare State? | 30 |
|  | Social policy and the Second World War | 32 |
|  | The transformation of social assistance | 36 |
|  | Beveridge and the Coalition | 42 |
|  | Was there a consensus? | 46 |
| 4 | The Selectivity Debate | 51 |
|  | First critics: the Conservatives in the 1950s | 51 |
|  | The Institute of Economic Affairs | 56 |
|  | The 'selectivity' debate | 61 |
|  | Selectivity and the Labour government | 66 |
|  | Conclusion | 72 |
| 5 | Extending Means Tests | 75 |
|  | The 'modernization' policy | 75 |
|  | Family income supplement | 79 |
|  | Rent rebates and allowances | 83 |
|  | Rate rebates | 89 |
|  | The Conservatives and other means-tested benefits | 93 |
|  | Conclusion | 95 |

6   Social Assistance                                          98
     National assistance                                        99
     Supplementary benefits                                    105
     The reform of supplementary benefits                      112
     Supplementary benefit in the 1980s                        116

7   Take-up                                                    122
     The level of non take-up                                  123
     Overall assessment of take-up                             130
     The reasons for non take-up                               131
     Models of take-up                                         139
     Methods for improving take-up                             140
     Conclusion                                                147

8   Poverty Trap                                               150
     The origins of the poverty trap                           151
     The poverty trap now                                      153
     How serious is the poverty trap?                          156
     Single parents and the poverty trap                       159
     Incentives and the poverty trap                           159
     Solutions to the poverty trap                             162
     Conclusion                                                174

9   Alternatives to the Means Test                             176
     Back to Beveridge                                         176
     Clean sweep solutions                                     182
     Conclusion                                                194

10  Conclusion                                                 196

*Bibliography*                                                 205

*Index*                                                        221

# Acknowledgements

The idea for this book came from Professor John Martin and Eric Briggs played an important part in the initial planning.

Alan Deacon is indebted to a number of colleagues for their advice and comments on particular chapters, including Tony Lynes, Kirk Mann, Adrian Sinfield, Carol Walker and Stephen Winyard. He is also grateful to Arthur Seldon who made detailed and constructive comments on Chapter 4. The Nuffield Foundation awarded a small grant to Alan Deacon which enabled him to gather much of the material for the first half of the book. Unpublished material in the Public Records Office is quoted with kind permission of the Controller of the Stationery Office.

Jonathan Bradshaw's interest in the subject has been sustained by the work of many students and colleagues, particularly Della Nevitt, Stuart Macpherson, Peter Taylor-Gooby, Keith Bradley and Anne Corden. He is also grateful for the stimulus provided by an association with the Child Poverty Action Group over many years. Some of the material in the later chapters draws on research in the Social Policy Research Unit funded by the Department of Health and Social Security and the Social Science Research Council.

We are grateful to Leisel Carter, Lorraine Winter, Jeanne Horsfield and Su Wompra for typing the manuscript and for the patient encouragement of Sue Corbett, our editor at Martin Robertson. Finally we are both grateful to Pauline Deacon and Nora Bradshaw for their help and patience whilst we were writing this book.

The book is a joint enterprise and we share responsibility for it — but Alan Deacon did most of the work for Chapters 2, 3, 4 and 6 and Jonathan Bradshaw for Chapters 5, 7, 8 and 9.

# CHAPTER 1

# Introduction

The means test has long been a central issue in British social policy. In the 1930s it was the focus of bitterness and conflict, and the popularity of the wartime Beveridge Report (Cmd. 6404) stemmed largely from the fact that it seemed to offer a realistic plan for the removal of the means test. The legislation of the 1940s did represent a significant shift away from the means test, but it re-emerged as a major issue within the 'selectivity' debate of the 1960s. That debate appeared to have lost much of its significance by the mid-1970s, but the number of people dependent upon means-tested benefits has grown rapidly during the last few years. Once again the means test is the vehicle for delivering benefits to a substantial minority of the British population, and once again it is at the centre of the debate about the purpose and scope of social policy.

There are now five or six times as many people receiving means-tested benefits as there were in the early years of the welfare state. At the end of 1948, there were only three benefits of any significance provided on a test of means: national assistance and non-contributory pensions, both of which were administered by the National Assistance Board (NAB), and free school meals. It is doubtful if there were more than 2 million people dependent upon means-tested benefits.[1] There are now over 12 million. In December 1982, 7 million claimants and their dependents were receiving supplementary benefit, the successor to national assistance. This is more than one in eight of the total population (DHSS, Quarterly Estimate). Another 5.4 million people were living in households receiving a rate rebate[2] (Cmnd, 8789, Table 2.12.3), and so nearly a quarter of the population was receiving one or other of these means-tested benefits.

The number and variety of means-tested benefits has also increased. A low-income family may now be eligible for the family income supplement (FIS), housing benefit, free prescriptions, free dental and opthalmic treatment and free school meals — all on a test of means. Only free school meals was a means-tested benefit in 1948. Neither FIS nor housing benefit existed at all, and the other services were free to everyone.[3]

The purpose of this book is to explain the growth of means testing, and to discuss the problems which have arisen as a result of that growth. We begin by tracing the origins of the means test and explaining why it was so hated in the 1930s. We show how the social conditions of the war years led to an enormous emphasis upon universalism in the post-war legislation. We then trace the re-emergence of the means test in the so-called 'selectivity' debates of the 1960s, before discussing the development of social assistance and the creation of new means-tested benefits in the 1970s. Finally, we review some of the problems of the modern means test, discuss the possible alternatives to it, and try to explain why these alternatives have been rejected by recent governments.

The book is concerned with benefits and services which are available only to people whose resources or means are below a specified level. These benefits may be contrasted with those which are provided for everyone in a particular category or group — such as the unemployed or the elderly — or in respect of specific needs, such as those arising from disability.[4] Means tests are used in one of two ways. The first is to decide whether or not the person concerned should be exempted from, or have refunded, all or part of a particular charge or levy. The obvious examples here are free prescriptions or free school meals. The second use is to allocate income maintenance benefits. The level of FIS or supplementary benefit which is payable depends upon both the needs of the claimant, as measured by the scale rates, and his or her resources as defined by the appropriate regulations. It is not possible to cover every means-tested benefit in a book of this length; instead we have sought to examine the most important problems and issues which are common to all such benefits, and to illustrate them by reference to the major national schemes: supplementary benefits, housing rebates, FIS, and exemptions from charges for prescriptions, school meals, or dental and opthalmic treatment.[5]

There are, of course, other ways in which means are taken into account in the allocation of resources. For example, there are various ways in which resources are channelled indirectly to poor people: housing subsidies, subsidies to deprived areas or regions or positive discrimination in favour of poor schools. These policies are not applied directly to individuals, however, and do not appear to give rise to the same problems and issues as personal means tests, and they are not discussed in this book. It could also be argued that income tax is a form of means test, since it is an assessment of income for the allocation of 'tax benefits'. It also imposes a particularly severe burden upon low-paid workers. Nonetheless it is not exclusive to the poor, and we do not consider it in the book except as a factor in the so-called poverty trap.

The book is about the means test in Britain. To set our experience in context it would have been illuminating to have studied the means test in other countries. Unfortunately this was beyond our resources. Certainly the means test plays an important part in the allocation of welfare in the US. Within Europe the literature does not exist to draw any firm conclusions about whether means tests are as prevalent as in Britain. Certainly we are not alone among our European partners in recourse to means testing but it does appear, at least as far as families with children are concerned, that no other country in the European Community has a system of child support so dependent on means-tested benefits (Bradshaw and Piachaud, 1980; HC 331–ii, pp. 112–16).

The importance of the means test within British social policy cannot be understood without reference to the past. Indeed there are many people for whom the means test is still inseparably linked with the 1930s, and it is with this period that the book begins.

*NOTES*

1. The National Assistance Board were paying benefit to 1.3 million people who had approximately 400,000 dependents (Cmd. 7767,

p. 5). In addition some 340,000 children were receiving a free meal at school, around 12 per cent of the total eating at school (Cmd. 7426, p. 57). In many cases, however, the parents of these children were claiming national assistance, and so are already included in the total of 1.7 million. About 200,00 children of national assistance claimants were of school age, though not all of them would be claiming a free meal.

2. 3.7 million households were receiving a rate rebate and about two-thirds of them were pensioner households. The number of people in those households has been estimated on the basis of 1.17 persons per pensioner household and 2.06 persons per other household.

3. The only exception was a charge for spectacles and other appliances broken through negligence (Maynard, 1980, p. 47).

4. The distinction is not always a clear one. In the 1930s, for example, school meals were provided only for children whose education would otherwise have been impaired by a lack of food, and the decision as to who was eligible was based solely on a medical examination. In practice, of course, the children all came from desperately poor homes, and, whilst this is an extreme example, it should be remembered that needs can arise directly from poverty.

5. In addition there are a large number of locally administered schemes such as higher education awards, local charges for residential accomodation for the elderly and handicapped and children in care, charges for home helps, meals, day nurseries, chiropody, convalescent homes, school uniform grants and educational maintenance allowances.

CHAPTER 2

# Bitter Legacy: The Means Test in the 1930s

Few issues in social policy have aroused as much bitterness as the means test in the 1930s. As Stevenson and Cook (1977, p. 68) have remarked, it became 'one of the most emotive symbols of administrative meanness', and the memory of its operation was to have an enormous influence upon popular attitudes in the post-war years. The intense reaction against the means test during the 1930s stemmed largely from its use in the administration of unemployment relief, and it is with this that Chapter 2 is primarily concerned. This is not to say however, that the means test was not important in other areas: on the contrary, it played a significant and highly controversial role in the allocation of secondary education and in the administration of rent rebates. Moreover, there remained the poor law, now much less significant in terms of the number of people which it provided for, but still an essential element in any explanation of the bitterness and resentment engendered by the means test.

## THE POOR LAW

The introduction of the New Poor Law in 1834 and its subsequent history has been discussed and debated at length (Poynter, 1969; Fraser, 1973; Brundage, 1978). The important point here is not that poor relief was subject to a means test,[1] but the manner and form in which it was provided and the stigma which was attached to anyone who received it. The poor law rested upon the assumption that destitution was due to personal failing. It followed from this that destitution should always be relieved in a way which would encourage self-reliance on the part of the pauper, and deter others from seeking relief. In short, poor relief should be so unpleasant and so degrading that people would turn to their families for support, or, if they were able-bodied, take the work which it was assumed was available. In practice the administration of the poor law varied considerably from one part of the country to another, but everywhere the pauper was an object of contempt: someone who was maintained at the expense of others and thus forfeited all status, all respect and any rights of citizenship. This meant that the 'respectable' working class would go almost any lengths to avoid the taint of pauperism, and those who could afford to do so subscribed to friendly societies, slate clubs, trade union schemes and commercial insurance companies in a desperate attempt to avoid recourse to the poor law (Gosden, 1973).

It was, of course, predominantly these skilled and better organized workers who were covered by the health and unemployment insurance schemes which were introduced by the Liberal government in 1911. The background to the Liberal measures was complex and it cannot be covered here (Gilbert, 1966; Hay, 1975; Burgess, 1980). What is important, however, is the way in which the distinction between contributory insurance and means-tested assistance emerged within the context of the Edwardian obsession with the deserving and undeserving poor. The chief characteristics of the deserving poor were thrift, sobriety, the absence of a criminal record and membership of a friendly society or similar body. The latter was particularly important, since someone who had taken steps to avoid becoming a burden to others did not deserve to be treated as a pauper. National insurance was clearly for the deserving, and the fact that entitlement to benefit rested upon the prior payment of contributions was believed to remove the need for explicit tests of moral character (Deacon, 1976, p. 11). It was true that claimants had to meet various conditions — such as a requirement to register for work in the case of unemployment benefit — but any contributor who was refused benefit had the right of appeal to a tribunal headed by a lawyer. It was this emphasis upon legal entitlement, irrespective of means, which made insurance benefits so attractive to claimants.

This is not to argue that non-contributory benefits necessarily acquired the full stigma of the poor law. The pensions introduced in 1908, for example, were non-contributory and means-tested, but they were drawn at the local post office and were quite separate from the poor law. They were also quite different from insurance, however, since the scheme incorporated a number of rules and regulations which were designed to ensure that pensions were not paid to the undeserving. Quite apart from undergoing a means test, claimants had to show that they had not been in prison within the previous ten years, were not aliens, were not paupers and had not been guilty of an 'habitual failure to work' (Collins, 1965). The inference, of course, was that anyone who could not meet these conditions was a suitable case for the poor law and thus there had developed something of a hierarchy. Insurance benefits had greater status than those subject to a means test, but anything was better than poor relief.

It is in this context that the subsequent expansion of social insurance must be seen. Unemployment insurance was expanded to cover some 12 million workers in 1920, and in 1926 contributory pensions were introduced for the slightly larger number who were already covered by the health insurance scheme.[2] Thus, by 1930 the great majority of workers had become accustomed to receiving insurance benefits when they were unemployed, sick or had retired from work. Moreover, they regarded such benefits as distinct from, and quite superior to, the poor law. It followed that any attempt to introduce a means test would be bitterly resented; not only because it would involve an embarrassing enquiry into the circumstances of the household and could lead to a reduction in benefit, but because it would symbolize a loss of status. Writing of the unemployed in the 1930s, Bakke (1935, p. 191) noted that the means test signified the entry into a 'less eligible and less secure class':

> The filling out of forms, the recurrent knocking of the
> investigator at one's door, the knowledge that all eyes

in the street are on the investigator, the close association
with the methods of the ... [poor law] ... the experience
of having the public eye on one's private affairs, all of
these are symbols of one's new status.

Two qualifications should be made before proceeding
further. The first is that the social insurance schemes of the
1920s were neither as comprehensive nor as uncontentious
as the above might suggest. In particular the onset of mass
unemployment in 1921 undermined the contributory basis
of unemployment insurance, and this led to the introduction
of a requirement that all claimants prove that they were
genuinely seeking work. Large numbers of claimants were
refused benefits on the grounds that they had failed to meet
this condition, and it was bitterly resented. Nonetheless
the scheme was still seen as one of insurance, and insured
workers were still in a separate category from those on the
poor law. Indeed it was because of this that the genuinely
seeking work test was so hated (Deacon, 1977).

The second qualification is that the stigma of the poor law
was beginning to break down in some areas. During the 1920s,
a minority of Boards of Guardians had openly defied the
Ministry of Health and had provided relatively generous
relief to the unemployed who were refused insurance benefits
(Briggs and Deacon, 1973). There were similar differences
between the Public Assistance Committee (PACs) of the
county boroughs and county councils who took over the
administration of the poor law in 1929.[3] Not surprisingly,
the taint of pauperism remained strongest where the PACs
were most harsh, and the introduction of supplementary
pensions in 1940 was to provide dramatic evidence of the reluctance of many old people to claim assistance in some
areas (p. 37 below).

The dislike of means tests was as strong in the case of
services as it was in respect of cash benefits. The 1929 Act
empowered the local authorities to take over the poor law infirmaries and run them as general public hospitals, and by
1939 there were more beds in municipal hospitals than in
poor law institutions (Gilbert, 1970, p. 233). In some cases
the improvement in standards was dramatic (Aronovitch,

1974, pp. 63–4, 75–80), but the Act also required the local authorities to recover the cost of the patient's maintenance. Anyone who sought exemption from these charges would have to undergo a means test (Cmd. 3273). Overall the amount paid in charges represented about 10 per cent of the total public expenditure on general hospitals (PEP, 1937b, p. 252). In a great many cases, however, the charges were covered by the patient's own insurance, and the growth of contributory hospital schemes was one of the most remarkable features of the inter-war period. The initiative for such schemes had come from the voluntary hospitals, who had been forced to introduce charges immediately after the First World War (Abel-Smith, 1964a, pp. 295–8). Typically a subscriber paid 3 pence (d) a week in return for free treatment in a voluntary hospital or reimbursement of local authority charges for a specified period. By 1935 there were 114 schemes making returns to the British Hospital Contributory Schemes Association. They had 5.25 million subscribers and, including dependents, covered around 10 million people (PEP, 1937b, p. 234). The popularity of this type of scheme was revealed by a survey of working class attitudes towards welfare which was carried out by Nuffield College in 1942. A 'typical' transport worker, for example, was found to subscribe to a Co-operative Society sick scheme, three slate clubs, a hospital scheme, a district scheme and the TGWU convalescent home (Harris, n.d, p. 20). Patients who had subscribed to these schemes did not necessarily receive better treatment, they just avoided the means test.

## OTHER SERVICES

The opposition to means testing was even greater in the case of services which had never had any connection with the poor law. The best examples of this were the furore which followed the abolition of free places in secondary education, and the attempt to introduce rent rebates for council tenants.

Elementary education had been free since 1891, but the great majority of secondary schools still charged fees. There was, however, a long tradition of local authority scholarships, and in 1907 Reginald Mckenna, then President of the Board of Education, announced an extra grant for secondary schools who were willing to offer 25 per cent of their places as free places to pupils coming from elementary schools (Simon, 1965, p. 270). By 1914, free places accounted for 30 per cent of the total, and the proportion rose steadily during the 1920s. In the peak years of 1931 and 1932 they represented 46 per cent of the annual intake in England, and over 70 per cent in Wales (Simon, 1974, p. 364). A third of local authorities imposed some kind of income limit upon those taking free places, but in the remainder they were still open to any child who had attended a public elementary school for at least two years.

The growth in free places was an obvious target for the May Committee, which had been established by Philip Snowden in February 1931 to make proposals for effecting 'all possible reductions in national expenditure'. The Committee recommended a substantial increase in fees — which then ranged from 3 to 30 guineas a year — and the remission of those fees only on proof of need (Cmd. 3920, p. 198). The idea was rejected by Labour ministers, but in September 1932 the National government issued Circular 1421. This required the local authorities to levy a fee of at least 9 guineas, and abolish free places. Instead there were to be special places, which would be filled by open competition, but would entitle the holder to a reduction in fees only if this was justified by the financial circumstances of the family. Herwald Ramsbotham, Parliamentary Secretary to the Board, told the Commons in November that the purpose of the circular was to raise extra revenue whilst protecting those who could not afford to pay an economic fee. Attendance at a public elementary school had been 'a fairly good criterion of poverty' in 1907, but there was no longer any guarantee that the free place 'goes to the child who needs it' (*Hansard*, 270, 1173).

The response to the circular was immediate. As Simon records (1974, p. 335), it 'resulted in the greatest mass of protests received by the Board on any issue in the inter-war years'. Ministers were unrepentant, however, and Ramsbotham made it clear that the government did not regard the provision of secondary education for all children to be one of its responsibilities. 'Where the parents' resources are not adequate for the educational requirements of the child, it is for the State to intervene, but, so long as the parent has those resources, it is his business to look after his own child and to be responsible for it' (*Hansard*, 270, 1171).

The most telling opposition, however, came from the local authorities, and the government was forced to make concessions on both the level of fees and the severity of the means test (Cmd. 4364, pp. 16–17). In addition, a growing number of schools were allowed to offer all their places as special places, and the overall effect of the circular was thus to stabilize rather than to reduce the numbers receiving free secondary education. By 1938, special places represented 70 per cent of the entry into secondary schools, and nearly half of the 494,000 children in secondary schools were exempt from fees (Cmd. 6013).

In stark contrast to the arguments about the place of the means test in education, the idea of rent rebates attracted a surprisingly broad measure of support. They were advocated by the Conservatives as a means of reducing public spending, and by the Labour and Communist parties as a measure of social justice. The only people to oppose them were the tenants.

There had been various housing acts since the war, but in each case the subsidy paid by central government to the local authorities depended upon the number of houses they built. The 1924 Act, for example, provided £9 per house *per annum* in urban areas, and this was fixed irrespective of the rent charged for the house. It followed from this that the local authorities could reduce the cost to their own funds by selecting, as tenants, those who could afford to pay a relatively high rent. The market for local authority houses was thus confined to a limited range of income groups: ... 'the small clerks, the artisans, the better-off semi-skilled workers with small families and fairly safe jobs' (Bowley, 1945, p. 129). The effect of this was to force many of the poorest families into privately rented accommodation often of a very low standard. Moreover, the rates which they paid on that accommodation were used in part to subsidize the rents of the council houses from which they were excluded. Even within the council sector, however, there was growing criticism of the practice of subsidizing the house rather than the tenant. A Fabian Society pamphlet, for example, claimed that:

> the practice of attaching a flat rate subsidy to a parti-
> cular house is both wasteful and unjust. Where the sub-
> sidy is attached to the house, the tenant gets the benefit
> of it, whatever his financial circumstances may be. It
> is wasteful in that, in many cases, a subsidy is given to
> a tenant who has no need of it, and it is unjust in that
> the money thus wasted is not being given to those
> who really need it (Wilson, 1939, p. 6).

The alternative was to raise the rents of all the houses to a level sufficient to cover costs, and to provide rebates for tenants in need. This policy had something for everyone. In 1934, the Labour Party Conference unanimously approved a policy statement which declared: ' "Each according to his need" is a good Socialist precept', and concluded that, 'it is, for the time being at least, quite out of the question to consider letting all local authority houses at the minimum rents necessary for the "poorest families" ' (1934, p. 33). Similar conclusions were reached − via a rather different route − by the Ray Committee. This was set up in 1932 to apply the same scrutiny to local spending as the May Committee had applied to national expenditure. It argued that 'every reasonable endeavour be made' to ensure that all those who could afford to pay a higher rent did so (Cmd. 4200, p. 65).

The sudden interest in rent rebates was prompted by a renewed emphasis upon slum clearance after 1930. As long as council tenants were drawn from a narrow range of income, the flat-rate subsidy did not cause any particular difficulty. Many of those rehoused from the slums, however, could not afford the usual rents − which was why they were in the slum in the first place. To meet this problem, the 1930 Act varied the subsidy according to the number of people re-housed, and encouraged the authorities to introduce rebate schemes. At first these schemes were confined to slum clearance, but after 1936 it was possible for an authority to pool all of its income from subsidies and introduce rebates for all its tenants.

In practice, however, relatively little happened. By 1938, 112 local authorities in England and Wales had introduced rebate schemes, but only in Leeds did it cover every tenant. Overall, around 10 per cent of tenants were included in a scheme and only 2 per cent were actually receiving a rebate (Wilson, 1939, p. 14). There were several reasons for this. First, any scheme involved the local authority in a considerable amount of work, since it was necessary to know the incomes and dependents of all those who were to be included. This was because each scheme had to be adapted to local circumstances. The subsidy from central government depended upon the number of people rehoused. It followed from this that the greater the proportion of these people who qualified for a rebate, the less money there would be for each one. In short, the greater the incidence of poverty in an area, the less generous was the scheme it could afford. Moreover, there was always the danger that a factory closure would suddenly increase the numbers eligible for a rebate, and thereby threaten the whole scheme. It is not surprising, then, that Wilson (1939, p. 14) found that the schemes differed 'in practically every respect possible'. The second reason why there were not more schemes was the hostility of the tenants themselves. The sight of a neighbour paying a lower rent for the same house was a new and not entirely welcome experience for many people. The major problem, however, was the means test, and the fate of the Leeds scheme was sufficient to deter many authorities.

Labour took power in Leeds in November 1933, committed to a massive clearance programme. In all, one-third of the existing housing stock was to be cleared. The most contentious feature of the plan, however, was that the rent of every council house in the city was to be raised to an economic level and all the tenants included in a rebate scheme. The new rebates were brought into operation in April 1934, although the legal position regarding such a comprehensive scheme was still uncertain at that time. The regulations governing who was eligible for a rebate were extraordinarily complex. The financial contribution expected of sons and daughters who were in work, for example, depended not only on their age, income and dependents, but upon whether or not they had their own room in the house.

To the Rev. Charles Jenkinson, the Labour leader and architect of the clearance programme, a policy of 'differential rents' was 'a logical working out of Christian principles' (Hammerton, 1952, p. 112). In any case, he regarded it as inevitable if the former slum dwellers were to be able to afford decent houses. Neither Jenkinson's principles nor his reasoning made much impression upon the tenants in the older estates who were now facing rent increases of between 70 and 100 per cent. Opposition to the scheme remained intense even though more than half of the tenants eventually qualified for a rebate, and one in ten paid no rent at all. In 1935 the Conservatives regained control of the council — against the national trend — and Jenkinson lost his own seat in the following year. There were, of course, other reasons for the unpopularity of the housing programme; many people simply preferred the convenience and community of the old slums to life on the new suburban estates. Nonetheless, Alison Ravetz (1974, p. 38) has demonstrated that it was the means test which was the dominant issue: 'More than any other aspect of their policy, differential rents were responsible for Labour's defeat in 1935'. Another all-inclusive rebate scheme in Birmingham in 1939 had to be abandoned in the face of a rent strike, and once again the means test was the main reason for the protest (Schiffres, 1975, p. 99). Writing in 1945, Marion Bowley (1945, p. 219) concluded that rent rebates were simply not worth the trouble they caused.

## TRANSITIONAL PAYMENTS

It was argued earlier that the main reason why the means test became such an important issue in the 1930s was its use in the administration of unemployment relief. In fact it is possible to be still more precise and to point to two specific episodes: the introduction of transitional payments in November 1931, and the early days of the Unemployment Assistance Board (UAB) in January 1935. These events had a profound impact upon hundreds of thousands of claimants and they gave the means test an emotional significance which was to last until the present day.

The origins of transitional payments lay in the rapidly mounting costs of unemployment insurance. Unemployment had remained over a million throughout the 1920s, and successive governments had been acutely conscious of the danger of unrest if such numbers had been thrown onto the poor law. As a result they had continually extended the length of time for which benefits could be drawn (Bakke, 1935, pp. 70–4). This had been extremely expensive, and neither the seeking work test nor higher contributions had prevented the insurance fund from sinking deeper into debt. By September 1931 the total deficit had reached £116 million and the total Exchequer contribution to the scheme accounted for nearly one-quarter of all government expenditure on the social services, compared with 3–4 per cent in 1920 (ML, 1932, pp. 381–3).

It was over this issue, of course, that the second Labour government fell. In August 1931 it became clear the the government needed to raise substantial loans in New York and Paris and that those loans would only be available if very considerable economies were made in public expenditure. Above all, the Cabinet would have to approve cuts in unemployment insurance. In the event, ministers agreed to the imposition of a means test upon those who had drawn benefits for more than 26 weeks, but an important minority refused to accept a 10 per cent reduction in the general level of benefits. On 24 August Ramsay MacDonald resigned as Prime Minister only to return at the head of a National government (McKibbon, 1975; Marquand, 1977).

One of the first measures of the new government was the National Economy Act, which empowered it to make economies in public expenditure by Orders in Council. Two such orders were made in respect of unemployment insurance. The first reduced benefits by 10 per cent and raised contributions, the second brought in the means test. Under the second order, insurance benefits were restricted to those who had paid 30 contributions in the last 2 years, and would, in any case, be limited to 26 weeks in any one year. Around 900,000 claimants would be excluded by one or other of these conditions, and they were to apply for transitional payments. This new benefit was to be paid at the employment exchange but would be subject to a test of means administered by the local PACs. The PACs were instructed by the government to assess claims for transitional payments in the same way as applications for poor relief, save that they could not pay more than the claimant would have received in insurance benefits (Cmd. 4044, pp. 87—92).

The new policy was justified on the grounds that benefit which has not been earned by contributions was really a form of poor relief. It was not being provided because people were entitled to it, but because they needed it. Hence there was nothing unreasonable in asking them to demonstrate that need. Milner Gray, Parliamentary Secretary to the Minister of Labour, told the Commons: '. . . you cannot allow people who do not need this money to draw it when they are not drawing it as a result of contributions paid. In that case it is really a form of public assistance. Let us accept that term, because it is the fact' (*Hansard*, 257, 313). This argument was far from new. As Skidelsky (1970, pp. 229—46, 263) notes, the need to distinguish between insurance and relief had become the 'accepted orthodoxy' by 1930. It had become the policy of both opposition parties, had been proposed by the May Committee and was one of the few points upon which contemporary economists — including Keynes and Robbins — could agree.

The need for such a distinction, however, would be somewhat less clear to the claimants. There were hundreds of thousands on the unemployment register in the Autumn of 1931 who saw themselves as insured workers and who had never been to the poor law. Indeed they probably despised anyone who had. Now, suddenly, they were told that they were to go to the PACs, and many would have had little idea of what was in store for them.

What did lie in store for them was the household means test. Under this, the resources of each member of the household were regarded as being available to meet the needs of the claimant, whether or not they were related. The usual procedure was to provide relief only if the combined resources of the household were less than its total requirements as measured by the PAC's scale.[4]

As a result many of the unemployed were told that they would now have to look for their support to parents, children, brothers or sisters, or even comparative strangers who happened to be living in the same household. Moreover, the other members of the household would be subjected to detailed enquiries into their private affairs even though they themselves were making no claim for assistance. This meant that some families were better off if the younger members left home, and 'collusive desertion' was to become a serious problem for the PACs. At first many Committees simply maintained the benefit deductions in such cases, while others made a discretionary allowance of so-called 'dignity money' — though such payments were technically illegal (PRO, 1935a). In later years the UAB evolved the doctrine of the 'constructive household'. Under this the assistance payable was reduced to take account of the resources of a person who was 'constructively a member of a household even though not physically present' (PRO, 1938).

The statistics give some idea of the impact of the household means test in the first weeks of its operation. Between 12 November 1931 and 2 January 1932 the PACs considered some 800,000 claims for transitional payments. One-fifth were disallowed completely and over one-third more had their payments reduced. In all, 440,000 claimants were made wholly or partially dependent upon the people they lived with. Each one of them would have been in receipt of benefit before 12 November and in every case the decision was taken solely on the grounds of household income (PRO, 1932a).

These figures are even more remarkable in view of the fact that the Ministry of Labour adopted an extremely cautious approach in its early dealings with the PACs. In December 1931, Wilfred Eady, a senior official in the Ministry, told a conference of General Inspectors that they should not push the PACs too hard, but should encourage them to use their discretion to avoid potential problems. 'The test is one that a Committee passes on the total marks, and not on the marks for each question.' The concessions were being made for a purpose, however, and Eady reminded the Inspectors of their overall objective in unusually frank terms:

> People have thought that benefit was so certain and so much of a right that they built up their lives on the certainty of getting money from the Employment Exchange on Friday. Their family life has centred round that principle. We cannot allow that principle to go on. If we relax on the proper treatment of a man's assets we must remember that we are doing that as part of an experiment . . . If we can get the idea that benefit does not run as a right forever, if we can get that idea exercised, we shall have won the first round (PRO, 1931).

Not everyone who supported the new scheme was as explicit as Eady. Nonetheless, *The Times* (2 February 1932) welcomed the numbers disallowed as clear evidence that the means test was long overdue. It reported that over 12,000 cases had been dealt with in the first two weeks in London alone, and in nearly 30 per cent of these the household income had been found to be sufficient to meet the claimant's needs. Numerous abuses had been exposed, particularly by men living in common lodging houses and by married women. The money saved would thus be a 'tonic' to public opinion, whilst the objections being raised against the means test would make little impression upon 'the millions whose means are subjected every year to the scrutiny of the taxing authorities'. In fact it is impossible to tell precisely how much abuse was prevented by the means test. This is because it was introduced at almost the same time as the anomalies regulations, which imposed severe restrictions upon the benefits paid to married women. The anomalies regulations did lead to both a sharp rise in the proportion of women's claims which were disallowed and a considerable drop in the number of women registering for work at the exchanges. The evidence suggests, however, that the great majority of those disallowed on the grounds of household income continued to sign on at the exchange, and it is quite wrong to assume that they were malingerers (Deacon, 1976, pp. 87–8).

The introduction of the means test seems to have provoked relatively little unrest amongst the unemployed. This was partly because the National government had won an over-whelming victory in the general election held on 26 October, and everyone knew that economies were inevitable. On polling day, for example, *The Times* (26 October 1931) had declared that the issue was whether Britain had 'the grit and pride and self-discipline to choose rightly between a comfort-able way that leads on to bankruptcy and an uncomfortable way that leads back to prosperity'. The mood of fatalism and resignation which such rhetoric engendered was reinforced by the revelation that the previous government had also de-cided to bring in a means test, and protest was also inhibited by the allegations of abuse.

Opposition did emerge during 1932, however, as long-term unemployment continued to rise and more and more house-holds came under scrutiny. Indeed, Miller (1974, p. 171) has argued that the protests had become so serious by the Autumn that the government feared that it would have to abandon the household means test. Some of these protests were made on humanitarian grounds, and came from a variety of civic and religious bodies. Others came from Conservative MPs who had been elected in normally Labour seats in 1931. By far the most significant opposition, however, came from the unemployed themselves and from the local authorities.

There had been relatively little unrest amongst the unemployed since the disturbances which had followed the onset of mass unemployment in 1921 (Deacon, 1977, pp. 11–13). In the Autumn of 1932, however, there was a wave of protest, and severe rioting occured in London, Belfast and on Merseyside. The trouble in Belfast — the last non-sectarian violence in the city — was over the general level of relief, but in London and on Merseyside the focus was the means test. In Birkenhead a protest march to the PAC precipitated several days of bitter fighting between police and demonstrators, and this was later repeated in Liverpool (Stevenson and Cook, 1977, pp. 167-73). The protests were nearly always organized by the Communist-led National Unemployed Workers Movement (NUWM), which had been founded in 1921 and reached a peak of 50,000 members during 1932. The NUWM's greatest success came in October with its first 'National Hunger March against the Means Test'. Contingents from 18 different areas marched to London to present a million-signature petition against the means test, and there were 30,000 people in Hyde Park to welcome them. The government was genuinely alarmed at the prospect of massive disorder, even to the extent of arresting the NUWM's leader, Wal Hannington, on the eve of the Hyde Park rally and of stealing the petition from the cloakroom of Charing Cross station (Stevenson and Cook, 1977, pp. 173–9).

These events were important, but they must be seen in perspective. After Hyde Park, the largest number attending any rally or demonstration was 12,000, whilst the unrest in Belfast and Birkenhead was undoubtedly exacerbated by local factors. In the case of Birkenhead, the crucial factor was the severity with which the means test was administered by the local PAC. This, however, was not typical. Indeed, the main reason why there was not more disorder was the relative leniency shown by a growing number of local authorities, and this was to prove the most difficult problem facing the central government.

It was always expected that the wide variations between different areas in the administration of the poor law would also occur in transitional payments. Indeed, ministers had been extremely reluctant to entrust the latter to the PACs. There was no time to establish alternative machinery at the exchanges, however, and it was also feared that the Minister of Labour would face a barrage of parliamentary questions on individual cases if his own officials had been responsible for the scheme (Briggs and Deacon, 1973, p. 54). In fact the problems proved to be far worse than had been feared. In January, Henry Betterton, the Minister of Labour, told the Cabinet that some PACs were being intimidated by local opposition and that 'guidance and admonition' were being given where appropriate (PRO, 1932a). By February, however, he was reporting the deliberate refusal of some PACs to conduct the means test properly (PRO, 1932b), and by

June the size of the resistance was becoming clear. Rotherham, for example, was disregarding virtually all of the income coming into the claimant's household, and paying the full allowance in 98.2 per cent of cases (PRO, 1932c). This was exceptional, but there were still inexplicable variations throughout the country. Among the counties, for example, the proportion of claims refused outright varied from 33.3 per cent in Lancashire to 1.5 per cent in Glamorgan; among the boroughs from 0.5 per cent in Merthyr and 6.0 per cent in Southampton to 37.6 per cent in Halifax and 34.8 per cent in Birmingham (Cmd. 4184, p. 62).

The government responded to this in two ways. It sought to clamp down on the most generous PACs, and appointed commissioners to take over in Rotherham and County Durham. At the same time it made significant concessions over the treatment of savings and income of various kinds. Thus emerged what Miller (1974, p. 171) has called a 'tacit compromise' whereby the local authorities 'recognised that they could ease some of the worst aspects of the test if they did it without openly challenging the principles of government policy'. Not all of the dissident PACs were under Labour control, though an increasing proportion of them were after Labour's recovery in the municipal elections of 1932 and 1933. Indeed, for many Labour members the means test posed a cruel dilemma: if they agreed to administer it, they could be accused of giving it legitimacy; if they refused, they were passing up an opportunity to secure extra money for some claimants (Brockway, 1932, p. 26).

None of this should be taken to mean that the household means test virtually disappeared or was applied very leniently after 1932 – far from it. The proportion of claims which were disallowed completely had fallen from 18 per cent to 14 per cent by 1934, but this was matched by a similar rise in the proportion given benefit at a reduced rate. The number paid benefit in full remained constant at around half the total (Cmd. 4861, p. 65). This points to a gradual easing of the means test, but not to a general defiance of the government. Above all, it must be remembered that many of the generous PACs were in areas of high unemployment, and such was the poverty in those areas that even the strictest regime would have saved relatively little. This was confirmed by Bowers, who as Accountant General in the Ministry of Labour had been the staunchest advocate of strict administration during the 1920s. In January 1933 Bowers examined the impact of the Commissioner appointed in County Durham, and concluded that even if every PAC was as lax as Durham, only £5 million a year would be saved by the appointment of a Commissioner in every area. This represented a cut of some 10 per cent in the total cost of the scheme (PRO, 1933).

Bowers's calculations, however, did little to alter the attitudes towards local administration held within Whitehall. This was especially true of Neville Chamberlain, whose experience at the Ministry of Health in the 1920s had convinced him that locally elected bodies could never be trusted to administer social security benefits (Deacon and Briggs, 1974). He believed it to be inevitable that candidates would seek election by promising more money, and the operation of the transitional payments scheme only reinforced his view. In December 1932 he told a Cabinet Committee on Unemployment Insurance that local government 'was being debauched; standards were being lowered and the trouble was spreading like a contagious disease' (PRO, 1932d). By this time, however, Chamberlain was Chancellor of the Exchequer, and in a position to propose a solution.

### THE UNEMPLOYMENT ASSISTANCE BOARD

The origins and purpose of the UAB have been discussed at length elsewhere (Millet, 1940; Briggs and Deacon, 1973; Miller, 1974). Chamberlain's original proposal was for a Statutory Commission which would be responsible for the relief of destitution in all cases, except those requiring institutional care. This amounted to a merger of transitional payments and the poor law, and was strongly resisted by Betterton. The new Commission, he argued, was bound to inherit the poor law taint, and it would be a political blunder to transfer to it people who had previously enjoyed the status of insured workers. The eventual compromise was the establishment of a Board, which was free from parliamentary control but was responsible only for the unemployed. The Board would be responsible for the decisions of its local officers, and so the Minister would not have to answer Parliamentary Questions on individual cases. More than anything else, however, the new Board was a centralizing measure. It was impossible to devise regulations which covered all the circumstances of every case, and so a measure of discretion had to be given to local officials. Now, however, these officials would be accountable to – and appointed by – a central authority.

In theory it was for the six members of the Board to determine both the scales of assistance and the details of the means test. They began work in July 1934, and submitted draft regulations to the new Minister of Labour, Oliver Stanley, in the following November. The whole point of the UAB, of course, was that these regulations would now be applied in a uniform manner across the whole country. It was only to be expected that claimants living in the areas covered by the more lax PACs would suffer some reductions when the new scheme went into operation in January 1935. Nonetheless, the total cost of unemployment assistance was expected to rise by £3 million or 7 per cent, as the cuts in South Wales and Glasgow would be offset by increases in Lancashire and London.

It came as a shock, therefore, when the introduction of the scheme provoked an unprecedented storm of protest across Scotland, Wales and Northern Ireland. The uproar and the panic which it induced in the government has been vividly described by Miller (1979). What was so alarming to the government was not simply the size of the demonstrations – 300,000 were involved in South Wales alone – but the fact that they were obviously spontaneous. By the end of January it had become clear that nearly half of the UAB's clients were getting less than they had from the PACs, and only 34 per cent were better off. Instead of rising by 7 per cent, the total cost seemed likely to fall by that amount, and the government now faced a barrage of complaints from its own backbenchers. On 5 February, Stanley announced a legal standstill, during which claimants would receive either their allowance from the Board, or the amount they would have been paid by the PAC, whichever was the greater. The stand-still lasted for nearly two years, and proved to be extremely effective in defusing the protests. Administratively, however, it was a nightmare, and it never ceased to enrage the Board. In its *Annual Report* for 1935, for example, the Board (Cmd. 5177, p. 15) complained that the standstill required 'the continuance of many of the anomalies in . . . transitional payments . . . whose abolition was one of the reasons for the creation of the Board'. Over half the claimants were in fact receiving a hypothetical PAC assessment, which often paid insufficient regard to the household income and in 'numerous cases' was 'simply an abuse of public money'.

Not surprisingly, there was a bitter argument over who was responsible for this fiasco. The Minister blamed the Board, and the Board blamed the Minister and the PACs who, it claimed, had become increasingly lax in the months prior to the changeover (PRO, 1935b, 1935c). It is more likely, however, that most of the cuts stemmed from the simple fact that working-class rents were lower than anyone in Whitehall had realized.[5] The Board had adopted an extraordinarily complex rule which was based on the assumption that be-tween one-third and one-quarter of any allowance would be spent in rent. When the actual rents proved to be lower than this, the allowances were adjusted accordingly. In theory the Board's officers could have used their discretionary powers to minimize the reductions, and the failure to do so was criticized at the time. Millet (1940, pp. 204–5) has pointed out, however, that the pressures on the local staff were all in the direction of economy:

The regulations themselves spoke of 'special circum-stances' and 'needs of an exceptional character'. Any implication that these words were not to be taken literally was very faint indeed in the early instructions of the Board . . . Is it any wonder the local offices decided to play safe and stick to the scale? The scale was objective. It could be calculated with mathematical precision. Discretion was subjective and the officers were confused as to just what was its purpose or how they were expected to proceed.

All of this changed, however, following the standstill. The Board issued its officers with a continuous stream of circulars illustrating the use which they should make of their discretionary powers and by the end of 1935, 20 per cent of claimants were receiving a discretionary addition. Around one-quarter of these were awarded to meet the costs of a special diet, but the additions were primarily granted to mitigate the impact of the rent rule (Cmd. 5177, pp. 12, 40–4). Indeed the increased use of discretion was to play an important part in the gradual liquidation of the standstill after November 1936 (Cmd. 5752, pp. 13–17).

Following the fiasco of the standstill, then, the tenor of the UAB became less severe than had been expected by either its critics or its creators in 1934. If it figured in controversy, it was more likely to be through allegations of laxity than of harshness. In 1938, for example, R.C. Davison (1938, p. 69) spoke of the Board encouraging its officers in 'a use of their discretionary powers which seemed to go beyond anything revealed in the original plan'. In the same year the Board had to defend itself against accusations that it was allowing young people to settle down on assistance and thereby become unemployable (Deacon, 1980, p. 63). Certainly the Board did not hound the long-term unemployed. As early as 1936 it conducted an enquiry in all cases where the claimant had been out of work for two years, in order to see if there was a need for an exceptional payment to provide such items as bedding. This was done because:

> experience showed that in some cases where hardship was being experienced the applicant himself made no request for special assistance, either because he was unaware of the Board's powers, or because of a reluctance to obtrude his need. It was thought, therefore, that where exceptional need was likely to exist, the Board should take the initiative (Cmd. 5526, p. 28).

Once again, however, the statistics serve as a reminder of the continuing impact of the means test. One-third of claimants in October 1938 had had their assistance reduced on the grounds of household income, and the proportion rose to

57 per cent in households of three or more persons without dependent children. There were 445, 000 new claims during the year, and just over 10 per cent of them were 'found to possess resources sufficient for their needs' (Cmd. 6021, pp. 60, 64). The Board did not carry the full taint of the poor law — as the wartime supplementary pensions scheme was to demonstrate — but assistance was still seen as grossly inferior to insurance. Why else would agricultural workers demand — and get — their own insurance scheme even though the benefits they received for their contributions were lower than the assistance they could have claimed anyway?

*CONCLUSION*

The passions aroused by the treatment of the unemployed during the 1930s have tended to distract attention from the complexity and significance of the debate over the means test in general. Throughout the decade, the use of the means test was defended on two main grounds. The first was the need for economy. Although the 'Keynesian revolution' in economic ideas was to begin during the decade, social policy was dominated by the belief that economic recovery would follow only a severe reduction in the levels of public expenditure, and particularly in spending on the social services (Winch, 1969, p. 98). The introduction of transitional payments, of special places, and of rent rebates all followed hard on the financial crisis of 1931, and in each case the arguments for a means test had been set out by the May Committee (Cmd. 3920). More than any other document, it was this report which established the context for social policy in the early 1930s. Not only because of its alarmist and exaggerated picture of the nation's indebtedness, but because of its analysis of how that debt had arisen. 'After the heavy sacrifices of the War', it argued, 'large sections of the nation' had anticipated an improvement in their living standards and this had tempted politicians into promising dramatic reforms. In fact these reforms were 'of the nature of privileges or benefits for particular classes at the cost of the general tax-payer.'

As a result candidates arrived at Westminster committed to a cause 'which on fuller knowledge they see to be opposed to the national interest'. 'Especially serious is this danger at the present time when the mass of the electorate still does not appreciate the true, economic position of the country and its problems' (pp. 12—13). Now Britain had to take its medicine, and the means test loomed large on the prescription.

Means tests were also supported as a way of maintaining a sense of personal responsibility amongst claimants. The more the state afforded protection against the contingencies of sickness, unemployment or old age, and the more it provided hospitals, schools and houses, the greater was the threat to self-help and self-reliance. The threat could be reduced, however, by an extension of social insurance — a form of collective self-help — and by ensuring that benefits and services which had not been earned by contributions were given only to people who could not afford to provide for themselves. It was seen earlier that special places were justified in those terms, and the growth of private medical insurance was seen as a clear example of the capacity of people to provide for themselves without state help.

Conversely, the opposition to means tests from the Labour movement and elsewhere was greatest in respect of benefits which were seen as fundamental rights. Few argued that subsidized housing should be available for all, but 'work or maintenance' had long been Labour policy, as had secondary education for all. The degree of opposition to a particular means test also depended upon whether or not it was based on the income of the household, or on that of the individual claimant. The personal means test for non-contributory pensions or some local authority welfare services aroused far less opposition than the household means test, and the Fabian pamphlet which advocated rent rebates was clear that 'every attempt' had to be made to avoid the impression of a household test (Wilson, 1939, p. 30).

It was the household means test which was remembered in later years. The enduring image of the means test in the 1930s was a young couple who were told that their savings would now have to go towards the maintenance of one of their parents, the family which was told to live off the pension paid to a war veteran, or the thousands of similar cases recorded by comtemporary observers and critics (Warburton and Butler, 1935). This was the legacy of the 1930s, and it was to be a potent influence upon the politics of the 1940s.

## NOTES

1. The first priciple of the poor law was that of family responsibility. The Act of 1601 had declared that it was the duty of 'the father, grandfather, mother, grandmother, husband or child' of a person who was destitute and unable to work to maintain that person. This was re-enacted in 1834 and 1930, when the list was extended to include stepfathers, married women with property and the mother of an illegitimate child. The Act of 1601 had assumed that the able-bodied would always be set to work, and so the liability to maintain did not extend to the relatives of the unemployed. In all other cases, however, the relatives were liable to contribute towards the cost of any relief provided, though these powers were not widely used in the twentieth century (Ford, 1939, p. 13). By 1937 the amount recovered from non-resident relatives represented only 3 per cent of the total cost of outdoor relief, and in the case of infirmaries and sick wards the figure was 8 per cent (PEP, 1937a, p. 252; Marshall, 1943, p. 43). Instead of a family means test, the great majority of Boards operated a household means test, and this is discussed later in the chapter (pp. 16–17).

2. Those not covered by the Act continued to receive the non-contributory pension which had been introduced in 1908. There were 750,000 receiving such pensions during the 1930s, and there were still 450,000 when their administration was transferred to the National Assistance Board in 1948.

3. The creation of municipal hospitals and the Unemployment Assistance Board (UAB) — discussed on pp. 22–3 — meant that the importance of the poor law declined during the 1930s. By the end of the decade, the responsibility of the PACs was limited to fatherless families, the old, and the sick and infirm. Even so there were still a million people living on poor relief in 1939.

4. The only sources of income disregarded under the poor law were small amounts of friendly society and health insurance benefit. Two days before the scheme started, however, the PACs were given a broad hint to go easy on capital assets and disability pensions.

5. The other major reason for the reduction was the rigorous way in which the Board set out to apply the household principle. Under its original regulations the parent or spouse of the claimant could retain only 5 shillings of any earnings, a son or daughter, brother or sister one-third of earnings up to 20 shillings and one-quarter thereafter, and other members one-third of all earnings. The Board significantly altered its definition of the household shortly before the standstill. Under the new rule anyone entering a household after reaching the age of employment was not regarded as a member of it if they paid an amount equivalent to board and lodging.

# CHAPTER 3

# A Universal Welfare State?

The welfare legislation of the 1940s led to a significant decline in the numbers receiving means-tested benefits. The 1944 Education Act, for example, abolished the free places scheme and made secondary education free for all children. Similarly the creation of the national health service meant the removal of virtually all charges for medical care.[1] Rent rebate schemes had all but disappeared by the end of the war (Parker, 1967, p. 42), whilst both the Conservative and Labour Parties entered the 1945 election committed to providing universal free school meals. Only in social security did the means test remain important, and even here the position was very different from what it had been in the 1930s. The numbers claiming national assistance in 1948 were little more than half those dependent upon the poor law and the Unemployment Assistance Board (UAB) immediately before the War.[2] More importantly, the household means test had gone and only the resources of the individual claimant and his or her dependents were taken into account in determining need.

The emphasis on universalism during the 1940s is often seen as stemming from the unprecedented sense of social unity which had developed during the war. The years of common effort and sacrifice are believed to have brought about a fundamental shift in public attitudes and created an atmosphere in which a return to the social divisions and inequalities of the 1930s would not have been tolerated. Peter Townsend (1973, pp. 2–3), for example, has recalled the belief in 'fair shares' which characterized the period: 'There was an attitude of trust, tolerance, generosity, goodwill

— call it what you like — towards others; a pervasive faith in human nature. Then there was a prevailing mood of self-denial, a readiness to share the good things in life and to see that others got the same privileges as oneself.' The dole queue and the means test became the twin symbols of the 1930s, and the focus for a collective determination not to repeat the failures and mistakes of those years. Two reasons are usually given for the importance attached to the means test. First, the public were now less inclined to see poverty as the result of personal failing or irresponsible behaviour. Second, there was a far greater awareness of the misery and hardship which it had caused in earlier years. This shift in public attitudes is seen in turn as forming the basis of a new welfare consensus; one in which both major political parties accepted that the widespread use of means tests was morally indefensible and politically impossible. As Derek Fraser (1973, p. 192) put it: |If the essential theme of the 1930s had been selectivity, that of the 1940s was universalism'|

It is not the purpose of this chapter to challenge the broad sweep of this interpretation. No-one would dispute the profound impact of the war, or question the importance of the 1930s as an influence upon post-war politics. Rather, the intention is to examine more closely the nature of the consensus as it related to the means test. Was there an all-party agreement that the role of the means test should be reduced to a minimum? If so, what had happened to those who had supported the means test in earlier years? Had they changed their minds, or were they simply remaining silent whilst public opinion was so obviously against them? Questions must also be asked of the left. Why, for example, did the Labour Party not object to over a million claimants being forced to resort to the National Assistance Board (NAB) in 1949 when it had consistently denounced its predecessor the UAB? The answers to such questions are central to this study. Indeed, the view which is taken of the war years largely determines the approach to subsequent events. Is it a question of explaining the collapse of a consensus based on feelings of obligation and expressed through universal social policies, or of charting the gradual erosion of a vague compromise in which Labour had conceded more than the Conservatives?

*SOCIAL POLICY AND THE SECOND WORLD WAR*

Academic discussion of wartime social policy was long dominated by Richard Titmuss's famous book *Problems of Social Policy* (1950). Titmuss argued that the circumstances of the war had a profound impact upon the British people and led them to accept and even demand social reform. Two episodes were particularly important: the evacuation scheme and the retreat from Dunkirk.

Pre-war estimates had greatly exaggerated the effects of bombing and plans had been made for the mass evacuation of women and children from the major cities. In the first three days of September — immediately before the declaration of war — nearly 1.5 million people were moved under the government scheme, whilst another 2 million had evacuated themselves privately. In terms of the number of people evacuated, the government's arrangements were highly successful, but little consideration had been given to the compatibility of the evacuees and those already living in the reception areas:

> The indiscriminate handing round of evacuees in the billeting of 1939 inevitably resulted in every conceivable kind of social and psychological misfit. Conservative and Labour supporters, Roman Catholics and Presbyterians, lonely spinsters and loud-mouthed, boisterous mothers, the rich and the poor . . . the sensitive and the tough, were thrown into daily intimate contact (Titmuss, 1950, p. 112).

The mutual hostility which this provoked was intensified by the fact that no bombs fell, and within a few days the great majority of the official evacuees had returned home. The immediate and most obvious result of the scheme was thus a flood of complaints about verminous children and feckless parents. More fundamentally, however, the evacuation had shattered the mutual ignorance of the social classes and people in the reception areas saw for the first time the effects of the unemployment and the poverty of the 1930s.

Titmuss went on to argue that a second, decisive change occurred in the aftermath of the retreat from Dunkirk. Now Britain stood alone and the possibility of invasion and occupation confronted everyone. The result was a sense of unity and common purpose, and a fierce resentment of privilege. 'If dangers were to be shared then resources were also to be shared' (p. 508). 'Fair shares' became both the official slogan and the dominant mood. It found expression in food rationing, in high taxation, and in a virtual transformation of social policy.

Nowhere was the change more dramatic than in the provision of school meals. Before the war, meals had been provided only after a medical inspection had confirmed that the child was suffering from malnutrition.[3] In 1938 there were around 150,000 such children receiving a hot meal in a 'feeding centre', and another 560,000 were being given 'milk meals' — usually a drink and a biscuit. It was not believed to be necessary to provide for children in general, although the Board of Education had come to recommend the introduction of school canteens 'at which normal children may receive nourishing dinners on payment of a moderate charge' (Cmd. 6013, pp. 42–4). During the war, however, the overriding priority was the need to ensure that every child had at least one nourishing meal a day. By 1945, the stigmatized and humiliating feeding centres had been replaced by school canteens, and the number of children eating at school had risen to 1.7 million (Gosden, 1976, pp. 185–209).

The changes made in the accommodation provided for the victims of bombing was another example. Accommodation was originally provided under the poor law, with predictable results. In 1939, for example, the London County Council was refused permission to provide blankets on the grounds that they would tempt people to stay in the centres (Titmuss, 1950, p. 53). The onset of the blitz, however, brought a torrent of protests as — contrary to official expectations — the centres came to be used by all social classes and not just the poor. By the end of 1941 'the transformation was complete' and the 'bleak inhospitable poor law standards' had given way to decent board and lodgings available to all without charge (p. 267). For Titmuss, the crucial point was that not even the staunchest champion of liberalism could hold someone responsible for the bombs which fell on their home:

> What this period of the war meant to a great many people was less social disparagement. There was nothing to be ashamed of in being 'bombed out' by the enemy. Public sympathy with, and approval of, families who suffered in the raids was in sharp contrast to the low social evaluation accorded to those who lost material standards through being unemployed during the nineteen-thirties (p. 347).

It was a similar story in social assistance, discussed in the following section, and in the provision of milk to children and expectant mothers. In nearly every case, the new initiatives and improvements were supported by all parties. Indeed, what impressed Titmuss most of all was 'the unanimity underlying policy and the speed at which decisions were acted on' (p. 514).

There was no doubt that it was the mood of egalitarianism which gave the Labour Party its overwhelming victory in the General Election of 1945. Nearly everyone had expected that the personal popularity of Churchill would ensure victory for the Conservatives, but in the event their association with the 1930s outweighed even this. It does not follow, however, that welfare legislation was itself a matter of party politics. Indeed, the 'underlying' unanimity emphasized by Titmuss could be seen as evidence of a consensus which embraced all parties, and would have led to the introduction of the same measures whoever had won the election. This theme has been developed in Paul Addison's controversial study, *The Road to 1945* (1977).Addison agrees that 1940 was the crucial year. 'It should . . . go down as the year when the foundations of political power shifted decisively leftward for a decade.' The immediate cause of this shift was the manner and terms of Labour's entry into the Coalition, but it was firmly rooted in the 'pervasive ideals' of egalitarianism and community feeling. 'The political influence of the ration book', Addison wrote, 'seems to me to have been greater than that of all the left-wing propaganda of the war years put together' (p. 18). He went on to argue, however, that it was the Coalition which responded to the radicalism of the war years, and that the Labour government 'had only to consolidate and extend the consensus achieved under the Coalition' (p. 261). Furthermore, the measures taken by the Coalition had their origins not on the political left but in the 'progressive centre' which had emerged in the 1930s. It was non-socialist intellectuals such as Keynes and Beveridge, and bodies such as Political and Economic Planning and the Spens Committee on secondary education, which provided the stimulus for the major innovations in economic and social policy. It follows that they were often closer to Conservative thinking than to socialism and Addison concluded that the 'consensus developed in the 1940s represented a dilution of Conservative rather than Labour politics' (p. 271).

Addison's interpretation has been challenged by a number of writers. Lewis Minkin (1981), for example, has argued that unity within the Coalition was maintained only by avoiding contentious issues such as the law relating to trades disputes and the nationalization of mines. Moreover, the behaviour of the Conservatives in opposition is not necessarily an indication of the stance they would have adopted had they won the election. 'Acceptance in the later 1940s of the changes that had already taken place – that was one thing. It should not be taken as synonymous with their willingness to carry through a similar reconstruction themselves in 1945' (p. 32). Criticisms have also been made of Titmuss's account. In particular, John MacNicol (1978) has shown that the introduction of family allowances in 1945 owed very little to a concern with social justice and a great deal to the belief that they would maintain work incentives and help to curb wage demands.

It would be wrong to try to evaluate either the Addison or the Titmuss books on the basis of only one aspect of social policy. Nonetheless a number of conclusions can be drawn from the evidence relating to the means test, and it may be helpful to state these at the outset. In respect of the means test, Titmuss's description of the changes in public attitudes was entirely accurate, but he exaggerated the extent to which those attitudes were shared in Whitehall. The verdict on Addison must be that he was right for the wrong reasons. There was a convergence of policy over the means test, but this was not due to a 'genuine fusion of purpose' (p. 165), but because the same policy was viewed in very different ways by Labour and the Conservatives.


*THE TRANSFORMATION OF SOCIAL ASSISTANCE*

Titmuss was primarily concerned with the emergency services introduced during the war, and he said relatively little about the changes which occurred in the established social services. In a perceptive footnote, however, he observed that a historian would find 'much material' in the work of the Assistance Board and in particular in its insistence that local officials adopt a more courteous and sympathetic approach than they had in earlier years (p. 297n). In fact the history of social assistance during the war not only provides strong evidence in support of Titmuss's interpretation of the period, but was also a crucial influence upon the shape of post-war policy. There were three developments which were important: the Prevention and Relief of Distress scheme (PRD) inaugurated at the outset of the war, the introduction of supplementary pensions in 1940 and the abolition of the household means test in 1941.

The PRD scheme was designed to cover those who were in need because of the war, and who would otherwise have been forced to apply to the poor law. It took the form of regulations which enabled the UAB to provide assistance to evacuees and others who had lost their livelihood but were not eligible for unemployment benefit (Cmd. 6883, pp. 7–9). The Board was also given the power to make immediate grants to people whose homes had been damaged by enemy action. The numbers involved were relatively small — no more than 48,000 PRD allowances were in payment at any one time — but the ability of the Board to provide prompt and generous help was believed to have played an important part in maintaining civilian morale (*The Times*, 31 May 1941).

The supplementary pensions scheme was much more

significant. Prices rose sharply at the beginning of the war and this led to strong pressure for higher pensions. The Treasury, however, argued that an increase in national insurance pensions would be wasteful since the great majority of pensioners had savings or other sources of income. The Chancellor, Sir John Simon, told the Cabinet in January 1940 that only 10.5 per cent were receiving a supplement from the poor law 'and it is difficult to believe that there are still any very large number who prefer destitution to the alleged indignity of applying for public assistance' (PRO, 1940a). If it was necessary to provide a more generous supplement then this could be done most easily through the UAB. The local authorities would object to any further burden on the rates, whilst the experience of transitional payments in the 1930s had demonstrated that some authorities could not be trusted with the administration of monies provided by central goverment. Simon's proposals were quickly accepted by the rest of the Cabinet. In all some 400,000 old people were expected to apply to the renamed Assistance Board (AB) for a supplementary pension, 125,000 more than had gone to the poor law. The scheme was thus seen as a very limited one even by the government, whilst the Labour opposition was furious both at the failure to provide an increase for all pensioners and at the use of the Board. Its chief spokesman Arthur Greenwood said that 'as one who dislikes the poor law system' he would 'prefer that to this new method'. Similarly the Clydeside MP George Buchanan declared that 'under the Bill large numbers will be worse off and . . . few will be better off' (*Hansard*, 357, 1479, 2305).

In the event the number applying to the Board was not 400,000 but 1,275,000, a figure which stunned contemporary politicians and observers. Moreover, the response varied widely from one part of the country to another. Overall the number of claims from people who had not previously sought poor relief was eight times that which had been expected, but this figure varied from twice as many in Glasgow to 24 times as many in Bristol (Deacon, 1981a). The reason, of course, was that the number of unexpected claims was greatest in the areas where the shame of the poor law was felt most keenly, and the reaction to the scheme was a remarkable demonstration of the extent to which the stigma of pauperism still survived in many areas.[4] Even more remarkable, however, was the response of the Board to its new clientele.

The Act which introduced supplementary pensions included provision that the Board should conduct its administration 'in such a manner as may best promote the interests of pensioners'. Such a requirement was rendered academic in the early days of the scheme by the sheer volume of claims, and the Board was forced to adopt some remarkable expedients to handle the new work. Relatives and friends were 'pressed into service as casual clerks', undergraduates were recruited for the vacations and 'flying squads' of experienced officers were formed to visit the more hard-pressed offices (Deacon, 1981a). Both the new and the existing staff, however, were told of 'the need for a special approach to pensioners' and it is impossible to tell how far the changes recorded below were due to the influx of new staff, or to a change in attitude on the part of the existing officials.

In the Autumn of 1941 the Board launched a detailed enquiry into the circumstances of the pensioners and particularly into the proportion who were infirm or were living alone. Individual members of the Board made their own investigations and it is clear that the conditions experienced by some pensioners made a deep impression. Following a visit to Chesterfield and Sheffield, for example, Violet Markham wrote that 'the poor quality of housing renders the more admirable the astonishingly high standard of cleanliness and order amongst the pensioners' (PRO, 1941a).

Similar comments were made by other members of the Board which came increasingly to see itself as the champion of the pensioners' interests. In 1942, for example, it launched a major enquiry into clothing needs, visiting all those who had no resources other than their pension — some 480,000 cases — and making additional grants to 70 per cent of them (PRO, 1942). By this time the Board had also begun to develop what it termed its welfare services. These included a programme of regular visits to pensioners who appeared to be particularly isolated — over 40 per cent of supplementary pensioners were women living alone — as well as encouraging the local officials to refer claimants to other agencies who might be able to help with particular problems. Examples given to the staff were voluntary organizations for a hot meal, the district nurse, or the local health authority in cases where a landlord refused to carry out repairs (Cmd. 6700, pp. 8–14). In 1943 the Board assumed responsibility for widows with dependent children, and the officers were told to be prepared to assist with applications for such items as utility furniture, free school meals, free milk or assisted holidays (Cmd. 6883, pp. 10–17). The Board itself had no doubts as to the value of this work, and it is clear that it wished to expand its welfare role in any post-war reconstruction. Violet Markham wrote in 1944, for example, that the Board should be given the task of 'administering a system of National Welfare available for all sections of insured persons'. Otherwise, she added, they could be left providing means-tested benefits to 'poor law toughs' and with nothing constructive to offer the staff (PRO, 1944). It is difficult to tell how far Miss Markham's enthusiasm for welfare work was shared by the pensioners. The Nuffield survey received conflicting evidence on the work of the Board, and found some suspicion of its attempt to introduce 'a social work element' (Harris, n.d., p. 16). This was in 1942, however, and there is considerable evidence that the standing of the Board had risen quite remarkably by the end of the war. Perhaps the best indication of this is the response to the introduction of higher national insurance pensions in 1946. When asked by the Board, two-thirds of those who had been receiving a regular visit said that they wished the visits to continue even if they were no longer eligible for a supplementary pension (Cmd. 7184, p. 10).

Another reason for the enhanced popularity of the Board was the fact that it was no longer administering a household means test. The household principle was virtually abolished by the Determination of Needs Act of 1941, and there is little doubt that this was largely due to the efforts of Ernest Bevin. As General Secretary of the Transport and General Workers Union, Bevin had been a prominent critic of the test in the 1930s and it was he who first raised the issue in October

1940 (PRO, 1940b). There were, however, a number of other factors. The introduction of supplementary pensions meant that the chief beneficiaries of any change would be the elderly and not the unemployed. Moreover, the administration of the test had been made much more difficult by the enormous movement of population — there were twenty million changes of address between September 1939 and June 1942 — and by the attempt to disregard war savings. *The Times* (7 November 1940) observed that 'so many modifications' had been made to the test that 'even those who stood by its principle' had 'come to see that its retention was politically impossible.'

.It is this combination of factors which explains why a regulation which had been at the centre of bitter controversy for a decade was finally withdrawn with scarcely a murmur of protest within Whitehall. Six days after Bevin's original memorandum, George Reid (Secretary to the Board) outlined an alternative set of regulations which were eventually to form the basis of the Act (PRO, 1940c). Where the claimant was living in someone else's household, the income of the other members was to be ignored unless they were the claimant's father, mother, son or daughter and the household income was more than £6 per head per week. In such cases benefit would be limited to 5 shillings a week pocket money. If the claimant was the head of the household, an income of 7 shillings a week was assumed from any non-dependent member who was in work and was earning over 55 shillings a week. In neither type of case would it be necessary for the Board to make detailed enquiries into the earnings or circumstances of the other members of the household. The administration of these regulations caused few problems, and around 240,000 claimants benefited immediately from the Act (Cmd. 6338, pp. 7, 10).

Thus, by the middle of the war both the regulations governing eligibility for social assistance and the manner in which they were administered had changed enormously. In January 1944 the transformation was completed by a substantial rise in the level of benefits. Once more Ernest Bevin played an important role. Encouraged by Bevin, the Assistance Board announced in the Spring of 1943 that it intended to simplify its regulations. In October it submitted to the Cabinet a set of proposals which included the abolition of Winter allowances and the withdrawal of its complex regulations on rent.[5] The Board recognized, however, that reform would be costly:

> So far as scales are concerned, simplicity consists of making the categories of people for whom rates are prescribed as few and as broad as possible. Such simplicity is expensive, because the broader the class the less homogeneous it will be, and the rate for the class must be appropriate to those with the greater rather than those with the lesser needs (PRO, 1943a).

It therefore recommended a substantial rise in the basic scales. On the basis of the official index of the cost of living the Board's proposals were 25 per cent higher than the subsistence scale set out in the Beveridge Report.[6] In fact, of course, the official index greatly underestimated the rate of inflation during the war, but even if the more accurate index produced by the London and Cambridge Economic Service (LCES) is used to measure price changes, the Board's proposals were still more generous than those of Beveridge. Indeed, the LCES index suggests that the 1944 scales were higher in real terms than those introduced in 1948. The Board justified its proposals in two ways. It argued that the old were 'peculiarly affected' by wartime shortages and difficulties in shopping, and that in any case it believed that 'something should be provided for old age pensioners' (PRO, 1943a). It would be wrong to see the Cabinet's acceptance of these proposals as having a decisive influence upon the subsequent relationship between insurance and assistance. Nonetheless the 1944 uprating did create an impression that the assistance scale was 'something more' than a poverty income, and this was to become extremely important a few years later.

In the context of the desperate shortages of manpower, materials and money occasioned by the war, the work of the Assistance Board was remarkable. By 1945 there were over 1.5 million supplementary pensioners, and together with their dependents they represented more than a quarter of all people over pension age. It was not simply a question of numbers, however, but of the attitudes held by the Board and, apparently, by its local staff. The resources devoted to ensuring that the lonely were visited or that the widow and her children had a holiday appear to confirm Titmuss's (1950, p. 508) description of 'the war-warmed impulse of people for a more generous society'. A very different picture emerges, however, from the official response to the Beveridge Report.

## BEVERIDGE AND THE COALITION

The main features of the Beveridge Report are well known. The centrepiece of Beveridge's plan for social security was a comprehensive scheme of social insurance providing cover against the loss or interruption of earnings due to unemployment, sickness or old age. The benefits were to be of unlimited duration and sufficient for subsistence, and this would ensure that means-tested assistance played only a minor role. It was, Beveridge wrote, 'first and foremost, a plan of insurance – of giving in return for contributions benefits up to subsistence level, as of right and without means test' (Cmd. 6404, p. 7). The public response to the Report is equally well known. As Jose Harris (1977, pp. 421–2) has remarked, it received a 'euphoric popular reception' when it was published in December 1942. This was partly due to the timing of its publication – a few days after the Battle of Alamein – but more than anything it reflected the fact that the Report seemed to offer a realistic plan for the removal of the means test. Indeed, there had been a remarkable measure of agreement on this question amongst those giving evidence to Beveridge (Harris, 1981, p. 251).

The popular enthusiasm for Beveridge was not shared by many in the Conservative Party or in Whitehall. Kopsch (1970), for example, has shown that the great majority of Conservative MPs were opposed to the payment of benefits at subsistence level. In December 1942 a secret committee was set up under the chairmanship of Ralph Assheton to ascertain the Party's views on Beveridge. Its report was presented to Churchill in the following month, and represented the views of around 90 per cent of Tory MPs. It emphatically rejected the idea of subsistence benefits. They would be too expensive and would undermine the incentive to work and to save. It also opposed the payment of unemployment benefit as of right for unlimited periods and argued that anyone out of work for more than six months should be subject to a means test. A means test was also believed to be essential to prevent waste. Kopsch (1970, pp. 119–20) records that 'the majority of Conservatives favoured the retention of a major role for Assistance, based on the means test, on the grounds that a test of need would ensure that income would not be redistributed to those who had sufficient resources for subsistence'.

Equally forthright criticisms were made by a committee of officials chaired by Sir Thomas Phillips of the Ministry of Labour. This reported to the Cabinet Reconstruction Committee on 9 January, and began by stating that it was quite unrealistic to attempt to provide subsistence benefits through an insurance scheme. The problem was that the benefits were to be paid at a flat rate, whereas the cost of subsistence varied widely from one claimant to another depending on the amount they paid in rent. This meant that Beveridge's scheme could only provide subsistence in cases where the rent was high by making excessive payments to the majority of claimants. Moreover, the contributions levied on people in work would not vary with their earnings but would also be paid at a flat rate. In consequence they would have to be fixed at a level which the lowest paid worker could afford, and this would impose a severe limit upon the benefits which could be provided out of the insurance fund. The committee concluded that claimants with higher rents would have to apply for a supplementary payment, and that 'the scheme does not itself avoid recourse to a means test to the extent one would assume from the opening statement of principles'. The numbers subjected to a means test were a matter 'more of judgement than of fundamental principle', and the officials went on to recommend that unemployment and sickness benefits be paid at a higher rate than pensions:

Attainment of the age of 65 is the inescapable fate of those who live long enough and it is arguable that there is nothing inherently unreasonable in basing a scheme on the assumption that many will make some provision on their own behalf against a circumstance which can be precisely foreseen.

The committee was adamant that there should be a limit on the duration of unemployment benefit, and it was scornful of Beveridge's assumption that post-war unemployment would not exceed 8.5 per cent — 'recollections of the actual course of events after the last war must obtrude themselves' (PRO, 1943b).

These two 'reports' do much to explain the negative stance of some Conservative ministers during the famous Commons debate on the Beveridge Report in February 1943 (*Hansard*, 386, 1613--94; 1765--1916; 1964--2050). The lack of enthusiasm shown on this occasion, however, had a marked effect on public attitudes and morale (Mass Observation, 1943) and criticisms of Beveridge became much more muted following this debate. As a result the Conservative Party Conference of 1943 was dominated by the pro-Beveridge Tory Reform Committee and this created a misleading impression of the attitude of the party as a whole (Kopsch, 1970, p. 146).

The White Paper on *Social Insurance*, which was published by the Coalition in September 1944, departed little from the proposals of the Phillips Committee. The principle of subsistence benefits was explicitly rejected. Instead, benefits were to provide 'a reasonable insurance against want', whilst taking account of 'the maximum contribution which the great body of contributors can properly be asked to bear' (Cmd. 6550, p. 7). Family allowances were to be introduced for second and subsequent children as Beveridge had recommended, but here too the principle of subsistence was rejected (p. 14). Unemployment benefit was to be limited to 30 weeks, and the White Paper also rejected Beveridge's proposal that the administration of insurance and assistance be merged in a single Minstry of Social Security. The government, it said, attached 'great importance to the preservation of the distinction between insurance and assistance' (p. 36). The level of pension was to be below that of unemployment and sickness benefit, but the new pensions were to be paid in full from the start of the scheme and not phased in over a period of 20 years as Beveridge had recommended. This latter decision was widely criticized at the time as being over-generous to pensioners, particularly as family allowances were to be well below the level proposed by Beveridge. *The Times* (26 September 1944), for example, remarked that it seemed 'to reflect the fact that pensioners have votes while children have none'. In part, however, the decision was forced on the government by the relatively generous level of assistance established in 1944. R.A. Butler, the Minister of Education, explained to the Commons that if the higher pensions had not been paid from the outset 'there would . . . [have been] . . . a greater need for pensioners to turn to assistance, and the Exchequer would have had to pay just the same' (*Hansard*, 404, 1110).

The election of the Labour government in July 1945 brought no dramatic change in policy. In February 1946, however, James Griffiths — the new Minister of National Insurance — announced that the principal rates of benefit would be 26 shillings a week for a single person and 42 shillings for a couple, compared with 24 shillings and 40 shillings proposed in the White Paper. The government, he claimed, had 'endeavoured to give a broad subsistence basis to the leading rates' (*Hansard*, 418, 1742). The grounds for this 'historic fluff sentence' (Abel-Smith, 1963) were the fact that a strict application of the rise in the official cost of living index to Beveridge's figures would have produced rates broadly comparable to those proposed by Griffiths. It has already been noted, however, that the official index grossly underestimated the rise in prices during the war, and in any case the 5 shilling family allowance provided nothing like a broad subsistence basis for children.[7] The position was obscured at first because the rates proposed for the insurance scheme were compared to the levels of assistance established in 1944. On this basis *The Economist* (2 February 1946) described the National Insurance Bill as the 'virtual abolition of the means test' and such statements appeared to be borne out when the new pension rates were introduced in advance of the main scheme in October 1946. The number of supplementary pensioners dropped from 1.47 million to just over 500,000, and the average supplement fell from 16 shillings to 5 shillings (Cmd. 7184, p. 8).

The government, however, faced a real dilemma when it came to decide what should be the level of national assistance when that scheme went into operation in July 1948. The price index was more accurate after June, 1947, and it rose sharply towards the end of the year. By the time it finally became necessary to fix the assistance scales in the Spring of 1948, the index was 8 per cent above its 1946 level. The Cabinet believed that it would be administratively and financially impossible to increase the insurance benefits further, and it was faced with the choice of either launching the assistance scheme with an effective cut in the benefits it provided, or accepting that the means test would play a greater role. It chose the latter.

The way in which the assistance scale was determined was somewhat complex, and has been described elsewhere (Deacon, 1982). The important point is that the new scales of 24 shillings for a single person and 40 shillings for a couple, exclusive of rent, were higher than the corresponding insurance benefits in the great majority of cases. In December 1948, some 675,000 claimants were having their insurance benefits 'topped up' by the NAB, and this figure had risen to over a million by the end of 1951.

## WAS THERE A CONSENSUS?

At first sight the system of social security introduced in the 1940s appears to confirm Addison's view of the essentially conservative nature of post-war social reform. There is no doubt that it was the emphasis placed upon means-tested national assistance which secured Conservative support for *Social Insurance*, and after 1944 it was the Tory Reform Committee which had to swallow its principles and remain silent (Kopsch, 1970, pp. 169–70). It is hardly surprising, therefore, that the Conservative Party as a whole found little to oppose in Labour's National Insurance Act.

And yet to speak of a consensus is profoundly misleading. It would be more accurate to say that the parties arrived at a common policy by different routes. The Labour Party genuinely believed that the means test was no longer a serious problem. The household means test had gone, and it was seen in the previous chapter that a personal means test was not viewed with anything like the same hostility. In 1947 the last vestiges of the household principle disappeared with the withdrawal of the £6 rule, and Aneurin Bevan told the Commons: 'I have spent many years of my life in fighting the means test. Now we have practically ended it. In future only the resources of the man and dependent children . . . will be taken into account in determining their needs' (*Hansard*, 444, 1606). This was not just political rhetoric, and the difference between the two types of means test was emphasized in academic studies. David Marsh (1950, p. 148), for example, wrote of national assistance in 1950: 'There is no real means test, in the sense of which that phrase was used in previous measures of Public Assistance'. Moreover, the experience of the Assistance Board seemed to show that the problem of take-up was confined to the poor law, and there was little reason to believe that old people would object to having to apply to the NAB. As far as the unemployed and the sick were concerned, the government's position was that it did not matter if people receiving short-term insurance benefits did not claim the supplementary payments to which they were nominally entitled. The UAB had tried to discourage such claims and it was assumed that similar restrictions would continue under the NAB.[8] This attitude rested in turn upon the belief that the assistance scale did not represent an official poverty line, and that someone living on a slightly lower income was not necessarily suffering hardship. Steele, Griffiths's Parliamentary Secretary, told the Commons in June 1948 that the new rates provided 'an appreciable margin over bare subsistence' (*Hansard*, 452, 564). This seemed to be confirmed by the results of Rowntree's third study of poverty in York. The proportion of the working-class population with an income below Rowntree's poverty standard fell from 31.1 per cent in 1936 to 2.7 per cent in 1950, and the new welfare measures were the biggest single cause of the fall.[9]

What emerged then was a policy which was all things to all men. An enormous shift towards universalism had occurred, and the areas of means testing that remained were seem as unimportant by Labour but were sufficient to reassure the Conservatives. The gulf between what was now common ground and what had existed in the 1930s was so wide as to make the remaining differences seem marginal. Indeed the whole debate was conducted with reference to the past rather than the future. It is striking, for example, that the withdrawal of the household means test in 1941 was discussed almost entirely in terms of the unemployed, even though the vast proportion of those affected were pensioners. As Bessie Braddock remarked on the second reading of the National Assistance Bill; 'I think of what we are repealing more than of what we are proposing' (*Hansard*, 444, 1631). The preoccupation with the 1930s created a defensiveness on the Right which meant that the welfare measures were subjected to strikingly little criticism. As Jose Harris (1981, p. 258) has noted, this represented a consensus of 'a rather peculiar kind. It was a consensus based not upon a reconciliation or compromise between conflicting ideas, but rather upon the falling away of certain interests and opinions that were powerful features of the normal peacetime spectrum of opinion in British political life'. All of this meant that the planning of post-war reconstruction proceeded relatively quickly:

> But it meant also that the kind of welfare state policies designed in the 1940s were ill-equipped to meet the criticisms either of free marketeers or of theoretical socialists or simply of moderate people who disliked paying taxes or who disliked excessive officialdom, when all these groups began gradually to resurface in the years after the war (p. 259).

This was particularly true of 'universalism'.

*NOTES*

1. The exceptions were private hospital beds, the repair of spectacles and other appliances broken through negligence, and domestic help provided for patients after discharge from hospital (Maynard, 1980, p. 47).
2. At the outbreak of war there were around one million on the poor law, and 600,000 receiving unemployment assistance. The number claiming national assistance was 842,000 in July 1948, and this figure rose to just over a million by the end of the year. (Dependents are excluded from each total.) There would have been a much larger fall in the amounts paid, since two-thirds of national assistance claimants were receiving a relatively small supplement to insurance benefits. In addition, the number receiving a non-contributory pension (Note 2, Chapter 2) fell from 650,000 in 1938 to 450,000 in 1948.
3. In County Durham, for example, as many as 17 per cent of the children in some schools were found to be undernourished, and the position was not much better in parts of South Wales (Cmd. 3307, p. 69).
4. Some of the additional claims would have been due to the fact that supplementary pensions were paid at a higher rate than that provided by most PACs. Nearly one-third of the initial claims were refused, usually because of the amount the claimant had in savings.
5. The original regulation was described in the previous chapter (p. 24). After January 1944, the scales were calculated exclusive of rent, and the rent paid by the claimant was simply added to his or her weekly benefit, save in exceptional circumstances where the amount was considered unreasonable.
6. Beveridge had estimated subsistence needs in 1938 prices, and hence the rate of inflation in subsequent years is crucial to any comparison. According to the official index Beveridge's scale for a pensioner couple represented 27 shillings and 6 pence a week plus rent in 1943, compared to the 35 shillings a week plus rent proposed by the Board.
7. The official index rose 29 per cent between 1938 and 1943, but was virtually stable for the rest of the war. The LCES index shows a rise of 42 per cent between 1938 and 1943, and then a further rise of 14 per cent between 1943 and 1947, giving an overall increase of 67 per cent. It should be emphasized, however, that the LCES index measured the change in the general cost of living, not in the cost of subsistence. When the Board's officials did calculate the cost of a subsistence diet early in 1948, their estimate was nearly double

that which they would have obtained by inflating Beveridge's figure by the official index, and 15 per cent above the figure which would have emerged from using the LCES index. The wide discrepancy with the official index is not surprising since that had been carefully manipulated during the war in order to reduce the pressure for higher wages (Deacon, 1982, pp. 298–9).

8. The power to make supplementary payments to those receiving unemployment insurance benefits had passed from the PACs to the UAB in 1937. The Board, however, had always sought to discourage such applications. It decided that no assistance would be payable for the first four weeks of unemployment, and then only if the claimant was entitled to at least 2 shillings and 6 pence a week (PRO, 1937). These restrictions were maintained throughout the war, and in 1947 there were only 9,000 claimants receiving assistance as well as insurance benefit (Cmd. 7502, p. 6)

9. Rowntree calculated that if the welfare measures of 1950 had been the same as those of 1936, then 22.2 per cent of the working-class population would have been in poverty. If there had been no food subsidies, the proportion would have been 13.7 per cent and if unemployment had been the same as 1936, 7.8 per cent would have been in poverty (Rowntree and Lavers, 1951).

# CHAPTER 4

# The Selectivity Debate

The 'peculiar consensus' of the war years remained largely undisturbed in the 1950s. True there were arguments over the introduction of charges into the health service, over the decontrol of rents and over the level and finance of pensions, but none of these represented a serious challenge to the structure or scope of the existing social services. By the end of the 1960s, however, the picture was quite different. On the one hand, the welfare state was being attacked as an expensive and wasteful anachronism which should be replaced as far as possible by private markets in education, housing, life assurance and medical care. On the other it was being criticized for its failure to achieve a more fundamental redistribution of income and wealth, which in turn was seen as requiring a much greater transfer of resources from private consumption to the public services. This chapter traces the emergence of these two critiques, and examines the so-called 'universality *versus* selectivity' debates of the 1960s. It shows how the rediscovery of poverty by those academics who sought greater redistribution had the paradoxical effect of appearing to confirm the criticism that universal benefits failed to channel resources to those who needed them most. Finally, the chapter examines the way in which the experiences of the 1964–70 Labour government gave rise to a further debate over the extent to which it was realistic to expect governments to adopt redistributive measures in periods of low economic growth.

## FIRST CRITICS: THE CONSERVATIVES IN THE 1950s

Labour's welfare legislation presented the Conservative

opposition with something of a dilemma. Many of the front-bench spokesmen had been involved in the planning of the measures during the war, and hence found it difficult to object to them in principle. Nonetheless, they were anxious to appear to be putting forward their own distinctive view, and the result was much vague and at times tortuous rhetoric on the need for priorities, the importance of economic growth and the extravagance of socialist administration. During the late 1940s, the party had been forced to reconsider its whole approach to economic policy, under the intellectual leadership of 'Rab' Butler and his protégés at the Research Department (Butler, 1971, pp. 126—53). Relatively little thought had been given to social policy, however, and the first real attempt to provide the Conservatives with a coherent approach to the social services was the pamphlet *One Nation*, published in 1950 by a group of younger MPs including Edward Heath, Iain Macleod, Robert Carr and Enoch Powell. This began with an emphatic declaration:

> There is a fundamental disagreement between Conservatives and Socialists on the questions of social policy. Socialists would give the same benefits to everyone, whether or not the help is needed, and indeed whether or not the country's resources are adequate. We believe that we must first help those in need. Socialists believe that the State should provide an average standard. We believe that it should provide a minimum standard, above which people should be free to rise as far as their industry, their thrift, their ability or their genius may take them (ONG, 1950, p. 9).

Behind the rhetoric, however, the pamphlet made no specific proposals for change, other than a reduction in food subsidies and the introduction of charges for medical appliances, hospital board and prescriptions (pp. 54—6). Even these were scarcely evidence of a 'fundamental disagreement' between the parties, since Sir Stafford Cripps, Labour's Chancellor, had issued dire warnings of the need to restrict spending in these fields in his budget speech in April 1949 (Dow, 1970, pp. 40, 45—6). The main concern in both parties was the escalating cost of the health service, and especially the phenomenal demand for teeth and spectacles (Watkin, 1978, p. 33). Bevan, as Minister of Health had averted the introduction of charges in 1950 by agreeing to the establishment of a special weekly Cabinet committee to scrutinize health spending, but the onset of the Korean War and the appointment of Hugh Gaitskell to replace Cripps led to the imposition of a charge for dentures and spectacles in May 1951 (Foot, 1973, pp. 320–9; Williams, 1979, pp. 249–55). For its part *One Nation* declared that defence had to be given priority over the social services, but shrank from pursuing the argument to its logical conclusion, calling instead 'on all those engaged in industry' for 'a great effort' to increase production in order 'to save the social services' (p. 92).

In 1952 Macleod and Powell published a subsequent pamphlet, *The Social Services: Needs and Means*. This also began with a flourish. The essential features of a social service, they argued, were that it was provided for an individual and that it contained an element of redistribution. It followed from this that:

> the general presumption must be that they will be rendered only on evidence of need, i.e, of financial inability to provide each particular service out of one's own or one's family's resources . . . The question therefore which poses itself is not, 'should a means test be applied to a social service?' but 'why should any social service be provided *without* test of need?' (1952, p. 5).

Once again, however, the remainder of the pamphlet proved to be an anti-climax. Indeed it contained only one significant suggestion, and that involved a reduction in the role of the means test. Since July 1948, the proportion of pensioners who were also in receipt of national assistance had risen from 14 per cent to nearly 23 per cent. Macleod and Powell declared this to be 'an entirely indefensible position', since a compulsory contributory scheme was now providing little more than a grant in aid towards a system of maintenance through means-tested assistance (p. 31). Their solution was to increase national insurance benefits, even though that would require what Powell (*The Listener*, 17 April 1952) later called 'a steep rise' in contributions.

There were always some members of the Conservative Party who viewed the collectivism of the post-war years with distaste, and who argued for a greater emphasis on individual rights and responsibilities (Hoffman, 1964, p. 213). The weekly meetings of the One Nation Group provided a forum for such views, and also for those who criticized the apparently indiscriminate nature of much spending on welfare. Wigs and spectacles were one example, and the allocation of council housing was another. In June 1954, *The Economist* wondered whether the means test was 'a dog that has been given a bad name':

> Anybody who lives near a post-war housing estate is familiar with the private cars parked outside, and with the television aerials that festoon the roofs of houses and flats whose occupants pay a half or even less of their cost. Resentment is building up (as can be seen from the local press) at the lavish benefits that are being enjoyed by people, some of whom so evidently do not need the help they get (5 June 1954).

For others the growing importance of assistance merely highlighted the impossibility of providing an adequate income for all, and this failure of Beveridgeism' was emphasized more and more as the future cost of pensions became clear. The debate over the future of the national insurance scheme is discussed in Chapter 6. The important point here is that, by the mid-1950s, it was widely assumed that the increase in the number of old people would impose an impossible burden on the fund unless assistance was allowed to play a substantial role.

Conservative governments in the 1950s did take some steps which could be said to have reflected these feelings, most notably the introduction of prescription charges in 1952 and the reduction of housing subsidies in 1956. In general, however, they showed little enthusiasm for change in the social services, and this is often interpreted by their critics as timidity. *The Economist* (5 June 1954), for example, was quite sure that 'the principle of requiring proof of need' was 'as morally sound' as it was 'financial imperative', but added that it took 'courage to advocate the simple principle that no-one should live on the taxpayer unless he needs to'. In fact, however, the attitude of successive Conservative governments stemmed largely from a general satisfaction with progress since 1951. As Gamble (1974, p. 63) has remarked, the 1950s 'were not a period when the party was much given to reflection. The post-war settlement worked, and it was Conservatives who were making it work'. Moreover policy making within the Party was stilll dominated by Butler and Macmillan who had been the chief architects of that settlement, whilst Macmillan's skill as a party manager was to prove most effective in forestalling criticism in later years. On several occasions he adopted the tactic of asking the most fervent advocates of economy to head high-spending ministries. Both Macleod and Powell, for example, served as Minister of Health — where neither showed much interest in change. Nonetheless the most important single factor was the legacy of the 1930s. As *The Times* (17 January 1952) remarked in an editorial on *Needs and Means*, 'in no country is the means test, as a condition of social aid, so widely resented as in Britain'. Indeed Macmillan's whole approach was based in part on the belief that any move towards means testing would be an electoral gift to Labour, and in part upon a personal revulsion against anything which could be seen as marking a return to the 1930s.

The opprobium attached to the means test was also recognized by those who were unsympathetic to universalist social policies. In 1953, for example, Walter Hagenbuch (1953, p. 9) argued that Britain was drifting towards 'a system in which everyone becomes permanently dependent on the State for certain basic needs and will inevitably become more and more dependent. Not only are the social services no longer self-liquidating; they are self-propagating'. One solution would be to confine the benefits and services to those unable to provide them for themselves, but the unpopularity of the means test made this impossible. Instead he proposed that national insurance be made 'more genuine . . . in the sense of saving up for old age' and 'less equalitarian, in the sense of being increasingly financed out of general taxation' (p. 14). Exchequer subsidies would be withdrawn and the national insurance scheme would operate along the lines of an enormous friendly society, a massive, state-sponsored exercise in self-help. This idea was subsequently taken up by the One Nation Group (1959, pp. 38–40), who argued in 1959 that a much greater proportion of the cost of both pensions and health services should be met out of the contributions paid by workers and employers. By this time, however, others were proposing more drastic solutions.

## THE INSTITUTE OF ECONOMIC AFFAIRS

The Institute of Economic Affairs (IEA) was established in 1957. From the outset it argued for a major reduction in the role of government in economic and social affairs, and a much greater reliance upon market forces. This made it an implacable opponent not only of state welfare, but also of the prevailing emphasis upon macroeconomic policy and in particular of the Keynesian theories which were becoming increasingly influential in Whitehall. Indeed, it is important to stress that the studies of social policy which have been published or prompted by the IEA are only part, and arguably the least successful part, of its activities. It was not until the abandonment of the national plan in the mid-1960s, and, above all, the collapse of the 'Barber boom' and subsequent revival of neo-classical economics, that the IEA began to acquire the credibility and prestige which it enjoyed at the end of the 1970s.[1]

The central argument of the IEA has always been that much of the welfare state is unnecessary and that everyone should be free to purchase medical care, housing or education in the same way as they already purchase food, consumer durables, holidays and a host of other goods. Such a system of private markets is seen as preferable to government provision for two main reasons. First, the market preserves the individual's freedom of choice in contrast to the compulsion and regulation which is inherent in state welfare. In an early pamphlet on pensions, Arthur Seldon (1960, p. 8) claimed that in 'a society which values personal liberty':

A man will be free to decide whether to spend most of
his income on himself or his family while young enough
to enjoy it and leave the future to take care of itself,
or to live modestly while he earns and looks forward
to years of carefree ease when he retires. This is an inti-
mate, elemental, personal decision, and a free society
will not lightly tamper with it.

At the same time the individual must be prepared to bear
the consequences or his or her own decisions, and not automatically look to others for support if things go wrong. Such
independence, however, is quickly eroded if every eventuality
is provided for by the government, and a 'welfare state',
established with the best of motives, 'ends up by under-
mining self-respect and endangering social cohesion' (p. 37).
The second argument which is put forward in support of
the private market is that it is much more efficient at providing people with the particular combination of goods and
services which they prefer. The central notion here is that of
consumer choice between the goods offered by competing
suppliers. In a competitive market, the consumer's expenditure will reflect the order of his or her preferences. Goods
and services which are in the most demand will attract the
highest prices and this in turn will encourage more suppliers
to provide them. The most important point, however, is that
so long as there is competition between suppliers, any firm
which does not provide the consumer with what he or she
wants will go out of business. The case is summarized in the
famous remark of Adam Smith that it 'is not from the bene-
volence of the butcher, the brewer, or the baker that we
expect our dinner, but from their regard to their own interest'.
It follows from this that the proper role of government is
to create the conditions in which markets can work properly.
It should establish and enforce laws to regulate trade and
take steps to deal with monopoly suppliers, restrictive
practices and the other 'market imperfections' which occur in
the real world. What it should not do is to use those imperfections as an excuse to remove the market altogether. Indeed,
from the perspective of the IEA, nothing could be less
efficient or less likely to satisfy consumer wants than the

social services as they had been established after the war. Both the health and education services, for example, were near monopolies, provided almost free of charge at the point of delivery and financed out of general taxation. No individual had the freedom to alter the balance of his expenditure between, say, health, education or national insurance.

During the 1960s the IEA produced a series of papers on different areas of social policy. National insurance pensions were to be virtually wound up, and replaced with a means-tested scheme for the current generation of pensioners. The long-term solution to the problem of old age, however, was to be found in an expansion of private pension schemes (Seldon, 1960). The health service was to be gradually dismantled. In time hospitals would become private institutions and both they and general practitioners would be entirely dependent upon fees from patients. The patients would be able to meet these fees because of the medical insurance which they had been obliged to take out by the government (Lees, 1961). Schools would also become private institutions. Parents of children of school age would receive a voucher from the government which they could spend at a school of their choice. Some schools would charge only the voucher, whilst others would be able to charge additional fees depending upon the facilities they offered, or the demand for their particular style of teaching (Peacock and Wiseman, 1964). Individuals would thus choose a hospital or their child's school in the way that they choose a hotel or car. Those institutions which provided what the customers wanted would prosper, those that did not would go out of business.

There were, of course, differences in emphasis and tone between one pamphlet and another. They all, however, shared a number of assumptions. The first was that there is no significant difference between welfare goods and other marketable commodities, and this is discussed in the next section. The second assumption was that economic growth and rising personal incomes would substantially reduce the problem of poverty. Seldon (1960, p. 40), for example, claimed that 'by definition, the old in need are a dwindling minority. In ten or twenty years those who follow them will have earned sufficient to have saved for retirement'. The increase in living standards would also enable more people to pay the full cost of services which had previously been subsidized or wholly financed out of taxation. There would always be some who could not, however, and the third assumption was that an extension of the market would have to be preceded by a redistribution of income. This point was made by all of the authors. Lees (1961, p. 25), for example, conceded that low-income families would not be able to afford adequate insurance, but insisted that the 'appropriate solution' was for 'the state to pay out cash to whatever extent is considered necessary and to leave the market free to settle the production and distribution of goods'. More generally, Harris and Seldon (1979, p. 186) argued that the government should not supply goods or services for everyone, but channel 'direct financial support to the minority with inadequate incomes. State education and the NHS are supply responses to a deficiency of demand'. Similarly, Peacock and Wiseman (1964, p. 21) maintained that those who objected to the distribution of income and wealth should seek to alter it directly: 'education policy becomes even potentially relevant only if such general redistributive policies are technically impossible'.

The problem for the IEA, however, was that it found it impossible to convince even sympathetic politicians that sufficient redistribution was indeed 'technically possible'. The proposed mechanism was that of a negative income tax (NIT), and this is considered in some detail in Chapter 9. The important point here, however, is that whilst a large number of Conservative MPs — and some Labour ones — were enthusiastic about the idea, most were sceptical about the chances of putting it into practice. Without NIT, however, neither the IEA nor its supporters could suggest a way of securing a redistribution of income which was sufficient to enable the poor to participate in welfare markets and yet did not require a substantial increase in taxation for the better off.

By the early 1970s, then, the lack of a workable scheme of reverse taxation had become something of an Achilles heel for the IEA. It was this above all which made it difficult to persuade even the most sympathetic MPs to support a decisive move towards education vouchers or the privatization of parts of the NHS. This does not mean, however, that the IEA's arguments had no influence. On the contrary, its ideas contributed to the decision of the Conservative Party to adopt a policy of much greater selectivity within the existing services. In the case of child support, for example, the IEA had consistently maintained that it was wasteful to pay family allowances in respect of second and subsequent children in every family. Instead the money that was spent in this way on comfortable and even wealthy families should be channelled directly to the poor. This could be done either by a limited scheme of NIT, or, if that was not practicable in the short run, by making family allowances subject to a means test. Similar arguments were advanced in respect of council house rents, school meals and milk, and prescriptions. Throughout the welfare state, it was claimed, money was being wasted on people who could afford to provide for themselves, with the inevitable result that less was available for those in need. Two factors appeared to reinforce this message. The first was the growth of private affluence, symbolized by the increasing ownership of consumer durables. The number of cars and vans on the road doubled during the 1950s and doubled again in the 1960s. In the same period, the proportion of households with a refrigerator rose from 8 per cent to 69 per cent, and those with a television and washing machine from almost nil to 91 per cent and 64 per cent respectively (Marwick, 1982, p. 121). The second factor, however, was even more significant. This was the re-emergence of family poverty as an important political issue.

It was seen in the previous chapter that Rowntree's third survey of York in 1950 appeared to demonstrate that the post-war measures had all but eliminated poverty. In particular, his findings seemed to confirm the success of the national assistance scheme in lifting people out of poverty. This conclusion was questioned at the time (Townsend, 1952), but such doubts were not widely shared. Most people took it for granted that a continuation of the welfare state, full employment and higher wages had solved the problem, especially amongst those in work. Everything depended, however, upon what was meant by poverty, and Rowntree's approach was increasingly attacked by Peter Townsend and others. Rowntree's poverty standard was supposed to represent the income necessary to maintain subsistence, but Townsend argued that the calculation of such a standard involved arbitrary judgments of what was and was not necessary. Moreover, Rowntree's focus on subsistence meant that he took insufficient account of changes in the living standards of the population as a whole. Instead, it would be more realistic to take the national assistance scale as the basis of the poverty line, since this represented the official operational definition of the minimum level of living (Townsend, 1954, 1962). The corollary, of course, was that anyone whose income was below that which they would receive on assistance could be said to be in poverty. The most likely case was the old person who was eligible for assistance but failed to claim it, and it was this problem which attracted most attention in the late 1950s and early 1960s. Indeed, it was not until the publication in 1965 of Abel-Smith and Townsend's *The Poor and the Poorest* that poverty amongst people in work began to be recognized as a problem. The detailed story of the gradual acceptance of the 'relative' definition of poverty and of the estimates made of its extent has been told elsewhere.[2] The point here is that poverty was rediscovered only after it had been redefined. As Banting (1979, p. 68) has emphasized, it did not become an issue because of unrest amongst the poor, dramatic exposures, or agitation by the Labour Party or the trade unions. 'In Britain "poverty" was essentially a statistical concept. The poor did not make themselves visible: they were discovered at the bottom of incomes tables by social scientists'. The irony, of course, is that the last thing those 'social scientists' wanted to do was to give encouragement to the IEA.

## THE 'SELECTIVITY' DEBATE

As early as February 1952, Richard Titmuss had argued that the definition of the social services which Macleod and Powell had employed in *The Social Services: Needs and Means* was too narrow. It was 'too simple a view' to see them as something which existed for a small proportion of the population and was financed by the remainder:

> We are all now so inextricably mixed up in a society of artificial prices, payments, and benefits, free contributory, and partly free services and open and concealed subsidies, that it is no longer possible to put the social services in a separate compartment and regard them as largely paid for by one social group for the benefit of another group (*The Listener*, 14 February 1952).

In December 1955 he set out his ideas more fully in the famous lecture on 'The social division of welfare'. This has subsequently become the best known article in the literature on social policy, and it is important to remember that its arguments were originally advanced in response to those of the One Nation Group, Macleod and Powell, and the other early critics of the welfare state. Titmuss (1958a, p. 38) commented at the outset of his lecture that they constituted its 'political frame of reference'. The essence of Titmuss's argument was that the social services were only one of three distinct but related systems of welfare. The other two were occupational welfare and fiscal welfare. The former included the pensions, medical benefits and numerous fringe benefits provided by some companies, while the latter consisted primarily of the allowances and reliefs against tax which were granted in respect of wives, children and dependents. These three systems of welfare had developed to meet similar needs: 'They all reflect contemporary opinion that man is not wholly responsible for his dependency, and they all accept obligations for meeting certain dependent needs of the individual and the family' (p. 53). It followed from this that the conventional social services could not be viewed in isolation, and that developments in the three systems must be seen as a whole. 'The definition . . . of what is a "social service" should take its stand on aims; not on the administrative methods and institutional devices employed to achieve them' (p. 42). Titmuss's point, of course, was that the overall effect of the three systems was much less redistributive than his contemporaries supposed. Far from the welfare state imposing an ever-increasing burden upon a hard-pressed middle class, the three systems together were 'simultaneously enlarging and consolidating the area of social inequality' (p. 55). It was this argument which provided both the frame-work and the stimulus for much of the work undertaken by Townsend, Abel-Smith and others. In particular, the rediscovery of poverty was part of a wider attempt to document the extent of social inequality in post-war Britain. As Banting (1979, pp. 69–70) has noted, Titmuss, Townsend and Abel-Smith,

> were convinced that myths about the generosity of the Welfare State had blinkered discussion of social policy, and in the late 1950s they set out to gather the evidence with which to challenge the comfortable assumptions of the day. Their research was explicitly political: they were setting out to reshape [the] policy-makers' interpretation of their environment.

The fact remained, however, that the evidence which they assembled could be interpreted in two ways. They saw it as pointing to the need for a renewed effort to achieve the aims of the welfare state, others saw it as calling into question the feasibility and even the continued relevance of those aims. In trying to dispel what they saw as the myths surrounding the welfare state, Titmuss and his colleagues also strengthened the hand of those who sought its abolition.

This paradox lay at the heart of the so-called 'universality *versus* selectivity' debate of the 1960s. There were several strands to this debate. First, the desirability of a return to private markets in welfare; second, the introduction or extension of means testing within existing benefits and services so as to confine them to the poor; third, the extent to which additional public expenditure upon welfare in any form should be dependent upon economic growth. This last issue was thrown into sharp focus by the failure of the Labour governments of 1964–70 to achieve the rate of growth which they had promised whilst in opposition.

The key issue in the debate surrounding the role of the private market was the extent to which welfare services could be regarded in the same way as other consumer goods.

Abel-Smith (1964b, p. 6), for example, conceded that many people had little knowledge of technical goods such as cars or cameras. 'But the harm to the individual from an unwise choice of these goods is of a very different order to the damage done by going to a shabby private school, an ill-equipped nursing home, a dishonest doctor or a bad insurance agent, broker or company.' The arguments were fiercest in respect of health. Titmuss (1968, p. 146) provided a list of reasons why medical care was different from other goods. Consumers did not know when they needed it, they could not always evaluate the treatment they received and would have great difficulty in returning it to the seller. 'For many people the consequences of consuming medical care are irreversible.' A requirement that everyone should take out medical insurance would not lessen the problems, since commercial companies would have to practise risk-rating. Just as someone with a long history of accidents or a conviction for dangerous driving would have to pay more to insure their car, so the chronically ill or others most likely to need medical care would have to pay a higher premium. The alternative would be to retain a separate service for the poor, but services for the poor were always poor services. 'Insofar as they are able to recruit at all . . . they tend to recruit the worst rather than the best teachers, doctors, nurses, administrators and other categories of staff' (p. 143). The critics of private medicine came increasingly to cite the American system as proof of the disastrous consequences of allowing the profit motive into medical care, and this gave rise to a further round of charge and counter-charge.[3]

Not surprisingly the IEA's critics were dismissive of the NIT proposal, and openly contemptuous of the 'computer-mania' which underpinned it.[4] Perhaps the most significant aspect of the debate over NIT, however, was the way in which it reflected the contrasting perceptions of poverty held by the IEA and their critics. The scheme was invariably put forward as a replacement for some or all of the existing benefits, and so each proposal contained a break-even point at which the value of NIT began to be offset by the loss of other benefits. This was often at very low levels of income, and the scheme put forward by the IEA study group was particularly ungenerous (Barker, 1971, pp. 62–5). Townsend (1968, p. 6) argued that such a scheme was based upon a view of poverty as the lack of a minimum income 'which requires little more than the diversion of a minute proportion of national income in an efficient manner to alleviate . . . It also assumes that the circumstances of the poor can be greatly improved without changing major social institutions.' The same criticisms were made of means tests in general. By definition, they were designed to confine benefits and services to the poor whereas, for Titmuss or Townsend, it was essential that they were provided for the whole community. Only then, they argued, could the social services foster social integration and a sense of community as they had done during the war.

Titmuss's own perception of the role of the social services was based upon the premise that they were a form of partial compensation, both for those with unmerited handicap and for those who bore the social costs of economic change. Titmuss was writing in the 1950s and 1960s when unemployment was low, and the pursuit of growth was generally accepted as the main aim of economic policy. The majority of the population, he argued, shared in the benefits of economic growth, and yet it brought with it a range of problems which fell disproportionately upon particular groups. Industrial injuries, adolescent skills, environmental pollution and urban blight were all the 'social costs and social insecurities which are the product of a rapidly changing industrial-urban society'. The social services thus represented a communal redress: 'They are part of the price we pay to some people for bearing part of the costs of other people's progress' (1968, p. 133). Several things followed from this. First, the social services were permanent, the need for them would not wither away with affluence. Second, they should be provided as of right, without means tests and free from any imputation that the individual's dependency arose from his or her personal failing. Third, the extent of social inequality and the imbalance between public and private consumption meant that additional spending on the social services should not be dependent upon the achievement of a particular rate of economic growth. If necessary, the resources should be made available through redistribution. It was this emphasis upon egalitarianism and 'social growth' which was to bring the Fabian writers into an open conflict with the Labour governments of the 1960s.

## SELECTIVITY AND THE LABOUR GOVERNMENT

The debate between the IEA and the Fabians figured prominently in the academic textbooks of the 1960s, and became 'one of the fashionable talking points in politically conscious circles' (Lapping, 1970, p. 129). Within Whitehall, however, the dominant issue was the implications for public expenditure of the Labour government's consistent failure to achieve its economic objectives. Labour had entered office in 1964 with ambitious, if sometimes vague, plans for the 'drastic reform' of the social services. Prominent amongst these was the ill-fated income guarantee scheme, discussed in Chapter 6, but the manifesto also promised a major expansion of Britain's 'tragically inadequate' spending on education, an increase in house building and the introduction of a number of new wage-related social security benefits. All of this assumed, however, that the necessary resources would be provided by a substantial improvement in Britain's economic performance. On social security, for example, Labour warned that, 'with the exception of the early introduction of the Income Guarantee, the key factor in determining the speed at which new and better levels of benefit can be introduced will be the rate at which the British economy can advance'. Not that there was any doubt that the advance would be rapid. Labour, it said, was ready, 'poised to swing its plans into instant operation. Impatient to apply the New Thinking that will end the chaos and sterility'[5] (Craig, 1970, pp. 229, 240).

This buoyant optimism was reflected in the National Plan, which was published in September 1965 and was 'designed to achieve a 25 per cent increase in national output between 1964 and 1970' (Cmnd. 2764, p. iii). Within a year of its publication, however, the plan had been completely abandoned. The economic record of the Labour government has been much discussed and debated, but the crucial factor was the decision to give absolute priority to the balance of payments — first to avoid a devaluation of the pound and then, once it had been forced upon the government, to 'make devaluation work' (Fry, 1975; Stewart, 1977). The important point here is that this strategy involved a prolonged squeeze on domestic consumption in order to divert resources into exports. Although public expenditure continued to rise between 1965 and 1967, the cuts announced in January 1968 heralded a period of severe restraint. The Gross Domestic Product rose by 7.7 per cent between 1967 and 1970, but private consumption rose by only 5.4 per cent and public consumption by less than 1 per cent. The volume of exports grew by 27 per cent (Stewart, 1977, p. 89). By far the most significant statistic, however, was the increase in the proportion of national income taken by the government in taxation from 32 per cent in 1964 to 43 per cent in 1970 (p. 102). In part this was required to finance the increase in expenditure in the early years of the government, but it was primarily due to the government's belief that it had to reduce dramatically the gap between its revenue and its spending. In 1967–8, the so-called public sector borrowing requirement was over £2,000 million, but by 1970 the government was actually running a surplus (p. 90). This turnaround was, of course, part of the overall strategy of restraining domestic consumption, but it was also a precondition of the international loans which the government had to raise to prevent further speculation over the value of the pound.

The voters, however, were not impressed, and ministers became increasingly convinced that the higher taxes levied on wage-earners had provoked a massive backlash amongst their own supporters. Richard Crossman noted after a meeting in his Coventry constituency that 'the trade unionists want to see us spending less on social services so there'll be more for wage packets' (Banting, 1979, p. 80). Similarly Denis Healey remarked that four-fifths of the complaints he received when visiting Labour Clubs in Leeds were 'that income tax is too high and that we should not pay out so much in family allowances' (MacGregor, 1981, p. 114). These were not isolated examples, and it was generally assumed within the government that further increases in personal taxation were politically impossible. It was unlikely, however, that there would be any reduction in the pressures for higher spending. Indeed, the increase in the number of old people and other dependent groups within the population meant that more money would have to be found simply to maintain the existing standards of service. All of this brought the issue of selectivity to the fore, and precipitated a spate of proposals for higher charges, more means tests and a greater reliance on private provision.

One of the earliest expressions of this thinking came in a lecture delivered by Douglas Houghton in April 1967. Houghton had only just resigned from the Labour Cabinet — where he had had overall responsibility for the social services — and the fact that his lecture was subsequently published by the IEA was significant in itself. The gist of Houghton's (1968) argument was that additional expenditure on, say, the health service would have to be financed by higher charges.[6] No Chancellor would be willing to raise the necessary money, and at present there was no way that people could provide for themselves without opting out of the health service completely. This was 'the worst of both worlds. The government cannot find the money out of taxation and the citizen is not allowed to pay it out of his own pocket' (p. 17). The only way to increase the resources devoted to health care was to let people 'spend more on themselves within the Health Service' (p. 16). In short, the task was to make 'more social expenditure an acceptable, even a positively welcome, part of personal expenditure' (p. 23). David Owen (1968) similarly argued that taxation had 'reached the highest tolerable level' in the 1968 budget, and proposed a range of charges, some of which had been canvassed by the One Nation Group nearly 20 years earlier.

The central issue, however, was that of family poverty, and here the political problems were exacerbated by the alleged unpopularity of family allowances. The newly formed Child Poverty Action Group (CPAG) was pressing for a substantial increase in family allowances, financed in part by the reduction or abolition of child tax allowances. This would be selective insofar as the tax allowances were worth more to the better-off and would not involve a traditional means test. It could scarcely be expected to be popular, however, and Crossman was told by his local party that it would cost thousands of votes (Banting, 1979, p. 91). Moreover the so-called 'clawback' proposal would disturb the internal equity of the tax system — by increasing the tax paid by families with children — and would reduce the scope of the Chancellor when he came to frame his next budget. For all these reasons clawback was fiercely opposed by James Callaghan at the Exchequer. There were two other possibilities: a straightforward increase in family allowances — which would either be very expensive or would provide little help — or an entirely means-tested scheme along the lines of the family income supplement introduced by the Conservative government in 1971. A majority of the Cabinet would not accept a means test, and at one stage it seemed that the deadlock would result in a general increase in family allowances, a move which few people had originally wanted. In November 1967, however, Callaghan resigned as Chancellor and his replacement by Roy Jenkins led to the eventual introduction of the clawback scheme in 1968.

Clawback was described by Roy Jenkins as 'civilized selectivity', but the Labour government had already extended and consolidated the scope of less 'civilized' means tests in a number of fields. The most important of these were social assistance — discussed in Chapter 6 — and housing. The Conservative Housing Subsidies Act of 1956 had withdrawn some Exchequer subsidies to local housing and had also made it possible for local authorities to stop subsidizing council house rents out of their rate income. This meant that when housing costs rose in the 1950s and 1960s — largely due to higher interest rates — those costs were met through increased rents. This, of course, had raised the problem of the low-income tenant who could not meet a higher rent, and successive Conservative governments had encouraged the local authorities to adopt rent rebate schemes. Between 1955–6 and 1963–4, the proportion with such schemes had risen from 15 per cent to 39 per cent (Parker, 1967, p. 47). The Labour government also saw rebates as the most effective use of subsidies (Hill, 1972, pp. 242–4). In 1967 it published a circular setting out a model scheme, and although it did not accept a recommendation of the Prices and Incomes Board that rebates be made mandatory on local authorities, it did everything it could to encourage their adoption.[7] By 1970, over 60 per cent of authorities had a scheme. It was a similar story in the case of rate rebates, as will be seen in the following chapter.

All of this was a far cry from the social growth envisaged by those who had helped to formulate Labour's plans in opposition, and their disaffection was to lead to a public confrontation between Peter Townsend and Richard Crossman. The essence of the argument was, of course, the government's failure to redistribute income and wealth. The government's critics accepted that there was working-class opposition to higher taxes, but argued that the burden on the average earner was too high in any case. The answer was to raise the money through graduated social security contributions, more progressive taxes on the better-off, and – above all – a wealth tax (Abel-Smith, 1968a, Meacher, 1972b). As early as November 1966, Abel-Smith had complained at the low priority accorded to the social services in the National Plan, and the subsequent curtailment of the growth of public expenditure only increased the frustration of the 'universalists'. The most powerful attack, however, came from Townsend (1967, p. 30). The government, he argued, did not have a coherent strategy for the relief of poverty, because it had failed to grasp the nettle of redistribution:

> If poverty is relative then standards are partly determined by the incomes, wealth, living conditions and expectations of the rich. The relief of poverty is secured by lower managerial and professional incomes, relative to the average, as much as by higher minimum wages and benefits. It is not that the rich can pay sufficient new taxes to finance, say, a major increase in the retirement pension. It is doubtful whether they could finance a five shilling increase. Their resources and incomes provide the starting point from which the rest of the social hierarchy unfolds, and this is crucial.

Crossman's reply was brutal. The strictures of Abel-Smith and particularly of Townsend were 'curiously remote from everyday reality' and served only to illustrate the gap 'between the socialist academic and the practical politician'. They failed to realize the central importance of securing an economic recovery. Without economic growth it would be impossible to get public support for redistributive measures:

> In war time it is just possible to persuade democratic communities to accept the fair shares of a rationed siege economy, and even to welcome the drastic restrictions and heavy sacrifices involved. But this readiness to share is only 'for the duration' . . . Indeed, I am prepared to assert against our critics that in peace-time the gap between private affluence and public squalor cannot be corrected without a fairly rapid rate of economic growth (1967, p. 90).

Crossman observed that he was surprised at the 'width of the gap that had grown up between us', and the gap between the government and the poverty lobby was to widen still further during the life of the government. Towards the end of 1969, CPAG produced a memorandum which was highly critical of Labour's record and called for a further increase in family allowances. This was later sent to the press along with a press release which was headed 'Poor Worse Off Under Labour'. Evidence to support the claim was subsequently produced by researchers sympathetic to CPAG's position (Townsend and Bosanquet, 1972), although Frank Field (1982, p. 32) — the Group's Director at the time — has since stated that the original memorandum did not contain this evidence. Not surprisingly, the press release enraged Crossman and by 1970, the 'fashionable talking point' was no longer universality and selectivity, but the conflict between the Labour government and CPAG. Moreover the assertion that the poor had got poorer under Labour provoked a long argument within the poverty lobby itself over both the validity of that claim and the strategy adopted by the Group. In March 1970, Abel-Smith and Titmuss refused to sign a letter to *The Times* supporting the Group's position and the rift became public. *The Sunday Times* (22 March 1970) observed that 'Titmuss, Abel-Smith and Townsend . . . the massive triumvirate of the 1950s – have parted company. Back in 1964, that was perhaps the least likely prediction as an achievement of Labour'.


*CONCLUSION*

There was never the slightest chance that either side in the selectivity debate would convince the other. Those labelled 'universalists' started from the premise that there was an overwhelming case for the redistribution of income and wealth. The social services would have to play a central role in the creation of a fairer and more equal society, and this in turn required a higher level of state intervention. Any attempt to minimize the role of the state could only preserve and safeguard the existing inequalities, whilst the suggestion that health or education should be marketed and sold like coffee or soap was morally offensive. For their part the selectivists began by pointing not to inequalities, but to an archaic and inefficient bureaucracy which took money from people with one hand and provided benefits and services on the other. This was not only wasteful but oppressive, since it robbed individuals of the right to choose how to spend their money and undermined their sense of personal responsibility. They were not egalitarians. The state should provide a basic minimum but no more. Above all the continued pretence that the laws of supply and demand did not apply to welfare goods was irrational and myopic. Very often the resistance to change stemmed, not from compassion, but from the self-interest of the bureaucrats and welfare professionals who were the main beneficiaries of the welfare state.

Within Whitehall the issues seemed less clear cut, and the scope for change more restricted. NIT was impractical in the short run, and the restoration of the market would lead to intolerable inequalities. This was the view of not only the Labour Cabinet, but also of its senior advisers. Lord Croham (1981, p. 214) – Permanent Secretary at the Treasury from 1968 to 1974 – has described the 'prevailing belief' within Whitehall 'that any significant departure from the framework we have known . . . will produce social inequality. This fear of producing social inequality is deeply ingrained in Whitehall, and so long as it remains so, civil servants are likely to be highly suspicious of proposals to reduce the role of the state.'

An expansion of universal services was seen as equally impractical in the economic conditions of the 1960s. The argument that more and better public services could only be financed through a higher rate of economic growth was accepted by a large majority in both parties, and the growing evidence of popular discontent at the level of taxation gave it added weight (MacGregor, 1981, p. 92). This does not mean, however, that the debate was not important. The fact that the failures of the Labour government in the social policy field were so extensively documented had a considerable impact upon the party outside Parliament. It strengthened the feelings of betrayal amongst many people in the constituency parties and was one of the factors behind the move to make future Labour governments more accountable to the party at large and especially to the Party Conference.

The Conservatives drew their own lessons from the debate and from the experience of the Labour government. Universalism had proved to be both expensive and ineffective. Selectivity, on the other hand, seemed to offer a means of abolishing poverty, while at the same time reducing public expenditure. By 1970, the Conservatives were convinced that if they were prepared to abandon their own inhibitions over the means test, they could have the best of both worlds.

## NOTES

1. The change in attitudes towards the IEA within Whitehall is described in a recent essay by Lord Croham (1981) while the 'Barber boom' and its aftermath is discussed in Deacon (1980). It should also be remembered that the IEA was run on a shoe-string in its early years, with a part-time General Director and one employee.
2. See in particular Bull (1971). It was argued that since many of those on assistance were receiving additional grants or had resources

which were disregarded, then the poverty line should be higher than the basic scales. The study by Abel-Smith and Townsend (1965), for example, took 140 per cent of the assistance scale as the poverty line.

3. In particular it was claimed that doctors in the United States performed unnecessary operations, and that a higher proportion of insurance premiums was wasted on administrative costs. For the controversy, see Titmuss (1968, pp. 247–68); Jewkes *et al.* (1964).

4. It is interesting that the Fabian writers differed over the importance of the incentives argument. Townsend thought the emphasis on preserving the incentive to earn more amongst low-paid workers was 'misplaced' (1968, p. 108); whilst Abel-Smith claimed that an extension of universal benefits was 'needed simply to reduce the existing disincentives on poor families' (1968a, p. 116).

5. The 1959 manifesto had dismissed as Tory propaganda the allegation that Labour would have to put up taxes to pay for better social services. This was 'quite untrue', since the finance would come chiefly through 'planned expansion' (Craig, 1970, p. 200).

6. Houghton envisaged charges for prescription and treatment in hospital with ability to pay assessed by the Inland Revenue. He argued that the computerization of PAYE opened up 'quite exciting' possibilities. The Conservatives had introduced prescription charges in 1952 and their initial operation is discussed by Martin and Williams (1959). The Labour government abolished the charges shortly after taking office, but reintroduced them in January 1968. Low-income groups were exempt, and so these and similar charges for school meals were usually regarded as examples of selectivity.

7. The circular made it clear, however, that the government did not approve of schemes which required every tenant to declare his or her income, nor did it envisage that rents would reach a level at which a majority of tenants were eligible for a rebate.

CHAPTER 5

# Extending Means Tests

The general election of June 1970 returned a Conservative government committed to the introduction of a much greater degree of selectivity within the social services. This commitment was itself part of a wider strategy which was intended to refashion the role of government in economic and social affairs. In their manifesto, the Conservatives had promised to reduce both public spending and personal taxation, to reform the law on industrial relations, to modernize the machinery of government and to curtail drastically the level of government interference within the economy (Craig, 1975, pp. 325–44). Much of this broader strategy was subsequently abandoned, particularly in the now famous 'U-turn' of 1972. The dramatic way in which the Conservative government changed course — and the even more dramatic events which led to its eventual defeat in February 1974 — have distracted attention from its earlier years. The fact remains, however, that during this period the government introduced three major new means-tested benefits: family income supplement (FIS), rent rebates and allowances, and rate rebates, and extended the scope and importance of others. In this chapter we shall discuss these changes in means-tested benefits and the efforts that the government made to make them work. We shall also see how the measures they introduced into social policy were not reversed and remain the basis of current provision.

## THE 'MODERNIZATION' POLICY

As we have seen in Chapter 4, the Conservatives' commitment to selectivity did not spring from nowhere in 1970. A section of the Party had long been attracted by the arguments of the Institute of Economic Affairs. In 1961, for example, a Bow Group pamphlet by Geoffrey Howe (1961) had quoted with approval Seldon's critique of state pensions and argued that over the whole field of social policy the firm aim of the Conservatives should be:

a reduction in the role of the State . . . People who are able and willing to provide for the education and health of their families should be in every way encouraged to do so. All this will involve a deliberate reversal of certain aspects of Conservative policy as it has been applied in recent years (p. 61).

As a first step, the policy should be to encourage private provision by means of tax concessions, to require parents to pay the full economic cost of such services as school meals and milk, and to confine housing subsidies to poorer tenants by means of a 'straightforward test of need' (p. 72).

None of this, however, had much impact on Conservative governments before 1964, and it was only after the party's defeat in the general election of that year that selectivity emerged as a major theme of policy. Indeed, the strength of the criticisms levelled at the existing policies was due in part to the frustrations engendered by the extreme caution of the Macmillan and Home governments. As early as 1958, Peter Goldman — Director of the Conservative Political Centre — had complained that they were 'inching along' towards a redefinition of the role of government 'with all the goodwill and serenity of a London 'bus in a pea-souper' (Goldman, 1958, p. 8).

The catalyst was, of course, the election of Edward Heath as leader of the Party in July 1965. Heath had become Chairman of the Advisory Committee on Policy nine days after the election and had immediately begun a fundamental reappraisal of party policy. By the Spring of 1965, 36 specialist groups had been established, usually chaired by a shadow minister and composed of MPs and outside experts in roughly equal numbers. The groups reported directly to Heath, and he retained personal control of policy making despite a heavy defeat in the 1966 election (Rose, 1974, pp. 392–7). By 1970 the work of the groups and various other *ad hoc* committees and research units had culminated in a comprehensive programme which is usually known as the 'competition policy'. The central theme of that policy was the achievement of a higher rate of economic growth through the creation of greater incentives for individual effort and the modernization of Britain's institutions and working practices. To a remarkable extent, the policy reflected the personality of the leader. Heath was relatively uninterested in philosophical discussion, and gave absolute priority to managerial efficiency and the solution of specific problems. As Gamble has noted, 'Heath's abiding commitment was to the ideology of growth. Like the Bow Group it was the heart of his political perspective, the triumph of pragmatic, problem-solving, non-ideological politics' (1974, p. 91).

One aspect of the new 'politics of technique' was an emphasis upon administrative change and the promise of a 'quiet revolution' in government (Fry, 1982). Another was the rejection of universal benefits as a wasteful anachronism, the retention of which was explicable only in terms of inertia and the refusal of previous governments to confront outmoded fears and prejudices. Selectivity, however, had another, crucial, advantage. It would enable the Conservatives to fulfill their election promise both to personal taxation and increase spending on defence. As Geoffrey Howe told the Party Conference in 1966:

> In almost every debate this conference has been urging us to spend more money on particular services. We have to face it. It is not possible to do these things and at the same time to implement our pledge to cut taxation unless we have the courage to work out radically new solutions across the board (Conservative Party (CP), 1967, pp. 131–2).

Many Conservatives also believed that the means test had lost its emotional significance. Mervyn Pike told the same conference that Labour was content to 'keep alive the bogey of the means test state':

we, for our part, are not afraid of telling the truth, and we are not afraid of using words precisely. We are not going to dodge words like 'test of means' and 'test of needs'. Why should we? we have got the measures to meet these needs and we do not need to be afraid of measuring need (CP, 1967, p. 134).

For all the prominence given to selectivity in Conservative rhetoric, there were few specific measures in the manifesto for the 1970 election. 'The proposals were for a strange hotch-potch of measures which in total did not add up to a startlingly new selectivist programme' (Bradshaw, 1972, p. 159). They included two-yearly reviews of pensions, improved benefits for the sick and disabled, a constant attendance allowance, pensions for younger widows, and the abolition of flat rate contributions for insurance benefits. All these proposals had already been in the Labour government's massive National Superannuation and Social Insurance Bill, 1969. The Conservatives did not approve of the rest of that Bill, but they were not very explicit about their alternative proposals for pension reform, only promising to provide pensions for the over-eighties.

However, their plans for tackling family poverty were much clearer. The Labour Party had merely promised to 'review the present system of family allowances and income tax child allowances' (Craig, 1975, p. 358). The Conservatives, however, were clearly committed to tackling family poverty with family allowances. Both in their manifesto and in subsequent correspondence between Macleod, Heath and the Child Poverty Action Group, they committed themselves to increasing family allowances by clawing back on child tax allowances (Field, 1971a, p. 30).

It was in the new government's White Paper (Cmnd. 4515) on public expenditure that the role of selectivity became clear. Introducing it in the House of Commons on 27 October 1970 Mr Barber, the Chancellor of the Exchequer, said: 'We intend to adopt a more selective approach to the social services. There will be increases in expenditure on basic structure — schools, hospitals, payments to those in need. But we aim to confine the scope of free or subsidized provision more closely to what is necessary on social grounds' (*Hansard*, 805, 37). School meals charges would be increased; school milk abolished for children over seven; cheap welfare milk abolished; prescription charges for dental and optical treatment would go up and be related to cost. Payment of flat rate benefit for the first three days of unemployment or sickness was abandoned. But in particular and more significantly, there were to be major new means-tested initiatives in support of low-income families with children and in housing finance. 'Instead of the present indiscriminate subsidies', Mr Barber claimed, 'help will go where it is most needed' (*Hansard*, 805, 41).

### FAMILY INCOME SUPPLEMENT

Given the government's manifesto commitment to family allowances, FIS came as something of a bombshell. It was also enacted and implemented very rapidly: the decision to introduce FIS was announced in October 1970, the Bill received its second reading in November, was immediately considered in committee on the floor of the House, received its third reading in December, regulations were published in February and payments started from 3 August 1971. There has been a good deal of discussion since about whether FIS would ever have been introduced if Iain Macleod, the original Chancellor of the Exchequer, had not died shortly after taking office. He had after all criticized the Labour Party for not spending £30 million on family allowances in their 1970 budget — out of tax cuts of £220 million. In his budget in October 1970, Mr Barber, who had replaced Macleod as Chancellor in July 1970, had given £8 million for FIS out of £300 million returned to the tax-payer. Sir Keith Joseph, Secretary of State for Social Services, justified FIS, not on ideological grounds, but largely in terms of the weakness of the available alternatives. He argued in the second reading debate that, on reaching office, he had discovered that tax thresholds were too near the poverty level to pay for increases in family allowances by clawing back on child tax allowance. Furthermore many poor families, particularly single-parent families, had only one child and would not benefit from an increase in family allowances.[1] It is probably the case that despite the constraint of clawback and public expenditure, the government would not have gone for a means-tested alternative if such a scheme had not already been waiting when Joseph arrived at the DHSS. It would certainly not have been introduced so quickly. It is now clear that the Labour Cabinet had considered a means-tested alternative to family allowances similar to the FIS scheme in 1967, and was only narrowly deflected from it by the determination of Margaret Herbison who mobilized backbench and trade union opposition to it (Banting, 1979).

Under the Family Income Supplement Act low wage-earning families with dependent children would be entitled to have their incomes brought up to half the difference between their gross incomes and a prescribed amount up to a maximum. Income would be assessed over a five-week period and claims could be made by post to an office in Blackpool. Benefit, once awarded, would last for six months regardless of changes in circumstances. Both two-parent and one-parent families would be entitled to FIS but in the case of two-parent families, the man had to be the bread-winner. It was envisaged that FIS would benefit 134,000 couples with children, including 24,000 families on supplementary benefits who were wage stopped,[2] and 54,000 single persons with children — a total of 190,000 households containing 500,000 children. This estimate was later revised downwards to 160,000 households.

Much of the important research on the take-up of means-tested benefits had not been completed by 1971, but by the late 1960s there was evidence that low-income families with working heads were not claiming many of the means-tested benefits they were entitled to (see Chapter 7). Much of the opposition to the FIS scheme from the Labour Party and the Child Poverty Action Group was largely on account of the belief that the new means test would deter claims, and take-up would be low. Sir Keith Joseph, in the Financial Memorandum to the Bill, asserted that 'the finances presume that we shall have 85 per cent up take. I will do my best to do that and better' (*Hansard*, 806, 218).

Families became eligible to claim in May 1971 (for payments to start from 3 August 1971) but by 6 July and despite a publicity campaign costing £60,000, only 16,844 successful claims had been received (*Hansard*, 21, 191). The government then decided to extend the publicity campaign to television and by December, at a cost of £310,000, 66,000 families had claimed FIS payments. Altogether, including those who benefited from the relief of wage stop, about 48 per cent of those eligible had benefited from FIS.

Sir Keith Joseph was disappointed by these results and made considerable efforts to improve take-up — even writing a personal letter to all social workers urging them to find FIS families and encourage them to claim. However, he was able to claim that, although less than half those eligible had claimed, the average payment had been higher than expected and as a result £5 million of the £8 million projected expenditure had been directed at the poor.

The problem of take-up was not the only one to emerge with FIS. Government spokemen soon found themselves accused of introducing a new Speenhamland system which undermined work incentives. How could they claim to have 'reduced the burden of taxation and to extend individual choice, freedom and responsibility' (Craig, 1975, p.344) when recipients of FIS lost 50 per cent of an increase in earnings? A paper by Piachaud (1971) inspired an article in the *New Stateman* by Field and Piachaud (1971) which first called the accumulation of taxes and benefits on the marginal incomes of low-paid families the poverty trap. They showed that by 1971, an increase in income from £16.50 to £20.00 would result in an increase in net income of only 90p for a one-child family — and this was before the introduction of rent rebates (see also Chapter 8). 'Hundreds of thousands of trade unionists are not getting what they bargained for. It is now a fact that for millions of low-paid workers, very substantial pay increases have the absurd effect of increasing only marginally the family's net income . . .' (Field and Piachaud, 1971, p. 772).

Stung by the criticisms about incentives and the failure to achieve the level of take-up he desired, Sir Keith Joseph extended payment of FIS from six months to a year regardless of changes in circumstances. Growing awareness of the defects of means-tested benefits began to undermine the government's commitment to them. When the proposals for a tax credit scheme were published in 1972, it was suggested that there would be 'no need to continue FIS except for the self employed and others who for one reason or another were outside the tax credit scheme' (Cmnd. 5116, pp. 23–4). By the time of the 1974 election campaign, it was being claimed by the Conservative Central Office (1974) that 'FIS was brought in only as a temporary first aid measure, pending more comprehensive arrangements for tackling poverty as a whole' (p. 337).

If the Conservatives had won the election in 1974 and pushed on with their tax credit scheme, it is improbable that they would have been able to afford to pay child credits high enough to abolish FIS without at least some families being worse off (see Chapter 9). In the event a Labour government was returned, and in spite of their earlier criticisms of the scheme, they retained FIS. 'We do not like FIS. As soon as it is economically and administratively possible we want to replace it by our own non means-tested scheme. In the meantime we must deal with the situation as it is. We cannot leave the poorest families without help, so an increase in FIS is necessary' (*Hansard*, 873, 646). But they never found it economically possible to replace FIS. The child benefit scheme which was phased in from April 1977 and combined child tax allowances and family allowances was not paid at a high enough level to replace FIS, and indeed in order to prevent FIS families being worse off, child benefits were disregarded in assessing eligibility for FIS. In 1979, following a recommendation of the Finer Committee, FIS was adapted to help single parents – the minimum number of hours lone parents were required to work to qualify for FIS was reduced from 30 to 24 per week. FIS was also used in 1977 and 1978 as a passport to the electricity discount scheme. FIS had become an established part of the social security system.

When the Conservatives returned to power in 1979 they had no plans to diminish the role of FIS. Tax credits were no longer in their programme and FIS was expanded. In 1979 and 1980, the prescribed amounts were uprated by an addition to cover the cost of fuel and in 1982, unlike many other social security benefits, retained their value in real terms. The number of families in receipt of FIS nearly doubled from 78,000 in 1979 to 140,00 in 1982, and a Treasury Select Committee considering the interaction of taxes and benefits found that the cost of abolishing FIS by increasing child benefits would be £8 billion (see Chapter 8).

## RENT REBATES AND ALLOWANCES

The second major new means-tested benefit introduced by the 1970–4 Conservative government was the national system of rent rebates and allowances. A mandatory national rent rebate scheme began in October 1972 for council tenants. This was followed in January 1973 by a national rent allowance scheme for tenants in privately rented and housing association unfurnished accommodation. The allowance scheme was extended to tenants of furnished accomodation in April 1973.

We have seen in Chapter 2 how rent rebates played a brief and unhappy part in the story of the means test during the 1930s. We have also seen in Chapter 4 how, encouraged by the Labour government, many local authorities had developed their own rent rebate schemes. Some local authorities adopted a scheme suggested by the Ministry of Housing and Local Government (1967), some adopted the statutory rate rebate means test when it was introduced in 1966, and others used a variety of other means tests of their own making. The huge variety of different rent rebate schemes was one of the factors that led Reddin (1968, pp. 796–8) to claim that there were over 1,500 different means tests in operation in local authorities. The result of this variation was that similar housing costs were receiving very variable rebates. In 1964 Reddin had estimated that 39 per cent of local housing authorities were administering rebate schemes but by 1970–1, 64 per cent had rebate schemes in operation (IMTA, 1972, p. 2).

Although this haphazard accumulation of locally administered rent rebate schemes was part of the policy context of the national rent rebate scheme, the immediate political context was rather different. The Conservative government came to power committed to cut public expenditure. One area where they sought to find those cuts was in the Exchequer subsidies paid to local authorities — the mini-budget in October 1970 envisaged savings of £100–200 million by 1974–5. If Exchequer subsidies were cut, rents would have to increase quite dramatically. In order to mitigate the consequence of these rent increases for low-income households, a rent rebate system was required. Thus, while FIS introduced a means-tested supplement to earnings, rent rebates introduced a means-tested benefit in order to ameliorate the effects of an increase in charges.

However the White Paper *Fair Deal for Housing* (Cmnd. 4728, paras. 42 and 47) claimed:

> The national [rent rebate] scheme will . . . be an important new weapon against family poverty. The Family Income Supplement was devised to help those whose incomes are low in relation to their family responsibilities. But people with low incomes and high rents need more help than those with low incomes and low rents. The national scheme and the Family Income Supplement scheme will in combination give effective help to people with low incomes who have children to support but who are not eligible for supplementary benefit because they are in full time work . . . To be fair the rent subsidy must not only be available to tenants whose income is at or below the minimum level judged to be tolerable for such purposes as supplementary benefit. It must also be available to tenants with incomes above this level, if the rent of their home would otherwise impose an unfair burden on the family budget.

The new national means test for calculating rebates took gross income after the deduction of certain limited disregards and compared this with a needs allowance: '. . . to allow for the basic cost of necessities for [the tenant] and his family' (Cmnd. 4728, Appendix 2, para. 2 and para. 43). If gross income equalled the needs allowance, then the tenant would pay 40 per cent of the rent of his house. For every £1 by which income exceeded the needs allowance, the rent payable would increase by 17p and for every £1 by which income fell short of the needs allowance the 40 per cent rent would be reduced by 25p. For very low incomes, this could mean that the rent payable would be nil.

The scheme was to be administered by local authorities, and to simplify the administration the scheme adopted the income evidence required for FIS of assessing income over the previous five weeks if paid weekly, or two months if paid monthly.

There were a number of other new elements in the means test. There was to be a maximum rebate payable of £6.50 (£8.00 in London) and a minimum of 20p. Normally the rebate for the council tenant was to be deducted at source, but the rent allowance would be paid to the tenant weekly. Rebate having been calculated on the basis of the income of the householder and his spouse, deductions were to be made for non-dependents at varying rates depending on age and source of income. The means test also introduced a new dilemma for tenants who were not in employment. Would they be better off claiming supplementary benefit (SB) or rent rebate? If SB entitlement was small, typically when the benefit was topping up national insurance benefits, it was not at all clear whether a tenant would be better off on SB or rent rebate. Burgess (1974, p. 535) estimated that some 600,000 (nearly 20 per cent) of SB claimants might be better off on rebates. This 'better off' problem, as we shall see, was the cause of a further major reform in housing rebates in the 1980s.

One of the most significant factors in the new rent rebate means test was that it incorporated a very large number of people who had never previously been covered by means-tested benefits. As Field (1971b) noted:

In 1975–76 up to 3 million heads of households might be paying 'fair rents' which will be so 'fair' that they will be eligible for a rent rebate or allowance . . . means-tested housing rebates [will] extend well beyond families thought to be living in poverty. 'Respectable' working class and lower middle class families will start to experience the treatment which has hitherto been reserved for the poor.

One reason why Field expected rent rebates to extend entitlement even up to the lower middle classes was because of the rent increases that were associated with the legislation necessary to bring in fair rents. One of the objectives of the Housing Finance Act was 'a fairer choice between owning a house and renting one' (Cmnd. 4728, para. 5). The legislation was designed to encourage home ownership as well as save public expenditure. 'Home ownership is the most rewarding form of tenure . . . satisfies a deep and natural desire . . . gives the greatest security against the loss of . . . home and . . . price changes' (Cmnd. 4728, para. 14). Thus local authorities had to increase rents by £1 in the first year and 50p each subsequent year until the fair rent for the dwelling was reached.

Another objection to the scheme was that the cost of paying rent rebates and allowances was to some extent to be met by other tenants because a subsidy was payable from Exchequer funds only if the Housing Revenue Account was in deficit. The rent increases and the cross-subsidization was likely to make owner-occupiers more eligible.

The government were determined to make the new means-tested benefit work. The legislation laid duties on local authorities to inform all their tenants of the details of the rent rebate scheme at least annually. For private tenants, advertisements should be placed in local newpapers annually and landlords were required to insert details of the rent allowance scheme into rent books. There is little evidence of the impact of these local efforts.[3]

However the government did not rely only on local efforts. They mounted the most extensive advertising campaign that has ever been mounted on behalf of a benefit — on TV and in the local and national papers. Between September 1972 and February 1974, the Department of the Environment spent £997,400 on advertising rent rebates and allowances (Lister, 1974). A survey of 3,000 tenants carried out by Marplan in early 1973 to evaluate the impact of this campaign concluded that knowledge of the fair rent laws, awareness of rent benefits and knowledge of the working of the scheme had not increased between November 1972 and March 1973, and the number of tenants intending to apply had fallen (Marplan, 1973, Vol. 1, pp. 7–9).

In May 1973, using data from the Family Expenditure Survey, the government claimed that the take-up of rent rebates was 70—80 per cent and about 10 per cent for rent allowances (*Hansard,* 861, 293—4). These figures were subsequently revised to 60—70 per cent for rent rebates and 20—25 for rent allowances when an analysis for the whole of 1973 became available (DoE, 1982, Table 125).

Once the scheme was introduced, the government expanded its coverage by increasing the needs allowance. Between October 1972 and October 1973, average earnings rose by 12.5 per cent and the national insurance pension rose by 15 per cent for a single person. During the same period the needs allowances were increased by 47 per cent for a single person, 40 per cent for a married couple and 33 per cent for a two-child family.

The Housing Finance Act was one of the most politically contentious issues during the 1970—4 Conservative government. The conflict between the government and the opposition and between the government and local authorities was centred on the increases to 'fair rents' and the removal of rent fixing from local authority control. The new means test caused relatively little resentment, and indeed it may have been the one factor that made the rent increases acceptable to both local authorities and tenants. The effects of the Act were also mitigated by the imposition in 1973 of a total freeze on prices and incomes which delayed the progress to fair rents.

The Labour government which returned to power in 1974 immediately set about dismantling the 1972 Housing Finance Act provisions. In the 1975 Housing, Rents and Subsidies Act, they repealed the provisions relating to 'fair rents', abolished the rent scrutiny committees, gave back to local authorities their freedom to fix 'reasonable' rents and make rate fund contributions and recast the subsidy arrangements. However they retained the rent rebate and allowance scheme. The Labour government had come to power with ambitions for a searching and far-reaching enquiry into housing finance. Crosland, the Secretary of State for the Environment, favoured a radical change replacing rent rebates and tax relief on owner-occupiers with a new non means-tested housing benefit. But he died and the *Housing Policy Review*, when it was published by his successor, Peter Shore, in 1977, failed to come up with changes to tax relief because 'rent rebate schemes . . . protect lower income tenants . . .' (Cmnd. 6851), p. 27), and because 'the decisions and family budgets of millions of households have been shaped by the expectations that existing arrangements will continue in broadly the same form' (Cmnd. 6851, p. 4). All the government offered was that 'the scope and coverage of the rent assistance schemes and their relationship with the supplementary benefit scheme are under review' (Cmnd, 6851, para. 12.09).

It was to be within the field of social security and particularly from the Supplementary Benefits Commission (SBC) that the arguments for rationalizing housing benefits were taken up and pursued most vigorously. In its annual reports from 1976, the Commission argued for a unified housing benefit primarily as a means of solving the 'better off' problem. It was to the review of supplementary benefits (see Chapter 6) that people turned for hope of further advance. But they were disappointed – opposition from the Department of the Environment (Donnison. 1982) prevented the DHSS coming up with a resolution. All the review team could do was to reiterate the arguments in favour of taking housing costs out of the purview of supplementary benefits.

When the new Conservative government which returned to power in 1979 had digested the results of the review, they became aware that apart from its own intrinsic merits, a new housing benefit scheme could lead to savings in civil service manpower. From these considerations emerged housing benefit and in housing benefit the system of means-tested rent rebates and allowances introduced by the 1970–4 Heath government has survived.

Indeed, 'new housing benefit' is something of a misnomer since the scheme effectively represents the unification of the administration of the existing housing benefits. Those currently receiving a rent rebate or allowance or a rate rebate will notice little difference, unless they are affected by the new tapers. For the great majority of people on supplementary benefit, this new scheme will mean that they will no longer receive money to meet their housing costs as part of their weekly allowance or pension. If they are council tenants, they will cease to pay rent and rates and will have their benefits reduced accordingly. If they are private tenants, they will receive housing benefits from the local authority, in the same way as those who are in work or are claiming insurance benefits now receive a rent allowance (Goss and Lansley, 1982).

*RATE REBATES*

When the Conservative government came to power in 1970, they found a system of means-tested rate rebates already in existence. During the 1960s as rates increased faster than incomes, there was growing disquiet about the rates burden faced by low-income households and more generally the inequitable nature of the rating system. The Allen Committee (Cmnd. 2582) reported in 1965 that rates took 2.9 per cent of net incomes of the average household compared with 8.2 per cent for lower-income households. In response to their report, in 1966 the Labour government introduced a means-tested rate rebate scheme. This scheme aimed to reduce the regressive nature of rates by relieving low-income households of up to two-thirds of their annual rate bill. When Richard Crossman presented the rate rebate scheme to Parliament, he said that it would be a temporary measure to prevent hardship in the period before the rating system could be abolished. While the Bill was before Parliament, a Green Paper was published which included further measures to reduce the impact of rates by increasing the rate support grant from central revenue. This was also described as a temporary reform until it was time to re-examine the whole position of rates in the light of the conclusions of the Royal Commission on Local Government (Cmnd. 2923) which had been established. But by the time they lost power, the Labour government had made no progress with local government or rating reform, and rate rebates still existed benefiting 795,000 households in 1971 at a cost of £16 million.

The Conservatives published another Green Paper in July 1971 (Cmnd. 4741). This discussed the advantages and disadvantages of rates and concluded that their main defects were that the yield from rates was not buoyant and 'their effect on individual ratepayers in some cases bears little relationship to ability to pay'. The Green Paper considered a number of alternatives to the rating system, including local income tax, a sales tax or value added tax, a local employment or payroll tax and locally levied duties. It also considered improvements to existing rates, including improvements to rate rebates.

There were many defects in the existing rate rebate scheme. It was limited in scope, helping only households with incomes up to about the equivalent of supplementary benefit level — well below the level at which rates continued to be a regressive tax. There was evidence that it had a very low take-up. For example, Meacher found a take-up rate of only 12 per cent of those eligible in low-income areas of Islington (Meacher, 1972a, p. 43). It appeared to be of most benefit to pensioners — 88 per cent of recipients were pensioners. Because of this factor, Bradshaw and Wicks (1970) suggested that the areas with the highest proportion of householders getting rate rebates 'reads like a list of seaside resorts boasting the longest hours of sunshine rather than a list of the centres of urban poverty'. Owner-occupiers were also more likely to be receiving rate rebates (5.9 per cent) than tenants (2.6 per cent) (Bradshaw, 1973). The rate rebate scheme also had a very sharp taper on extra earnings of 25 per cent. This meant that the means test operated in such a way that a family not eligible for a rebate could be worse off than a family receiving one (Meacher, 1972a). In the light of these defects, the Green Paper outlined ideas for a possible new rate rebate scheme designed to extend relief to 3 million people at a cost of about £65 million per year.

Following the introduction of rent rebates in 1972, logic demanded that, if a new scheme of rate rebates was to be devised, it should follow a similar pattern. This was achieved in the Rate Rebate Act 1973. This Act replaced the old rate rebate scheme with one modelled on the rent rebate scheme. The same income and needs allowance was used and when income equalled the needs allowance, the same proportion of rates as rent was payable. The only substantial difference between the two schemes was that the taper on income below and above the needs allowance was different.[4] This difference ensured that as far as possible at similar incomes the same proportion of rent and rates was payable.

The new scheme had a number of advantages over the old. The rate of taper was lower, the average rebate was higher, but above all, many more low-income households obtained relief from the burden of rates. In 1974, the last year of the old rate rebate scheme, 910,00 households had received an average rebate of £30.77 — at a total cost of £28 million. By 1976, the second year of the new scheme, 2.6 million households were receiving an average rebate of £45.50 at a total cost of £117.4 million per year. Thus this Conservative government reform resulted in more than twice the number of households receiving nearly five times the amount of help. Take-up was estimated at 65–70 per cent (DoE, 1982, Table 125).

As soon as the Labour government returned to power in 1974, they established a complete review of local government finance by a committee chaired by Frank Layfield, QC. This committee produced its report in 18 months (Cmnd. 6453) and concluded that the regressive nature of rates, which had been the main reason for reform in the 1960s, was no longer a problem. They argued that domestic rate relief provided through the rate support grant (RSG) had had an effect on the distribution of rate burdens. The RSG had grown from 3.6 per cent of average bills in 1967–8 to 27.5 per cent in 1975–6. However, the more important factor was rate rebates. 'We believe that the present rebate scheme, although expensive to administer, is a necessary feature of rating. It is in our judgement generally satisfactory in content. The problem is to ensure that those entitled are aware of their rights and encouraged and aided to exercise them' (Cmnd. 6453, p. 161) '. . . rates help to make taxation progressive at lower levels of income' (p. 159).[5]

The Layfield Committee did consider alternatives to rates and rate rebates. They were most enthusiastic about a local income tax, but admitted that it would take five years to introduce, involve 12,000 additional staff and cost £50 million. Instead they gave rather lukewarm support to local income tax as a supplement to rates.

In May 1977, the Labour government responded to the Layfield Report with yet another Green Paper on local government finance (Cmnd. 6813). This rejected the idea of a local income tax on the grounds that it would impose unacceptable burdens on national taxation. They proposed modest changes to rates but left rebates alone:

> It is alleged that rates bear no relationship to ability to pay. . . The Committee examined the criticisms and concluded that they were based on misconceptions. Rates are in fact progressive for lower income earners, due largely to the assistance given to nearly one-third of households by the rate rebate scheme and in supplementary benefit . . . the rate rebate scheme alleviates the hardship which might otherwise by imposed on the poorest (Cmnd. 6813, pp. 16—17).

So the Labour government, with the evidence of Layfield, turned their backs on the reform of local taxation and accepted means-tested rate rebates as a permanent part of social provision.

There is now no doubt that Layfield was wrong about the efficiency of rate rebates. They established that take-up was 75 per cent only by excluding those eligible for less than £10 per year. Yet there was no justification for this — £10 was a quarter of average rates in 1975 and for many low-income households a more substantial proportion of the rates they paid. If these households had not been excluded, take-up would have been about 55 per cent. More recent official estimates of 65 per cent take-up indicate that Layfield was over-optimistic.[6]

The Layfield calculations of the burden of rates were also based on the assumption that all those eligible for rate rebates were receiving them, which from the above discussion is far from the truth. They also determined that all recipients of SB had nil rates to pay because they received money for rates with their benefit. While it was true that almost all SB recipients received an allowance to cover their rates in full, rates still represented a call on their income at least until the introduction of housing benefit. To claim that rates were a nil burden for SB recipients, as the Layfield Committee did, was to underrate the regressive nature of this indirect tax.

The Layfield Committee's assurances on both the take-up of rate rebates and the impact of rates on low-income households misled the Labour government. Rates remain a burden on low incomes which means-tested benefits are failing to mitigate.[7]

## THE CONSERVATIVES AND OTHER MEANS-TESTED BENEFITS

FIS, rent rebates and rate rebates were the major innovations in means testing by the 1970—4 Conservative government. The role of other means tests was also enhanced — particularly by the policy to increase charges for services. However the most important means-tested benefit — supplementary benefit — remained relatively unchanged by the Conservative years (see Chapter 6). The new social security benefits that were introduced had no real impact on the number of supplementary beneficiaries and there were roughly the same number on SB at the end of the Conservative term of office as there had been at the beginning.

The main extension in means testing came in the improvement in exemptions for increased health charges and education benefits. The government abolished cheap welfare milk in April 1971, and in compensation increased the income levels for free welfare milk. The price of prescriptions was increased from 2 shillings and 6 pence to 4 shillings and the cost of dental and optical treatment were increased. The price of school meals was increased from 1 shilling and 9 pence to 2 shillings and 10 pence. The arrangements for exemption from prescription, opthalmic and dental charges remained unchanged, but the gross income levels for entitlement to free welfare milk and exemption from charges was increased by 30 shillings.

These changes were accompanied by a major advertising campaign. A press release issued in April 1971 announced that: 'The Government has now embarked on the biggest campaign of its kind ever launched in an attempt to reach every family and individual in need with all the benefits they are entitled to . . . What we would like to see are new records being set in the levels of take-up'.

By July 1973, £970,000 had been spent advertising FIS, free welfare milk and remission from health service charges (Lister, 1974, p. 20). The results were quite impressive: in August 1970 1,509 families had been receiving free welfare milk; by September 1971 this had increased to 65,907. But the increase was not sustained; by November 1972 the number had fallen back to 26,269, and as 340,000 families were estimated to be eligible, the overall take-up achieved was not great (Lister, 1974).

Similar results were achieved for free prescriptions. The number of people receiving free prescriptions on income grounds rose from 15,000 in 1970 to 69,000 in 1971, but fell back to 38,000 in 1972. There was no official estimate of the numbers entitled to free prescriptions but Meacher (1972c) estimated that, prior to the 1971 advertising campaign, 44 per cent of those eligible were receiving them and after the campaign in 1971 this proportion had increased to 49 per cent.

The number of people receiving remission of dental and optical charges also rose following the campaign and in this case the increase was sustained, but Meacher estimated that take-up rose from only 6 per cent to 15 per cent following the 1971 campaign.

The position with regard to free school meals is more difficult to assess because after the introduction of FIS in 1971, all families claiming FIS had an automatic passport to free school meals. The proportion of children who received free meals increased from 12.2 per cent in 1970 to 17.3 per cent in 1971, but had fallen back to 14.7 per cent by 1973. These shifts were partly a function of the numbers staying at school for meals — the price increases in 1971 led to a drop in the proportion of children staying for meals from 67.9 per cent in 1970 to 59.8 per cent in 1972.

In a pre-budget memorandum to the Chancellor of the Exchequer in October 1973 the Child Poverty Action Group stated:

the implications of these figures should be as deeply disturbing to the Government as the realities behind them to the poor themselves . . . on its own criteria, and despite a determined attempt to concentrate help selectively on the poor in work, the Government has managed to reduce the total in poverty in two years by only 13,000. This finding, more than any other, should lead the Government to question the correctness of its present strategy (Field, 1973).

*CONCLUSION*

The means test was not an important issue in the general election of February 1974. This is scarcely surprising in view of the unique circumstances in which that election was held. The miners' challenge to the Conservative government's incomes policy meant that the campaign was dominated by the twin issues of 'who governs Britain' and the causes and control of inflation. The lack of interest in means tests, however, also reflected the fact that there was less divergence between the policies of the two major parties than either was prepared to admit.

The Conservatives appeared to have lost much of their earlier enthusiasm for means tests by the time they left office. In part this was because they had already taken steps to rectify what they saw as the worst examples of waste and extravagance. The introduction of FIS and of a national system of rent rebates and allowances represented a significant extension of means testing, and meant that other more comprehensive measures were discussed with less urgency. Another reason, however, was the Conservatives' own experience of means-tested benefits. The failure to achieve a satisfactory take-up of FIS was a considerable setback, and they were also disappointed by the number of administrative objections which were raised to their tax credit proposals. (These proposals are discussed in Chapter 9). The most important factor, however, was the dramatic change which occured in the government's attitude towards public spending. For all his abrasiveness Edward Heath was not an advocate of *laissez-faire*, but a conservative in the tradition of Butler and Macmillan. The central objective of his policies was a prosperous and growing national economy, and he regarded the maintenance of a high level of employment as one of the major tasks of government (Rhodes James, 1972, p. 121). During the winter of 1971–2, unemployment rose to nearly a million and the response in Whitehall was something close to panic (Cosgrave, 1978, p. 91).

In March 1972, Anthony Barber announced a massive expansion of the economy which was designed to achieve a growth in output of 5 per cent a year. The eventual collapse of this strategy and the political repercussions of its failure have been discussed elsewhere (Deacon, 1980). The important point here is that the 'Barber boom' was fuelled in part by a considerable growth in public spending. Keegan and Pennant-Rea (1979, p. 199), for example, have described how the various government departments 'saw their chances: all manner of extra spending plans were dusted off the shelves; stress was put on how they would create extra jobs; and Treasury and ministerial resistance was seldom forthcoming'. In such an atmosphere, ministers had little incentive to propose new means-tested benefits, especially as they were also trying to secure trade union support for the prices and incomes policy they had introduced in the Autumn of 1973.

The commitment of the Heath government to selectivity proved to be less radical and far-reaching than its rhetoric sometimes suggested. With the important exception of FIS, the new means-tested benefits were an extension and rationalization of those which were already in existence when they took office. Even FIS, moreover, had been considered by the previous government, and was retained by various Labour ministers in subsequent years. Indeed, if the Conservative measures were less innovatory than some of its supporters may have wished, they proved to be remarkably durable. The contribution of the Heath government to the growth of means testing in Britain is more accurately seen as that of a catalyst than a watershed.

*NOTES*

1. Family allowances were then payable only to second and subsequent children.
2. The wage stop was a rule that ensured that if any family, by claiming

supplementary benefit, would be better off than they had been in work, their benefit was restricted to the level their income had been in work.

3. If landlords knew of their duty to put the 'statutory particulars' into rent books (or indeed to provide rent books), they would have found it difficult to reduce the details to a small enough size for rent books.

4. For every extra £1 income below the needs allowance 8p was added to the rebate, and for every £1 above the needs allowance 6p was deducted from the rebate.

5. For evidence for these conclusions the committee drew on the results of a special re-interview survey of households in the second quarter of the 1974 Family Expenditure Survey. Based on the assumption that all those entitled to rate rebates were claiming them, and those receiving supplementary benefit were receiving help with their rates, the study concluded that *gross* rates represented 3.1 per cent of average disposable income and 7.5 per cent of the disposable income of the lowest income group (12.2 per cent of households). But *net* rates represented 2.3 per cent of disposable income of the average household and *nil* per cent of the lowest income group. The committee also concluded that taking rate rebates and SB together, one-third of all households were eligible for help with rates, and 85 per cent of those eligible were receiving it. The take-up of rate rebates was estimated to be 75 per cent.

6. There is also evidence that some types of household – private tenants and non-pensioners – have much lower levels of take-up than this (see Chapter 7).

7. The Central Statistical Office (1982, Table 5, p. 96), in their regular analyses of the distributive impact of taxes and benefits, now present two figures for rates as a proportion of net income: one which assumes that households on SB pay nil rates, and the other which calculates rates paid as a proportion of all income. Even when the former method is used, rates take a smaller proportion of the disposable incomes of households in the top two quintiles than in the bottom two.

# CHAPTER 6

# Social Assistance

In few areas of social policy have the hopes and expectations of the 1940s been so totally confounded as in the case of social assistance. When the National Assistance Board (NAB) began work in July 1948 it had 842,000 clients, and this figure rose to just over a million by the end of the year.[1] This was more than many people had expected, and was some way from the role which Beveridge had envisaged for the Board. Even so, the majority of claimants were old people, and the Assistance Board had proved extremely successful when looking after a much larger number of pensioners during the war. The new Board would adopt the same approach and there was little reason to doubt that it would be equally popular. The home visit would still be the cornerstone of the service, and local officers would retain the power to pay additional benefits to claimants with special needs. Few doubted that those eligible for assistance would apply to the Board, or that claimants would be willing to declare additional needs. The work of the Board aroused little controversy amongst politicians or claimants, and Adrian Webb (1975, p. 467) has accurately described 'the quiet obscurity, into which the administration of national assistance had sunk in the mid-fifties.

'Quiet obscurity' would not be an accurate description of social assistance in the 1980s. In December 1982 there were not 1 million but 4.25 million people claiming supplementary benefits — which had replaced national assistance in 1966. This figure does not, of course, include the dependents of those claiming and all told some 12 per cent of the population relied upon means-tested social assistance for all or part of their income (DHSS, Quarterly Estimate). In addition it is estimated that there are over a million people who are eligible for supplementary benefit but do not claim it. Of those that do claim, less than half are pensioners. Over one-third are unemployed – they were 4.6 per cent of claimants in 1948 – and the majority of the remainder are one-parent families, who did not even appear as a discrete category in the statistics in 1948. Successive attempts to adapt the scheme to this new role have reduced the discretionary powers invested in the local officers, but have failed to produce rules and regulations which are easier for the staff to administer or simpler for claimants to understand. The emphasis upon domiciliary visiting and welfare has been reduced, and many local offices are struggling to cope with a mounting workload. For claimants, the difficulties of living on a low income are exacerbated by harsh or delayed decisions, lengthening queues in the office and mounting tension between staff and claimants. At the end of 1982, over 800 staff in local offices in Birmingham and Oxford had been on strike for 12 weeks in protest over the pressure of work and staffing levels. It was an event which would have been quite inconceivable in 1948.

These changes cannot, of course, be explained solely in terms of social assistance. The number of claimants, for example, is determined by a combination of political, economic and demographic factors, not the least important of which are the decisions which have been taken as to the scope and level of various contributory benefits. This chapter, then, has two purposes: to account for the growth in the number of people forced to apply for means-tested assistance, and to examine the changes which have been made to the scheme in response to that growth.

*NATIONAL ASSISTANCE*

The number of claimants receiving national assistance rose from 1 million in December 1948 to just under 1.8 million by the end of 1954. The total then fell by some 200,000 during 1955, only to rise gradually to around 2 million by the time the NAB was abolished in 1966. This pattern was the result of the interplay of four factors: the attraction of the scheme compared to public assistance, the increase in housing costs, the relationship between the levels of assistance and insurance benefits, and demographic change. It is likely that a considerable number of widows, separated wives and disabled people were prepared to apply to the Board, although they had previously avoided recourse to the public assistance committees.[2] This, however, would be a significant factor only in the early months of the scheme. Housing costs, on the other hand, became increasingly important as the proportion of claimants who were council tenants rose from 21 per cent to 43 per cent between 1954 and 1965. Council rents rose more quickly than other rents and so the net effect was to increase the proportion of insurance beneficiaries who were eligible for a supplementary payment. Much more important, however, were the changes which occurred in the relative value of insurance and assistance benefits.

The picture here was one of total confusion. Between 1948 and 1965 there were ten upratings of assistance and six of insurance. Roughly speaking, the Board's scales were raised in line with prices until the 1959 uprating, when there was a significant increase in their real value. The policy with regard to insurance, however, was much more erratic and so there was little in the way of a consistent pattern between the two. Sometimes insurance was increased more than assistance — at which point the government claimed that it was reducing the role of the means test and the opposition complained that help was not going to those who needed it most. On other occasions, assistance was increased more and then exactly the same debate was held in reverse, with the government extolling the virtues of selectivity and the opposition complaining about the means test. Two upratings, however, were particularly important: those of 1954 and 1959. The 22 per cent increase in insurance rates which took effect in February 1955 marked the only real attempt to reduce the numbers on national assistance. The Minister, Osbert Peake, told the Commons when the new rates were announced: 'That is the yardstick by which our policy in this matter should very largely be guided. It has been very distressing to see year by year a growth in the numbers having to seek help from the National Assistance Board'

(*Hansard*, 535, 2679). The very sharp increase in supple-
mentation worried everyone in the early 1950s. In a second
edition of *Needs and Means* Macleod and Powell (1954,
p. 31) had attacked the 'wholly illogical position' whereby
a compulsory insurance scheme provided only a grant-in-aid
towards maintenance by national assistance. As Macleod said
in the Commons, 'this was not what any member of any
political party who has thought deeply about this hoped for
when these great schemes were planned' (*Hansard*, 474, 1843).
This, however, was not the only reason for objecting to a
higher scale for assistance benefit. *The Sunday Times* regarded
it as iniquitous that the 'best type of man or woman' who
strove to avoid going to the National Assistance Board should
receive much less than the 'feckless type' who sought as
much as he could get on assistance (Seldon, 1981, p. 245).

The other factor behind the 1954 uprating was the very
healthy state of the National Insurance Fund (NIF), which
amassed large annual surpluses until 1952–3. This was largely
because unemployment was much lower than had been
allowed for when the contribution rates were set and because
large numbers of people chose to defer their retirement. The
effects of these surpluses was virtually to eliminate the
Exchequer subsidy to the NIF. Attitudes were to change
dramatically, however, as the cost of pensions rose, and,
more importantly, the future cost of pensions was appreciated
more widely. The number of people receiving a retirement
pension grew rapidly during the 1950s and this meant that
the number applying to the Board would continue to rise,
even if the proportion receiving a supplement remained
relatively stable.[3] Even this, however, appeared unlikely
as the prospective cost of pensions began to create something
of a panic within Whitehall (Titmuss, 1958b). Not only was
the number of pensioners increasing, but in 1958 people who
had contributed for only 10 years became eligible for a
pension. At the same time those who had deferred retirement
were finally stopping work, and would be entitled to an
enhanced pension by virtue of the extra contributions they
had paid. These additional demands on the Fund would require
either a substantial rise in the contributions paid by workers
and employers, an increased payment from the Exchequer, or

both.[4] The eventual solution was, of course, the introduction in 1961 of a graduated pension scheme which was specifically designed to increase the income from contributions and thereby stabilize the burden on the Exchequer (Lynes, 1963). Before then, however, it had been explicitly acknowledged that assistance would have to play a greater role in respect of the elderly. In 1954, for example, the Phillips Committee argued that 'an attempt to provide a subsistence rate for all without regard to need would appear to be an extravagant use of the community's resources', and proposed that pensions be supplemented through assistance in a 'moderate percentage of cases' (Cmd. 9333, pp. 56–7).

All of this ensured that, when the Conservative government decided upon a major increase in pensions prior to the 1959 election, that increase took the form of higher assistance scales rather than more generous insurance pensions. The 1959 uprating was a major improvement in the real value of assistance; the scales rose by over 11 per cent at a time when prices were stable. Insurance benefits were unchanged, and so the numbers applying to the Board were bound to increase. The irony is that this shift towards the Board occurred at the very time when its image began to turn sour.

The central issue was, of course, take-up. There was always an element of ambiguity in the praise heaped on the Board in the early years. The Attlee government, for example, did its best to ensure that the unemployed would never have to apply to it (Deacon, 1981b), while Enoch Powell for the Conservatives opposed the use of the Board as the agency for free teeth and spectacles (*Hansard*, 487, 1199). In general, however, it was assumed that the means test had lost its former significance, and in January 1951 *The Economist* told its readers that a 'fundamental change' had taken place. 'The fundamental change is that the stigma, which was formerly attached to the receipt of poor relief, whether indoor or outdoor, has gone' (20 January 1951). By the mid-1950s, however, there was growing evidence from voluntary societies and others in the field that many old people were reluctant to claim assistance. The problem was mentioned briefly by the Phillips Committee as early as 1954 (Cmd. 9333. p. 57) and was acknowledged by the Minister of

Pensions and National Insurance, John Boyd Carpenter, during the debate on the 1959 uprating. Boyd Carpenter conceded that it was now 'often alleged' that old people were reluctant to apply, but added that whilst it would be foolish to deny 'that such feelings existed', he was sure that they had 'enormously diminished' in recent years. The reluctance which remained, he went on, had three causes. The first was ignorance, and some people still believed that a person had to be penniless to be eligible for assistance. Second, there was a serious misconception as to the procedures adopted by the Board, which were believed to be much more humiliating than they actually were. Finally, the service was regarded in some quarters as charity because it was not paid for by contributions. He believed that there was a case for modifying the order books and for making other minor changes to lessen the distinction between insurance and assistance, but not for changing the name of the Board: 'I do think that as long as the Board's functions remain broadly the same we should not be dealing intellectually and honestly with our fellow countrymen if we were to change the name whilst retaining the organization and the system' (*Hansard*, 607, 1228). For its part the Board was convinced that the problems of take-up and stigma were not serious. The removal of the household means test meant that many pensioners were nominally eligible for assistance even though they lived with close relatives in what it regarded as comfortable circumstances. The Board assumed that these were the people who were not coming forward, and there is some evidence that this was largely correct. In a fascinating re-analysis of Rowntree's 1951 results, Atkinson and his colleagues (1981) found evidence of substantial non take-up, but also that 81 per cent of those failing to claim lived with relatives. A similar pattern emerges in the studies which finally confirmed the existence of the take-up problem, particularly that of Cole and Utting (1962) and the Ministry's own survey conducted in 1965. The latter found that around 850,000 pensioners in 710,000 households were failing to claim assistance, though over half of these were actually living at or above assistance level, either because they had resources which the Board would have disregarded, or because they were living within a larger household (MPNI, 1966, p. 84). The important fact, however, was that less than two-thirds of the pensioners who should have been receiving assistance were in fact doing so, and take-up became a major political issue.

The Labour Party's attitude towards the Board began to change after 1955, and it became increasingly critical of the stigma which it believed was attached to the receipt of assistance. In 1957 it published its proposals for a national superannuation scheme which was designed to remove pensioners from the scope of the Board, and delegates to the Party Conference in 1960 condemned assistance as a continuation of the poor law which 'had no place in a real affluent society' (Heclo, 1974, pp. 261–70; Webb, 1975, pp. 416–7).

The results of the 1965 survey came as a shock to many members of the Board, and their senior advisers. If people did regard assistance as charity, then the solution would be to make it more similar to national insurance. This, however, would involve the removal of those features of the scheme which had hitherto been held to be its greatest strength, most notably the home visit and the scope for adjusting benefit to meet the circumstances of each case. In the early 1960s, the Board began to improve its publicity material and extend and refashion the training it provided for its staff. This, however, was opposed by some of its senior officials who were still committed to the procedures and practices which they believed to have been so successful in the earlier years. The home visit was also changing. Although the welfare function remained important (Cmnd. 3042, p. 24), visiting became increasingly focused upon the assessment of claims for exceptional circumstances additions (ECAs). These were additions to the weekly benefit granted at the discretion of the local officer in respect of special needs such as laundry, fuel or a special diet. The proportion of claimants receiving these additions rose from 27.5 per cent in 1948 to 59.9 per cent in 1965, and the use of discretion on such a scale was criticized as both a waste of administrative resources and a further cause of stigma.

It is, of course, highly unlikely that the National Assistance Board had ever worked as well as its staunchest advocates believed. Nonetheless it is quite possible that its approach was more successful in the early years before the wartime atmosphere and attitudes began to fade. It was one thing for a claimant to have to tell the Board that he or she needed extra money for clothes or bedding when friends and neighbours were in a similar position and when the cause of the need was so obviously beyond the control of any one person. It was quite another to have to show worn clothing to a visiting officer when everyone else had 'never had it so good'. Moreover the Assistance Board had been distinct from and obviously superior to the poor law, and after 1948 there were many pensioners who felt that it was humiliating to have to go to the same office as people they regarded as down and outs. These problems, however, were exacerbated by the fact that facilities at many of the Board's offices were grossly inferior to those in national insurance offices, by the use of separate payment books for insurance and assistance, and by a range of other procedures which highlighted the difference between the two benefits. It was these latter factors which attracted the most attention, and there were many in the mid-1960s who believed that the problems of means-tested assistance could be greatly reduced by a new name, a new image and better publicity.

### SUPPLEMENTARY BENEFITS

National Assistance was renamed supplementary benefits (SB) by the Social Security Act of 1966. The background to this Act has been discussed elsewhere, most notably by Webb (1975). The important point is that the Labour government turned its attention to the reform of assistance only after it had been forced to abandon plans for an 'income guarantee' for pensioners. Labour had entered office committed to the view that assistance was essentially a 'pensioner problem'. Its long-term solution was its proposed scheme of national superannuation. That scheme, however, would take years to mature, and could do nothing for those already on pensions. A major increase in the basic pension was ruled out as too expensive. Geoffrey Gibson, secretary to the study group which devised the guarantee, wrote that to remove 'any significant proportion of pensioners from national assistance would mean a prodigious waste of re- sources. It would mean giving a gigantic and unnecessary increase to the three-quarters not on assistance to help the quarter who were' (1964). The short-term solution was to use the basic machinery to raise the incomes of the poorest pensioner households to a level above the prevailing assistance scale, a negative income tax for pensioners. In the event, the scheme quickly foundered in the face of the opposition of the Inland Revenue and mounting uncertainty as to its cost. This left a major election pledge unfulfilled, however, and having failed to remove the need for means-tested assistance, Labour sought to make it as acceptable as possible to the pensioners. Under the Act, the Ministry of Pensions and National Insurance and the National Assistance Board were merged to form a new Ministry of Social Security. Within the new Ministry there was to be a Supplementary Benefits Commission (SBC). This would be responsible for the day-to-day administration of the scheme, although the fiction that it had been the NAB which had determined the level of assistance was not continued. Pensioners would no longer need separate books for their insurance pension and assistance, and the two sets of offices were to be com- bined within a single building. There was also to be a long- term addition to the basic rates which, it was hoped, would remove the need for many of the ECAs then in payment. This new addition was to be paid to all claimants who had been in receipt of benefit for more than two years, with the exception of the unemployed. The latter were excluded on the grounds that they were unlikely to be in receipt of benefit for the rest of their lives, and that in any case they did not normally receive the discretionary payments which the new addition was designed to replace (Sinfield, 1982). The Act also made the receipt of supplementary benefit a legal right, although in practice the Commission could reduce or withhold benefits paid to people below pension age.[5]

The 1966 Act appeared to have a marked effect on take-up. By the end of the year, the number receiving benefit had risen by 365,000 and few of the new claimants had received national assistance in the past (Cmnd. 3338, p. 53). These figures, however, were subsequently shown to be misleading, because the Act also increased the scale rates and thus made more people eligible for benefit. Indeed, Atkinson (1969, pp. 75–6) argued that between half and two-thirds of the increase in pensioner claimants could be attributed to the more generous scales, and that those claiming after the Act probably represented a smaller rather than a larger proportion of those eligible. The other major objective of the Act was to reduce the role of discretion within the scheme and minimize the differences between it and national insurance. In this it was a total failure.

The numbers receiving SB rose by 12 per cent between 1966 and 1975. What was much more important than the overall figure, however, was a marked shift in the balance between the different groups of claimants. The number of supplementary pensioners actually fell, and the proportion of retirement pensioners who were receiving a means-tested supplement was lower in 1975 than for nearly 20 years. In contrast the number of unemployed claimants rose from 172,000 in 1966 to over half a million — 20 per cent of the total — in 1975. Over the same period, the number of one-parent families on benefit more than doubled to 276,000. The reasons for this change are clear. The development of occupational pensions lifted more pensioners above the SB scale. Conversely, the increase in claims from the unemployed reflected both the growth in unemployment generally and the limits placed upon insurance benefits for this group. Under the National Insurance Act of 1966, unemployment benefit could not be drawn for more than one year. Moreover, spells of unemployment not separated by more than 13 weeks counted as one, and once benefit had run out, it could not be drawn again until the claimant had worked for at least 12 weeks. The rise in long-term unemployment thus meant that an increasing number of unemployed people exhausted their entitlement under the insurance scheme, and there was also a growing number of unemployed school-leavers who had never paid contributions.[6] There was no insurance benefit at all for one-parent families, other than those headed by a widow. The increasing incidence of marital breakdown thus led more and more women with dependent children to apply for supplementary benefit.

By the mid-1970s, then, the SBC's clients were very different from those of its predecessor, and the consequences were profound and far-reaching. First, the administration of benefit became much more complicated; the workload on the local offices increased and the quality of service to the claimant declined, despite a 100 per cent increase in staffing between 1966 and 1975 (HC 535, 1976–7, p. 400). This was largely because single parents and the unemployed moved on and off benefit with a greater frequency than did pensioners or the long-term sick. The unemployed, for example, constituted 22 per cent of the people drawing benefit at the end of 1977, but they had accounted for 67 per cent of the claims made during the year (SBC, 1979, p. 5).

The unemployed and single parents were also less likely to attract public sympathy, and the second consequence of the changing balance between claimants was that the scheme became the focus of an extraordinary series of allegations of fraud and abuse in the mid-1970s (Deacon, 1978; Golding and Middleton, 1982). The 'scroungerphobia' of this period forced ministers to introduce a number of measures to detect and deter malingering which could not fail to affect the manner in which benefit was administered. More fraud investigators were appointed and fraud awareness packages were issued to all local offices. Both ministers and the Commission continued to stress the need for the local staff to treat the great majority of claimants with courtesy and respect. In practice, however, it was impossible for either the NAB or its successor to control the way in which local officers handled individual cases, and there was considerable scope for what Michael Hill (1969, p. 82) has termed 'mucking applicants around'. One example of this in national assistance was the avoidance of the official procedure for dealing with suspected fraud by simply cutting off the allowance:

If the person stayed away one assumed the procedure was justified; if he, or she, came back for more, then one would have to make a further payment and start the

laborious process of accumulating evidence . . . This
tactic was particularly used with unmarried mothers or
deserted wives where they were suspected of a continuing relationship with a man, the aim being to make
it more difficult for the woman to get money from the
NAB than the man . . . In this type of case inevitably
the woman often came back for more Assistance, hence
'mucking around' consisted of giving small payments,
after a long wait in the office, the inadequancy of
which forced her continually to re-apply for Assistance.

It was the unemployed and single parents who were most
vulnerable to 'mucking around', and it was these groups who
were growing in number in the 1970s. The third consequence
then of the scheme's new clientèle was that the manner of
administration became a major issue. The problem was
graphically described in an internal report by an official of
the DHSS who had spent six months working as an executive
officer in a local office:

> . . . concern to prevent abuse was probably the most
> significant influence on staff's attitudes to and dealing
> with claimants. The prevalent view was that abuse,
> whether trivial or serious, was rife throughout the
> scheme . . . Questioning a claimant with one eye on his
> welfare needs, and the other on the possibility of fraud,
> was an impossibly schizophrenic role. And with some
> staff, the suspicious eye became much the sharper of the
> two (Moore, 1980, p. 69).

What was equally significant, however, was the way in
which those attitudes were reflected in the distribution of
discretionary additions to the weekly benefits. The number
awarded varied not only between different groups of claimants but from one local office to another (Cmnd. 6910,
p. 111; Donnison, 1982, pp. 44, 63).

Such inconsistencies afforded a ready target for the welfare rights movement which emerged in the late 1960s. The
objective of the welfare rights campaign was benefits 'as
of right'. The argument was that if benefit was paid according

to unpublished rules and at the discretion of a local official, then claimants could not learn about, and insist on, their entitlement. A central demand was thus the publication of the 'A' Code, the voluminous guidance which the Commission issued to its local staff on the use of their discretionary powers. Tony Lynes, for example, wrote in 1969 'the real reason for keeping the A Code secret, I suspect, is that supplementary benefits are for the poor and only for the poor. They are a form of communal charity . . . To publish detailed rules about the administration of the scheme would conflict with this view of its essential nature' (1969, p. 6).

The arguments which were usually advanced in defence of discretion were that it was necessary to ensure flexibility and responsiveness to individual needs. In a seminal article, Richard Titmuss (1971) condemned the 'pathology of legalism' under which legal rules set out in minute detail what claimants were and were not entitled to. 'A definition of entitlement in precise material and itemised terms . . . would mean that whatever the level of provision it would become the maximum which no official or tribunal could exceed' (p. 126). Nonetheless, he added that deciding 'where the line should be drawn between legalised basic rights and discretionary additions' was a 'constant challenge' to the supplementary benefit scheme (p. 127). He also added that the Commission was in danger of being 'overwhelmed. Already it has too many claimants, too many callers, too many clients, too large a caseload' (p. 131).

Titmuss's article was published in 1972, when there were 2.9 million claimants and 15 per cent of them were receiving an exceptional circumstances addition. The proportion had been 57 per cent in 1965 and the decline followed the introduction of the long-term addition — discussed earlier — and the Commission's policy of standardizing the circumstances in which such payments should be made. The trend was dramatically reversed in 1973, however, and 40 per cent were receiving an addition in 1975 and 60 per cent in 1979. These additions were paid primarily to the old, and the main reason for the increase was the rising cost of fuel.[7] There was a similar increase in the number of exceptional needs payments (ENPs), from 580,000 in 1971 to 940,000 in 1975 and

1.2 million in 1978. These were lump sum payments, granted for the purchase of such items as clothes and bedding, and received most often by lone parents and other families with children (DHSS, 1978, p. 72).

The enormous increase in the number of discretionary payments could only exacerbate the problems of inconsistency and prejudice against particular groups of claimants. In an attempt to secure greater conformity, the Commission issued more and more guidance to its staff. In 1975 alone, over 10,000 pages of new or revised instructions were produced (HC 535, 1976–7, p. 399). This did not solve the problem, however, partly because of the complexity of the instructions and the attitudes of the staff and partly because of the intervention of the appeal tribunals. A claimant could appeal to a tribunal against any decision of the Commission. The tribunal was bound by the 1966 Act, but not by the Commission's policy as expressed in its instructions to its staff. This meant that a tribunal hearing often became a 'second look at the facts, in effect a second claim rather than an appeal as normally understood' (DHSS, 1978c, p. 86). The number of appeals heard rose from 22,420 in 1971 to 55,125 in 1976, and 42 per cent of the latter related to ENPs.[8] More than a quarter of those appeals were successful, and this was said to undermine both the morale of the staff and the attempt by the Commision to regulate the use of discretion.

There was another reason why the growing reliance on discretion was such a problem: it was labour intensive and the government was seeking to reduce the level of staffing. In 1975, the DHSS was asked to reduce its administrative costs by £5 million in 1977–8 and by £14.4 million in 1978–9 (at 1975 prices), and substantial savings would have to be made on supplementary benefit (HC 535, 1976–7, p. 952). It was hardly likely that the number of claimants would fall by a commensurate amount, nor that the staff would accept such an increase in their workload. The only possibility was to simplify the scheme and to make it easier and cheaper to administer.

By the mid-1970s, then, the pressures upon the SBC were intense: from claimants faced with a deteriorating service, from a public genuinely alarmed at the spectre of abuse, from staff resentful at the complexity of their instructions and the attitude of some claimants, and from politicians anxious to reduce the number of staff. There was a general conviction in Whitehall, the relevant pressure groups, and in the Commission itself, that the existing scheme would not be able to cope for much longer. There was no such agreement, however, as to what should replace it.

## THE REFORM OF SUPPLEMENTARY BENEFITS

In September 1976 David Ennals, Secretary of State for Social Services, announced the establishment of a review of the supplementary benefits scheme. This review was to be undertaken by officials of the DHSS, working closely with the Commission. The review team's report was published in July 1978, and became the subject of an unusual exercise in 'open government'. Over 65,000 copies of the full and an abridged version were distributed free of charge, comments were invited from all interested parties and 37 public meetings were held in different parts of the country. In November 1979, the new Conservative government issued a White Paper which adopted most of the review team's proposals and which in turn formed the basis of the Social Security Act 1980.

The work of the review team and the debate which it aroused has been described elsewhere, and these accounts will not be repeated here.[9] The initial impetus for the review came from David Donnison, who had been appointed Chairman of the Commission in October 1975 and had quickly become convinced that the scheme was in danger of breaking down:

> Pretty soon the more hard pressed officers would be having to make their own simplifications in order to cope with the work . . . We had perhaps a couple of years in which to achieve some nationwide agreement which would lead to constructive and orderly changes. After that it would be too late (1982, p. 46).

In a series of speeches and articles, Donnison set out the

case for a simpler system, based upon legal entitlement and relying far less on discretionary additions. For Donnison the advantages of a review by civil servants were speed and expertise, while the open government strategy was designed to secure a sufficiently broad measure of support to enable any proposals to survive a change of government. There was considerable opposition within Whitehall to the idea of a public review. The decisive factor here, however, was Donnison's earlier success in securing approval for the publication of an independent *Annual Report*, since the work of the review could not be kept secret if the Commission was free to discuss the issues which it raised (Walker, 1982, pp. 2—4). Two crucial concessions, however, were made by the advocates of a review. First, it was agreed that the review should be confined to supplementary benefit and should not consider other areas of social security. Second, it was accepted that the review team would not make any recommendations which would lead to a net increase in expenditure or manpower requirements. As Carol Walker (1982, p. 2) has shown, the nil cost approach and the narrow remit were necessary to secure Treasury approval for the establishment of the review. They meant, however, that 'the review team was asked to examine the internal structure and operation of the SB scheme with a view to producing financially feasible options for change'.

The review team themselves were quite explicit as to the approach which they had adopted. Their report, *Social Assistance* (DHSS, 1978c) began by saying that it had been the policy of successive governments to reduce the numbers on means-tested benefits:

> But against the background of continuing restraint on public expenditure and public service staff, there is no prospect of finding the massive sums for national insurance benefits or the services that would be needed to reduce the number of supplementary benefit claimants . . . In our view the most realistic aim is to fit the scheme to its mass role of coping with millions of claimants in known and readily-defined categories for the foreseeable future (p. 5).

The report recognized that this was bound to involve 'some element of rough justice', since it would be unrealistic to expect that 'extra money would always be found . . . to ensure that nobody would ever be worse off than now' (p. 5). It has been suggested that the review team spelt out the implications of their remit in such stark terms in the hope that this would generate pressure for additional resources. Nonetheless, their report stands in sharp contrast to the stance adopted by the Assistance Board during the 1944 'review' (p. 41 above).

The most important requirement if the scheme was to be adapted to its mass role was the introduction of a new legal structure 'with clearer and more public rules and based on simpler criteria covering the common and predictable needs . . . of claimants' (p. 5). These rules would apply equally to the staff and the appeal tribunals[10] and would make clear, for example, the circumstances in which an addition to the weekly benefit could or could not be awarded. It was envisaged that lump sum payments in respect of items already covered by the scale rates would stop. Such payments, however, constituted over half of all ENPs, and the review team did not think it would be possible 'simply to discontinue' them 'without causing considerable hardship for some claimants'. They suggested, therefore, the introduction of a system of regular lump sum payments at intervals of six months, the level of the payment depending upon the size of the household (p. 83). The report also outlined various ways in which the scheme could be simplified, including the alignment of the scale rates with the corresponding national insurance rates, the withdrawal of benefit from school-leavers until the end of the first vacation after leaving school, and the adoption of a greatly simplified procedure during the first weeks of a claim. Indeed the review team claimed that underlying 'all the possible changes we suggest is one common theme – a need for simplification' (p. 3).

The nil cost assumption was opposed by many of those who submitted written comments upon *Social Assistance*, and by the SBC itself (Walker, 1982, pp. 11–16). Nonetheless, it was accepted by the Conservative government and the review team's proposals formed the basis of the 1980 Act.

Under the Act the responsibility for determining eligibility for benefit passed to the local officials. Hitherto they had been acting on behalf of the SBC, and had reached their decisions on the basis of the advice and guidance issued by the Commission. Now they were to assess claims according to the rules drawn up — and published — by the Secretary of State.[11] The most important difference between these new regulations and the policies formerly adopted by the SBC was the virtual abolition of ENPs for items covered by the scale rates. This had been envisaged by the review team, but they had also proposed that all claimants should automatically receive a lump sum payment every six months. This proposal was not accepted, however, and nor were the scale rates increased to compensate claimants for the reduction in ENPs.

The government argued that the various changes represented a 'carefully balanced package . . . a small number will lose, and others will gain by varying amounts' (Cmnd. 7773, p. 2). In fact the original estimate was that 1.75 million claimants would lose and 0.75 million would gain, although the individual losses were generally smaller than the gains (*Hansard*, 975, 371—4). Overall the effect was to redistribute resources in favour of families with children at the expense of supplementary pensioners (Walker, forthcoming Donnison, 1982, pp. 177—81). All claimants, however, were expected to 'reap the benefits of the emphasis on legal entitlement and published rules, and on simplification' (Cmnd. 7773, p. 2).

Before the new scheme had even gone into operation, however, a second Act had nullified the alignment of the insurance and assistance scales. This later Act was designed to reduce public expenditure and safeguard work incentives, two objectives to which the new government was to accord a markedly higher priority than the simplification of the scheme. Short-term national insurance benefits and invalidity benefits were increased by 5 per cent less than the rate of inflation, while the earnings-related supplement to insurance benefit was abolished with effect from January 1982. This may have come as something of a surprise to any claimant who had read the White Paper, since this had argued that the alignment of the benefit rates would make it easier for them to see 'how the earnings related component of national insurance benefits helps to lift people above the supplementary benefit level' (Cmnd. 7773, p. 3).

*SUPPLEMENTARY BENEFIT IN THE 1980s*

In 1981, the DHSS argued that it would be 'at least another year, maybe even longer' before firm conclusions could be drawn as to the success or failure of the new scheme. Until then it would be impossible to distinguish between 'those problems which have arisen from the new scheme itself', and those which are 'associated with the fact of its introduction' (SSAC, 1982, p. 40). It is certainly true that the speed with which the changes were introduced has increased the problems of both staff and claimants. Nonetheless, the major obstacle to any assessment of the changes is the way in which the scheme has been overwhelmed by the tremendous upsurge in claims since 1980. However serious the problems with the new scheme, it can always be argued that they would have been even worse if the old system had remained in operation. The important point, of course, is that the scheme is currently subject to pressures which make it impossible for it to meet the needs of claimants whatever the legal structure.

The number of claimants rose from 2.85 million to 4.14 million between December 1979 and December 1982. Pensioners accounted for only 10,000 of this increase, whilst the number of one-parent families rose from 306,000 to 420,000. The dramatic change, however, was in the number of unemployed claimants which leapt from 56,000 at the end of 1979 to 1.7 million in December 1982. On the latter date there were over 1.3 million unemployed with no entitlement to national insurance benefit, and the collapse of the insurance scheme has been dramatic. Between November 1980 and February 1982, the proportion of those registered as unemployed who were wholly or partly dependent upon supplementary benefit rose from 46.2 per cent to 57.3 per cent. The proportion receiving national insurance benefits alone fell from 39 per cent to 28.1 per cent (DHSS, 1982b, Table 1.32).

All of this has intensified the pressures and tensions discussed in this chapter, and the most obvious manifestation of this has been the prolonged strile of office staff in Birmingham and Oxford in protest at the levels of staffing (*New Society*, 28 October 1982, 16 December 1982. An additional factor has been the phased introduction of the new housing benefit in November 1982 and April 1983. In the long run this will lead to a very substantial fall in the workload of the benefit offices and the amounts paid in benefit will fall by 30 per cent. Indeed it was the Commission – and especially David Donnison – who led the campaign for its introduction (Donnison, 1982, pp. 184–93; Cmnd. 7392, pp. 56–9). The single housing benefit will solve the problem of claimants having to make complicated calculations to decide if they would be better off on insurance benefits and rebates rather than claiming supplementary benefit. It should also increase work incentives and improve take-up. None of these advantages, however, is the reason for its introduction. The sole purpose of the new scheme is to save on staffing – an estimated 10 per cent of local staff time was formerly taken up with the calculation of benefits related to housing costs. Like the new supplementary benefit scheme, it is being introduced on a nil cost basis, and, again like the SB changes, this is giving rise to complexities and anomalies.

The rise in the number of claimants has distracted attention from the impact of the 1980 Act, and indeed has made it more difficult to assess the precise effects of that Act. Some problems, however, have emerged already. Carol Walker (forthcoming), for example, has pointed to the difficulties encountered by claimants or their representatives in obtaining copies of the regulations, and understanding them when they have. As she has noted, the complexity of the regulations stems from the need for very precise definitions of entitlement. If simplicity would have been expensive, economy is proving to be very complicated:

> There is an essential conflict between trying to contain
> the availability of additional payments to the minority
> for whom they are intended and trying to keep the

system simple. By catering for the exceptional cases, the regulations have to be extremely precise and over-definitive and can themselves give rise to new anomalies.

The most immediate problem, however, is the impact of the curtailment of ENPs, now called single payments. The SBC had always recognized that the larger number of ENPs awarded reflected the inadequancy of the scale rates, especially for families with children. This led it to urge that the change to six monthly payments be a gradual one. 'In some . . . [areas] . . . claimants have long relied so heavily on exceptional needs payments that an abrupt withdrawal of this help would cause severe hardship. In such places the transition should be brought about in stages' (SBC, 1979, p. 31). Instead ENPs for such items as clothing were withdrawn immediately. In addition, the DHSS had gone to some lengths to ensure that relatively little use is made of regulation 30. This permits an officer to make payment for an item not specified in the regulations if there is a serious risk to health. In evidence to the Social Security Advisory Committee (SSAC), however, the Department said that it had been successful in restricting this regulation to 'extreme cases' (Walker, forthcoming).

The fundamental question which arises from the recent history of social assistance is whether such a scheme could ever be satisfactorily adapted to play a 'mass role'. There is no doubt that the attempt will continue to be made. The introduction of the new housing benefit will lead to a revival of interest in the review team's proposal that a highly simpli-fied form of assessment should be used for new claimants who are judged to be unlikely to remain on benefit for a long period (DHSS, 1978c, p. 53). Greater use may also be made of computers (Lynes, 1982). None of this, however, would remove the need for a substantial increase in the scale rates, especially those paid in respect of children.

There is no doubt that since 1948, recipients of assistance have experienced a real improvement in their living standards. The scale rates have more than doubled in real terms. Never-theless with large numbers dependent on supplementary benefit, there has been growing concern as to whether the scale rates are adequate. Studies of the standard of living of claimants suggest that the scale rates provide enough for a boring life style for a good manager with no vices. Research by the DHSS found that it is particularly families with children who are most hard pressed and Piachaud (1979) has demonstrated that the child scale rates need to be doubled in order to meet the costs of a bleak modest modern minimum life style.

Since the introduction of the long-term scale rates, there has been a growing gap between the living standards of other claimants and the long-term unemployed who are never eligible for the long-term rates however long they remain on benefit. By 1982, the difference in the benefit for a couple was £10.60 per week and both the SBC and the SSAC have been particularly vocal in calling for entitlement to the long-term rates to be extended to the unemployed. The cost of doing this would be relatively modest: £325 million a year or £125 million a year if it was restricted to those with children (HC 123, 1983, para. 28). The argument against paying the higher rate to the unemployed has always been that to do so would undermine both the incentive to seek work and the contributory basis of the national insurance scheme. The first argument, however, loses much of its force at a time when there are no jobs for the unemployed. As the Commission pointed out, to 'increase incentives while unemployment accelerates upwards is like trying to encourage somebody to jump into a swimming pool while the water is drained out' (Cmnd. 8033, p. 41). The argument that there is a need to safeguard the incentive to contribute to national insurance has also become increasingly hollow in recent years. Nonetheless, the fact remains that increases in the rates of SB will draw people into means tests, with all their disadvantages, unless insurance benefits are also increased. Thus it is to benefits other than SB that one must look for the best chance of both reducing dependence on means-tested assistance, and improving the living standards of those who remain dependent on it. We return to discuss these changes in Chapters 8 and 9.

*NOTES*

1. This figure does not include those claiming non-contributory pensions, which were also administered by the Board.
2. In July 1948, for example, the Board assumed responsibility for 14,561 separated wives and 323 unmarried mothers. By the end of the year the numbers had risen to 31,867 and 4,495 respectively (Cmd. 7767, p. 23).
3. Between December 1953 and June 1965 the number of retirement pensioners rose by nearly half, from 4.31 million to 6.19 million. The proportion applying to the Board rose from 14 per cent in December 1948 to 27 per cent in December 1954, but then fluctuated between 24.7 per cent and 20.4 per cent.
4. The basis of the national insurance scheme was still the age 16 contribution. This was the contribution which would be needed to provide a person who contributed from the age of 16 with the benefits of the scheme if it were invested for this purpose. It was not, of course, an actuarial contribution in the strictest sense, since the benefits would have been increased substantially by the time the 16-year-old reached retirement age. Nonetheless the existence of the rule was an important constraint on the level of benefits provided. In practice the government of the day would take a decision as to what level of contribution was politically acceptable and then calculate what rate of pension could be afforded under the rule. This also influenced public attitudes. The Phillips Committee commented that contributions provided 'an important measure of social discipline since everyone is aware that higher rates of pension must at once be accompanied by higher contributions (Cmd. 9333, p. 44).
5. The Act distinguished between supplementary pensions and supplementary allowances, which were paid to those below pension age. Supplementary pensions did provide a guaranteed income equivalent to the scale rates. An allowance, however, could be reduced or withheld where, for example, a single parent was alleged to be cohabiting with someone in full-time work or an unemployed person was deemed to have left his or her job voluntarily. Decisions on individual cases were taken by local officers who acted on behalf of the Commission and received detailed advice and guidance from it. A full description of the 1966 Act may be found in Appendix A of the Commission's *Report for 1976* (Cmnd. 6910, pp. 209–10).
6. The number of people out of work for over a year rose from 48,000 in 1966 to 161,200 in 1975. There were 55,500 unemployed

school-leavers in August 1972, and nearly 200,000 in July 1977 (Cmnd. 7392, Table 8.5). The number claiming supplementary benefit as a supplement to unemployment benefit also rose, from 77,000 in 1966 to 135,000 in 1975.

7. In 1975, for example, ECAs were being received by 66 per cent of supplementary pensioners, 30 per cent of lone parents and 19 per cent of the unemployed (DHSS, 1978c, p. 72). Fuel prices rose sharply following the Conservative government's decision to phase out subsidies to the gas and electricity industries from 1973. Under the National Insurance and Supplementary Benefits Act 1973, the long-term additions were abolished and there were to be two scale rates: a short-term rate and a long-term rate. The difference between the two, however, was not to be offset against the costs of extra heating. The number of heating additions doubled almost immediately, and by 1975 they were being paid to 47 per cent of pensioners (Cmnd. 6615, p. 22).

8. A large number of appeals were lodged but not heard by a tribunal, either because the claimant withdrew the appeal or because the local officer revised his decision. In 1976, for example, a total of 101,112 appeals were lodged (Cmnd. 6910, p. 175).

9. The major sources are: Bull (1978), Donnison (1982), and Walker (1982, 1983). The authors are very grateful to Carol Walker for making available the manuscript of her forthcoming study *Changing Social Policy: The Case of the Supplementary Benefits Review.*

10. The review team found 'great attraction' in the idea of a Code of Practice, which would not be fully binding, but to which the officers and tribunals 'would be required to have regard' (DHSS, 1978c, p. 24). This was eventually rejected, however, in favour of legal rules.

11. The effect of this was to remove the executive functions of the SBC, and a new body, the Social Security Advisory Committee (SSAC) was set up to replace both the Commission and the National Insurance Advisory Committee.

# CHAPTER 7

# Take-up

From one perspective it is really quite extraordinary that large numbers of those eligible for means-tested benefits do not claim them. It appears that a beneficent government, recognizing the needs of its people, enacts rights and establishes machinery to help meet those needs, only to be faced with a population which stolidly refuses to utilize them. From the perspective of the claimant, things may appear different; far from government being beneficent it has established a residual hotch-potch of benefits designed to protect the interests of the tax payer and which provide marginal improvements in income to selected groups of people. Moreover, these people may obtain benefits if, and only if, they subject themselves to an assault on their privacy and sense of worth and if they can find their way through a maze of office visiting and form filling. Formal rights may exist, but procedures of administration are designed in such a way as to deter claims.

To understand the nature of the problem of take-up helps to position one between these competing perspectives. Take-up is not just a technical issue concerned with the effective delivery of welfare — it may help to answer questions about the nature and function of social policy.

In this chapter we start by assessing the latest evidence on the level of take-up of means-tested benefits; next we review the research on the reasons for non take-up that has accumulated particularly over the last decade; and finally we evaluate the methods that have been used in the attempt to improve take-up.

## THE LEVEL OF NON TAKE-UP

In order to establish the rate of take-up of any benefit or service, it is necessary to know how many people are eligible and how many are claiming. These apparently simple demands are in practice not easy to fulfill. The problems differ from one benefit to another but generally, because of technical problems, estimates of the take-up of means-tested benefits are out of date, subject to large errors and often inconsistent. In order to demonstrate both the level of take-up and the difficulty there is in arriving at satisfactory estimates, it is worth rehearsing the evidence for some of the most important means-tested benefits.

### Supplementary benefits

Estimates of the take-up of supplementary benefits (SB) are derived (now every two years) by statisticians in the DHSS using the Family Expenditure Survey (FES). The FES is an annual survey of about 7,000 households which collects detailed information on income and expenditure. When DHSS statisticians receive the data tapes they carry out a complex analysis for each family unit to assess whether they are eligible for SB. The estimates derived are grossed upwards for the population and compared with administrative statistics on the claiming population to establish what proportion of those eligible are claiming. There are a number of possible sources of inaccuracy in this process.[1] Over the years, the DHSS statisticians have considered and reconsidered these sources of error and concluded that they are either not very large or cancel each other out and that the estimates derived from the FES are fairly robust (DHSS, 1978a). At any rate they are the best that exist.

The latest estimate is derived from the 1979 FES and was first published in *Hansard* in April 1982 (an indication of how out-of-date estimates are), and is given in Table 1.

The Table shows SB was being claimed by 70 per cent of those eligible in 1979. Over a million families were foregoing an average of £5.60 per week. There was considerable varia-

*Table 1 Estimates of take-up of supplementary benefit for 1979*

|  | Numbers ('000) | | Proportion claiming (%) | £ million (per annum) unclaimed | Average weekly amount unclaimed (£) |
| --- | --- | --- | --- | --- | --- |
|  | eligible | not claiming |  |  |  |
| Pensioners | 2,590 | 900 | 65 | 145 | 3.10 |
| Sick and disabled | 300 | 110 | 63 | 90 | 15.40 |
| Unemployed | 700 | 130 | 81 | 70 | 10.50 |
| One-parent families | 370 | 60 | 85 | 30 | 10.20 |
| Other | 50 | 10 | 80 | 20 | — |
| Total | 4,010 | 1,210 | 70 | 355 | 5.60 |

Source: *Hansard*, 21, 248

tion in take-up and the amount unclaimed by different groups of claimants. Only 65 per cent of pensioners were claiming their entitlement, but because the vast majority of them were already receiving a national insurance pension, the average amount unclaimed was relatively modest. In contrast, take-up among one-parent families, most of whom do not have an entitlement to another social security benefit, was much higher at 85 per cent and the average amount foregone by those who failed to claim was also much more — £10.20 per week. The highest average amount foregone and the lowest take-up was among the sick and disabled.[2]

Between 1977 and 1979 the proportion of those eligible receiving benefit fell from 75 per cent to 70 per cent with the fall most marked among pensioners (from 72 per cent to 65 per cent), but the DHSS estimate that most pensioners with unclaimed entitlement to SB are receiving housing rebates. Certainly the average amount unclaimed by pensioners did not increase in real terms between 1977 and 1979 (*Hansard*, 21, 248).

Since 1979, the date of these estimates, two major changes have taken place which may have affected take-up. First in November 1980, following the review of supplementary benefits, a reformed scheme was introduced. Although one of the principal aims of the reform was to simplify supplementary benefits with the intention of making it easier for the claimant to understand, it is unlikely that these changes had a major impact on take-up — most of the measures introduced to simplify the scheme were concentrated on the discretionary elements which would not have affected take-up.

Since 1979 there has been an enormous increase in the number of the unemployed and particularly of long-term unemployed people — those most likely to be eligible for SB. We saw in the previous chapter that 57 per cent of those registered as unemployed in February 1982 were wholly or partly dependent upon SB. In 1979, take-up of SB by the unemployed was relatively high at 81 per cent, but it is possible that the massive increase in unemployment and the abolition of the earnings-related supplement from January 1982 may have brought into eligibility a new type of claimant who is less familiar with the benefit system or more reluctant to claim.

From November 1982, the new scheme of housing benefits will lead to a reduction in the numbers eligible for supplementary benefit and to a reduction in the amount of potential entitlement of those still eligible. Thus the number of those least likely to claim will have been reduced as well as the incentives to claim of the remainder.

## Family income supplement

Family income supplement (FIS) is a trival benefit in comparison with supplementary benefit — both in terms of expenditure and the numbers of people involved. Nevertheless it is of particular interest in any discussion of take-up: this is partly because it is a benefit of great value to those who do claim it, partly because the take-up of FIS appears to be particularly low, and partly because FIS holds a rather strategic position in the selective/universal debate. If the take-up of FIS was much higher than it is, then there would certainly be less reason for maintaining a non means-tested system of child support or, conversely, 'if it could have been shown that a very simplified means-tested scheme could not work, then means testing could be regarded as a failure in social policy' (Stanton, 1977, p. 27).

It is particularly difficult to assess the take-up of FIS. Until 1981, using estimates derived from their own analysis of the FES the DHSS claimed that take-up was about 75 per cent of those eligible. But the FES is not a good vehicle for assessing the take-up of FIS,[3] not least because FIS is awarded for 52 weeks regardless of changes in income or other circumstances. At any one time there will be families receiving FIS who, on the basis of their incomes or other circumstances, are no longer eligible and, more important, there will be families who are not receiving FIS who are not currently eligible but who during the previous year had been eligible and should therefore be counted as eligible non-claimants.

Until 1981, the DHSS assessed take-up of FIS by relating the numbers in the FES receiving the benefit at a given date to the number entitled 26 weeks previously 'on the assumption that, on average, this would be the number entitled at the given date' (Elton, 1974, p. 24.9). The 75 per cent take-up rate was in fact derived from an analysis in 1975 which estimated that take-up had risen from 'about half' in 1972, to 'about two-thirds' in 1973, to 'about three-quarters' in 1974 and 1975 (DHSS, 1978b, Table 32.15). In 1981 these estimates were revised in the light of findings from the Family Finances Survey. This survey, carried out between October 1978 and September 1979, had duplicated the methods of the FES but had been restricted to a sample of families with dependent children living at or below 140 per cent of supplementary benefits level. The basis of the calculation of take-up was also changed.[4] Take-up was assessed at 51 per cent among employees. Evidence from the survey suggested that for the self-employed it was probably much lower. It was also concluded that, if the more satisfactory method used to assess FIS take-up in the Family Finances Survey had been used in 1974 and 1975, then take-up would then have been about 50 per cent (*Hansard*, 6, 113–4; also DHSS, 1981).

Despite the advantages of the Family Finances Survey over the FES, estimating the take-up of FIS remains very difficult and subject to error. Even in the Family Finances Survey with a sample of 3,200 low-income families with dependent children, the estimate of 51 per cent take-up was based on only 69 eligible non-claimants (and had a sampling error of ± 8 per cent). Also, because of the small numbers, very little is known about the characteristics of non-claimants. It is known that non-claimants of FIS tend to be eligible for smaller amounts than those in receipt — although only 51 per cent of those eligible were claiming, they were estimated to be taking up 56 per cent of the money due to have been taken up.

Since 1978—9 there has been a substantial increase in the number of families claiming FIS and this *may* be evidence that take-up has increased (SSAC, 1982, p. 52), or that real improvements in the FIS prescribed limits, the change in the hours limit from 30 to 24 for single parents, increased rates of marital breakdown, reduction in overtime and increases in short-time working have increased the number eligible.

## Free school meals

The latest official estimate of the take-up of free school meals is based on a survey carried out in association with the Family Finances Survey in 1978—9 (Wilson, 1981). At that time, families could be eligible for free school meals either because they received SB or FIS or because they had low incomes in relation to a national scale. This national scale was abolished in the Education Act of 1980 and, though a number of local education authorities have continued to operate separate assessment scales, effectively and formally eligibility is now limited to those in receipt of passport benefits. In 1978—9 of the eligible *children*, 61 per cent were receiving free school meals. Among eligible *families*, 57 per cent were taking up free school meals. The take-up rate was much higher among families receiving a passport benefit (74 per cent) than those eligible by reason of low income (36 per cent). Of the eligible families not taking up free meals, 40 per cent had no children who stayed at school, but the rest were paying unnecessarily for their meals — 26 per cent of the whole sample. Take-up was found to be higher for one-parent families and large families. The eligible families not taking up free school meals were found to have a slightly higher level of net disposable resources, were more likely to be middle class and more likely to be in employment.

There was of course no variation in take-up according to the price of school meals because at that time, though not today, the price of meals was a standard 25p. Thus those not claiming their entitlement to free meals were paying £48.75 per child school year more than they needed to. One other study in November 1978 found a take-up rate of free school meals of 34 per cent among families with an unemployed head (Millar, 1982).

## Housing rebates (including rent rebates and allowances and rate rebates)

No official estimate of the take-up of the new housing benefit will become available until 1985 but, because the new scheme is not fundamentally different from rent rebate and allowances and rate rebates, estimates of the take-up of these benefits still have relevance.

The FES is also the source of official estimates of the take-up of these benefits. Statisticians in the Department of the Environment use the FES to estimate the size of the eligible population and compare this with the number of recipients derived from statistics provided by local authorities. The problems of using the FES to assess eligibility for other benefits apply equally to housing rebates, and no estimates of the take-up of rent allowances by furnished tenants have ever been produced because the sample is so small and because of the assumptions it would be necessary to make about the value of furnishings.

There is also some reason for anxiety about the accuracy of the administrative statistics of those claiming provided by local authorities. Tenants no longer eligible but receiving rebates may be included in the figures and there may also be double counting of rate rebate recipients who claim for two half-year periods. Both these factors would lead to exaggerated estimates of take-up. The Department of the Environment have adapted their procedures and given assurances that these are no longer problems (Cmnd. 7175, Appendix 7) but the official take-up rate of rent rebates was consistently higher than that found in a number of local studies carried out in the 1970s. At a time when the Department of the Environment was claiming a take-up rate of 70 per cent for rent rebates from FES data, Page and Weinberger (1975) found 49 per cent of those eligible claiming in Birmingham, and Taylor-Gooby (1976) found 48 per cent of those eligible claiming in Batley. This finding led the National Consumer Council (NCC) in their discussion paper on means-tested benefits to conclude: '. . . it seems that if we are to argue on the basis of official estimates of take-up then we are likely to be erring on the side of optimism (NCC, 1976, p. 26).

A study of a large sample of the unemployed in November 1978 found a take-up rate of only 20 per cent of those eligible for housing rebates. This report suggested, once again, that local authority returns exaggerated take-up by including those who are no longer eligible (Millar, 1982).

The latest official estimates (1980) of the take-up of rent rebates is 70–75 per cent and for rent allowances 60–65 per cent. Since 1975 rent rebate take-up has remained more or less constant, but there was a marked improvement in the take-up of rent allowances after 1975 – which has been difficult to explain because it post-dated the major advertising of the benefit (DoE, 1982, Table 125).

What evidence there is about the characteristics of non-claimants suggests that take-up was higher (78.3 per cent) amongst households without children – mostly pensioners – than households with children (54.3 per cent) (*Hansard*, 22, 117–8). The two largest groups of eligible non-claimants of rent allowances are thought to be unfurnished tenants over 60 and childless furnished tenants, particularly those under 30 (Ritchie and Matthews, 1982).

The official take-up rate for rate rebates is 'about 65 per cent' for 1981 (DoE, 1982, Table 125). Again households with children have a much lower take-up rate at 37.8 per cent than others with 78.7 per cent (*Hansard*, 22, 117–8). It is probable that private tenants are least likely to claim rate rebates because they are often not aware they are paying rates.

*Free welfare foods and exemption from prescription, dental and optical charges*

Again there are no very satisfactory or up-to-date estimates of the take-up of these benefits. We have to rely on such studies as the 1972 survey by Purnell (1973) of 452 housing association tenants in Wandsworth or the 1974 study by Syson and Young (1975) of 525 households in Bethnal Green. Neither of these or other studies were designed to assess the take-up of these benefits which call for rather carefully designed and detailed questioning to assess eligibility. Given these reservations it is probably best to indicate only the broad conclusions of these and other studies. These are that the take-up of these benefits and exemptions on grounds of low income is very low indeed — probably less than 10 per cent, but the take-up of these benefits by those who have a passport entitlement is much higher — probably between 75 and 85 per cent.

## OVERALL ASSESSMENT OF TAKE-UP

Over the years, various attempts have been made to assess the total value of means-tested benefits foregone. While it is possible (though not simple) to calculate for any *individual* how much they would benefit by taking up their entitlement, it is much more difficult to calculate an aggregate loss for the whole population because of the inadequacy of the estimates of the number of eligible non-claimants and the vagueness of estimates of the average amount of benefit foregone.

The first systematic attempt to estimate the amount of unclaimed benefit was by Field (1975) using data for 1973. He claimed that £416 million was being foregone in that year in unclaimed FIS, SB and housing rebates. Using Field's method (of assuming unclaimed payments were the same as the average claimed) the National Consumer Council (1976) arrived at a figure of £645 million for 1975—6. However the Supplementary Benefit Commission (DHSS, 1978a) criticized this method of calculation, arguing that there was clear evidence, for SB and FIS at least, that the average amount of benefit unclaimed is considerably less than the amount

*Table 2 Estimate of the non take-up of the principal means-tested benefits (1979) Great Britain*

| | Take-up rate (%) | Number eligible not claiming ('000) | Average weekly unclaimed (£) | Annual total unclaimed (£m) |
|---|---|---|---|---|
| Supplementary benefit [a] | 70 | 1,177 | 5.60 | 343 |
| Rent rebate [b] | 75 | 361 | 3.60 | 68 |
| Rent allowance [b] | 55 | 183 | 3.60 | 34 |
| FIS [c] | 51 | 77 | 3.85 | 15 |
| Free school meals [d] | 60 | 702 | 58.50 (annual) | 41 |
| Rate rebate [b] | 70 | 1,269 | 56.00 (annual) | 71 |
| Total | | | | 572 |

*Sources*:  a *Hansard*, 21, 248
　　　　　 b DoE, 1982, Table 125 (assumes average amount unclaimed is equal to average amount claimed)
　　　　　 c DHSS, 1981
　　　　　 d Wilson, 1981; DES, 1981

claimed and that the amount of unclaimed benefit in 1975 was nearer £200 million than that estimated by the NCC.

Bearing in mind these arguments, Table 2 provides a summary of non take-up for some of the benefits discussed in the first part of this chapter, together with an estimate of the revenue foregone by non-claimants and saved by the Exchequer. These calculations are necessarily crude but they give a general indication of the overall value of the benefits that some of the poorest people in the UK are failing to claim.

## THE REASONS FOR NON TAKE-UP

Although the evidence on take-up reviewed in the previous section is always uncertain and often conflicting, there is no doubt that the cumulative picture that emerges is that for all benefits there are considerably fewer people claiming than there could be. Why is this?

We now know a great deal more about the reasons why people do not claim means-tested benefits than we did in the early 1970s. But the steady stream of research that has emerged has, if anything, complicated the picture. It has shown that there is no simple explanation for non take-up. Early research on take-up was more preoccupied with estimating non take-up than exploring reasons for it and when eligible non-claimants were asked why they had not claimed, their answers tended to be organized into a simple classification of reasons:

*Ignorance* – absence of information
*Complexity* – difficulties with the claiming process
*Stigma* – or attitudes

As studies began to accumulate, it became clear that the non take-up of means-tested benefits is a much more complex phenomenom than this type of simple categorization suggests. First, there were clearly other factors at work not covered by ignorance, complexity or stigma. Second, each of these simple 'explanations' hid and confused a variety of different elements. Third and most important, it became clear than there was a good deal of interaction between the explanations.

Research workers began to expand the classification of reasons for non take-up and explore their interaction. A number of taxonomies of the reasons for non take-up have been produced in the literature from the relatively cryptic:

. . . reluctance to claim appears to come from some mixture of pride, ignorance, a sense of stigma, reluctance to make the efforts which a claim calls for, a desire for self-sufficiency on the part of an individual or family, an unwillingness to become involved with a government agency and a feeling that the whole business is not worthwhile (DHSS, 1978a, pp. 7, 8).

to the elaborate and comprehensive 'obstacle course' (Allison, 1982).

Below we consider in a little more detail some of the evidence for the most important explanations evinced for non take-up.

## Ignorance

Ignorance can be ignorance of the existence of a benefit or ignorance or misconceptions about eligibility or the process of claiming. Ignorance of benefits of one kind or another has been found to be a significant factor in almost all studies of take-up. For example, although all the families in Wilson's (1981) study had heard of free school meals, only a third of non-claimants eligible on income grounds thought they were eligible. Two-thirds of Taylor-Gooby's (1976) sample gave ignorance of rent rebates as reasons for not claiming. But respondents to surveys who give answers such as 'we did not know about it' may have additional, less easily articulated reasons for not claiming. Questions about knowledge tend to be asked first in surveys on take-up. Ignorance is a rational explanation which respondents appear easily to be able to admit. A number of studies have found that, although eligible non-claimants may explain their behaviour in terms of ignorance, they will fail to apply when provided with information. Taylor-Gooby (1976), for example, found that two-thirds of eligible non-claimants of rent rebate who blamed ignorance still failed to claim after being given explicit information and advice about it. This led him to conclude: '. . . practical problems of communication and application are intertwined with attitudes and beliefs about benefits' (1974, p. 130). Similar findings were reported by Meacher (1972a) in an action research project on rate rebate take-up in Islington, and by McDonagh (n.d.) and Walker (n.d.) in a series of studies designed to find ways of improving the take-up of rent allowances.

So research shows that many eligible non-claimants are ignorant about benefits, but it also shows that they are not very receptive to information — why is this?

*Stigma/attitudes*

Klein (1975, p. 5) believes:

> Stigma is the phlogiston of social theory: a label
> attached to an imperfectly understood phenomenon
> — when low take-up of means-tested benefits can be
> explained just as well, perhaps better, by the informa-
> tion costs involved, by the fact that expense in time,
> trouble and travel may outweigh the value of small
> benefits and by the ability of some people to manage
> on a given amount of money better than others . . .'

There is a good deal of conflict of evidence on the impact of
stigma on claiming. Allison (1982, p. 100) concluded in her
study that stigma was virtually of no consequence as a reason
for non take-up — 'a trace element in the chemistry of the
non take-up of welfare benefits' — something to be experienced and endured in the claiming process but not itself a
serious deterrent to claiming. Yet other studies point to a
variety of negative feelings about claiming means-tested
benefits. Taylor-Gooby (1976) distinguishes between felt
stigma, the subjective feeling of humiliation and stigmatiza-
tion, and the process of being treated as inferior. Stigma has
been used to describe a sense of pride, embarrassment, personal failure; an unwillingness to associate with or be
associated with claimants; a reluctance to expose private
matters to public scrutiny; a desire to be independent and a
fear of loss of dignity in the process of claiming.

Taylor-Gooby (1974) in a review of the theoretical literature suggests that stigma exists partly because means-tested
benefits conflict with the market norms that dominate and
regulate exchange relationships between strangers in our
society. With means-tested benefits there is no exchange of
goods and services, not even gratitude. On proof of need, the
individual receives an unreciprocated present — a gift from
the community. 'The relevance of means testing lies in the
situation of the individual who must receive and cannot pay.
He is by definition unable to maintain equality' (p. 113).

Deviancy theory may also contribute to understanding

stigma. Recipients of means-tested benefits are an 'out group' which are punished as a threat to 'a consensual symbolic universe' (p. 114). Stigma is the subtle and efficient sanction, and it remains today, not just as a hang-over from the days of the Victorian workhouse and the inquisitorial methods of the 1930s, but as a functional mechanism of regulation in society.

Reference group theory may also help in understanding the process by which individuals are prepared to recognize their eligibility for benefits or feel stigma in claiming. They may or may not want to associate themselves with a group who claim benefits. The non-claimant may defend his status by perceiving claimants as scroungers, undeserving or feckless. They are a normative reference group. To join them as a claimant is to remove the availability of this scapegoat.

Certainly there is evidence that people in the UK more than other countries tend to blame the victims of poverty themselves (CEC, 1977). The Schlackman Research Organization (1978) in detailed interviews with claimants and non-claimants for the Supplementary Benefits Review found that the epithet most commonly used to describe the process of claiming supplementary benefit was 'degrading'.

Although these theoretical perspectives may help us to understand the concomitants and meaning of stigma, the concept remains very difficult to investigate in empirical practice. In most studies only a small proportion have attributed their non-claiming behaviour to stigma. (However, it is interesting that more than a quarter of Taylor-Gooby's (1976) study are prepared to attribute it as a cause of other people's behaviour.) An exception to the general rule is free school meals where stigma or at least fear that their children would be identified and victimized as a 'free dinner child' is often given as the reason for not claiming (Wilson, 1981). There is also a good deal of qualitative evidence that discriminatory practices in the administration of school meals is a reason for not claiming (Bissett and Coussins, 1982).

Clearly for many people, feelings of stigma are an unpleasant concomitant to claiming. It is possible that as time passes, as people become more familiar with the modern means test and as memories of the pre-war means test fade, the importance of stigma will diminish. There is evidence that take-up of some, but not all, benefits has improved over time. One or two studies have suggested that loss of pride, self-respect or independence was less often offered by younger respondents as a reason for not claiming (see Page and Weinberger, 1975). The take-up of supplementary benefits appears to be lower for pensioners than for other groups. (But families with children seem to be less likely to claim housing benefits and very reluctant to claim FIS).

*Difficulties with the claiming process*

The evidence that difficulties in the process of claiming may be deterring claimants comes from two sources. First in almost all the research studies of take-up, difficulties in obtaining or filling in forms are recorded as a reason for not applying. There is probably a reluctance in many non-claimants to betray a lack of competence and those who state that 'it is not worth it' or 'too much bother' may be deterred more by this 'hassle' factor than the limited value of the benefit to be obtained. The second source of evidence comes, as we shall see, from the success of the experiments to simplify the process of claiming.

*Lack of incentive*

Lack of incentive may be a more important reason for not claiming benefits than is often realized. It is explicitly mentioned as a reason in most studies. For example Knight (1976) found in a follow-up study of claimants of FIS that of those who had not re-applied, 8 per cent said it was not worth it because the amount they would get was too small. There is evidence in the case of FIS and SB that eligible non-claimants are entitled to smaller benefits than claimants and Millar (1982) found the same applied to housing benefits. The SBC suggested in 1975 that about a third of eligible non-claimants were entitled to less than £1 per week or had an entitlement which lasted less than a month (DHSS, 1978a). Ritchie and Matthews (1982) found the ability to cope or manage on existing levels of income was an important factor in not claiming rent allowance. People wanted to see themselves as managing and not being in need.

The 'hassle' and incentive factors in decisions to claim means-tested benefits can be viewed as 'trade-offs'. Each individual decides whether or not to claim by trading off the utility of the benefit that would be obtained against the disutility of hassle and stigma and comes down in favour of that with greatest weight. How individuals assess the utility or disutility will vary, but there is some evidence that when the price of school meals or prescriptions goes up, so does the number of people claiming exemption.

## Family budgeting patterns

A number of studies have suggested that eligible families may be deterred from applying for benefit if they challenge or conflict with normal budgeting patterns within the family. Taylor-Gooby (1974) for example suggested that if the wife was given a 'housekeeping wage' which included the rent, she might be reluctant to persuade her husband to obtain certificates of earnings in order to claim a rent rebate because it might imply that the housekeeping was insufficient. It is possible that when the 'budgeting' and 'providing' roles are clearly separated there may be a number of problems in applying for benefit. The person responsible for budgeting may have no knowledge of the income level of the provider and the provider may have little understanding of the needs or pressures on the budgeter.

## Reluctance to approach landlord or employer

There is evidence of a reluctance to approach the landlord where this is necessary to claim rent allowance, and an employer where this is necessary for a number of benefits to obtain evidence of earnings. Meacher (1972a), for example, found that some tenants feared that they might be given notice to quit if the landlord found out they had applied for rate rebate. Taylor-Gooby (1974) found cases where employers had been reluctant to provide earnings slips —

possibly because of the low wages they were paying – and Corden (1983) found claimants of FIS who had delayed their claim, for fear that if they asked their employer for wage slips it might be taken as evidence of dissatisfaction and they would lose their jobs.

## Previous claiming experience

A number of studies have noted that people appear reluctant to claim a benefit because of previous experience trying to claim that or another benefit. Evason (1980) has also pointed out that information about benefits is often passed by word of mouth and a previous experience of claiming benefit might affect the subsequent behaviour of not only the individual but also their friends and relatives as well.

## Instability of circumstances

A number of studies have shown that those eligible for means-tested benefits are a very volatile group, subjected to repeated changes of residence, jobs, income, of employment status, marital status and household composition. Studies that have been able to look at a cohort of claimants over time have particularly pointed to this factor of instability in affecting claiming behaviour. These studies include Nixon's (1979) follow-up of FIS families, Corden's (1983) examination of the status of FIS claimants and Walker's (undated) temporal study of rent allowance claimants. Walker distinguished between a small 'core' of claimants of rent allowance and a large 'penumbra' who were only occasionally or temporarily eligible. The movement between employment and unemployment may particularly result in delays in claiming – Richardson (1978), for example, found that unemployed men 'put off' claiming supplementary benefit until it became absolutely necessary in the hope that they would find a job. Millar (1982) found that half the families receiving FIS, nearly half those receiving free school meals and a third of those receiving housing benefit were no longer eligible by the time they were interviewed.

## MODELS OF TAKE-UP

These are some of the ways in which simple explanations for non take-up have been developed into a more disaggregated classification in subsequent research. The other major advance in take-up research has been the development of models or hierarchies of how the process of claiming takes place. Kerr (1982a, pp. 505–17), who developed and tested a model of the take-up of supplementary pensions, has taken this approach furthest. His model has already been adapted by Corden (1983) to examine the process of claiming FIS and it represents a substantial contribution to the clarification of ideas about the barriers to claiming a means-tested benefit as well as being the first real assessment of the relative importance of different factors. Drawing on previous research, Kerr differentiated between six conceptually distinct reasons for claiming.

(1) *Perceived need* – the individual's perception of the extent to which he or she is having difficulty making ends meet;
(2) *Basic knowledge* – the individual's awareness of the existence of a benefit;
(3) *Perceived eligibility* – the individual's perception of the likelihood that they are eligible for the benefit;
(4) *Perceived utility* – the individual's perception of the utility of the benefit in meeting his specific needs;
(5) *Beliefs and feeling about the application procedure* – 'the sum of all negative and positive forces exerted by an individual's beliefs about the application procedure and how he or she feels about these beliefs' (p. 507);
(6) *Perceived stability of the situation* – the extent to which beliefs about the instability of the individual's situation prevents him from applying.

Kerr suggests that these six main 'constructs' comprise a series of thresholds and that to apply for a benefit a claimant has to achieve all six. Perceptions of need, eligibility, utility and stability are necessary to claim, but each taken alone is not sufficient reason for claiming. He is not particularly adamant about the order of the thresholds, but nevertheless suggests that there is a definite order: 'perceiving some utility . . . is contingent upon perceiving some probability of eligibility . . . both of which, in turn, are contingent upon some basic knowledge of the existence of supplementary pensions' (p. 509).

Kerr (1982b) validated four dimensions of his model in his study of pensioners receiving rent rebates who would be better off on supplementary benefits.

Much of the earlier research on take-up used standard structured questionnaires in local or national surveys. These have proved an unsatisfactory method for exploring the nature of the interrelationships of the key elements involved in the decision to claim. Kerr's and Corden's work, the first using experimental methods and the second small-scale detailed interviewing, have been attempts to overcome this problem. Ritchie and Matthews (1982) have also used small-scale methods — group discussion with claimants and non-claimants followed by detailed interviews. They produced conclusions that were very similar to those of Kerr and Corden, viewing claiming as a pathway.

## METHODS FOR IMPROVING TAKE-UP

We have seen that take-up remains a problem and shown how research has revealed that the reasons for take-up are very complex. Certainly no single factor is responsible for non take-up. Therefore no one means is likely to be effective in promoting take-up. But can take-up be improved? Is enough being done to encourage take-up? What more might be done? Below we briefly discuss each of the efforts that are being made and appraise their results.

### Information

There is a steady effort made by central government and local authorities to provide basic knowledge about the availability of benefits. The amount of effort varies from time to time: for example, FIS advertising is concentrated on the period of the year following the uprating. As we saw in Chapter 5, information campaigns have often been associated with the introduction of new benefits. The amount of effort also varies from benefit to benefit: for example, FIS is the focus of a major advertising campaign organized each year by the Central Office of Information (costing £476,000 in 1981—2). In contrast, rate rebates are very poorly marketed by both central government and local authorities who in some areas restrict their efforts to a note on the rates bill: 'You may be entitled to a rate rebate'. A very considerable effort has been made by DHSS in recent years to improve the clarity of leaflets, forms and standard letters to make them less off-putting. It is estimated that two million people have a reading age of less than nine and the NCC estimated that some basic application forms required reading ages of up to 25 (Vernon, 1980). Greater efforts are also being made to ensure that up-to-date leaflets are available in post offices and social security offices.

No doubt more can be done to improve the information provided about benefits. For example Corden (1983) and Ritchie and Matthews (1982) both suggest changes and improvements in the information presently provided on FIS and rent allowances respectively. However, while information may be a necessary condition for improving take-up, it is certainly not a sufficient condition. We have seen from the research on non take-up that the absence of basic knowledge is probably not a very important reason for non take-up. The inability to recognize eligiblity is much more important. Of course, better information can make an impact on this. However, there is also the evidence from a variety of experiments that providing information has very little impact on take-up (Bradshaw, Taylor-Gooby and Lees, 1976; Walker, n.d.).

There is also a constraint on information as a strategy to improve take-up. Information efforts need to avoid encouraging too many unsuccessful applications which create extra burdens for the administration and may engender disappointment and a sense of rejection in the claimant. The SBC reported in 1978 that about a third of applicants were unsuccessful (DHSS, 1978a) and over a half of new and repeat FIS applications fail to 'stick'.

## Advice

We have seen that the barrier to claiming is not the absence of basic knowledge but the inability of potential claimants to recognize their eligibility. This is why advice is so important. The provision of well informed advice and assistance is a vital point on the path to claiming. Such assistance is and always has been available from the agencies administering benefits. The efforts that these agencies make to advise claimants about their own benefits are very variable and certainly more effort could be made in informing claimants of one benefit about their entitlement to others. A study in Harlow by their welfare rights officers found that out of 3,737 households already receiving a rent or rate rebate, 613 were eligible for supplementary benefit or FIS. By sending those people a letter advising them of this fact, about half of them were encouraged to claim a total additional benefit of £52,000 per year (Bennett, 1981). This kind of effort could be duplicated by housing authorities all over the country. Corden's research on FIS showed the potential for improving take-up by advice from agencies. Her respondents were not isolated from such agencies but there had been many lost opportunities for advice-giving from formal agencies — social services and probation and after-care were particularly disappointing in this respect, but even DHSS unemployment review officers were not systematically advising their clients to claim FIS as they moved into work.

The main difficulty with improving the advice-giving of existing agencies is the very complexity of the system of means-tested benefits. Staff administering benefits may be equipped to advise about their own benefit but not equipped to advise about others. Social workers and other professionals in touch with claimants — even if they have had any training in welfare rights (and on social work courses the time devoted to this is still inadequate) — have only limited opportunity to practise their skills and keep up to date. In an effort to improve welfare rights advice-giving, three developments have taken place in recent years. First, the range of welfare rights handbooks has been improved in both coverage and quality. These are published by government departments (for example the *Supplementary Benefits Handbook*), commercial publishing houses ( such as the *Penguin Guide to Supplementary Benefits*), or voluntary bodies. Among the latter perhaps the best known is the *National Welfare Benefits Handbook* which has been published annually by the Child Poverty Action Group since 1970 and now has a monthly welfare rights bulletin associated with it.

Second, in many areas full-time welfare officers have been appointed. The role of the welfare rights advocate was first developed by the Child Poverty Action Group which was influenced in this by the American War on Poverty. The first local authority welfare rights officer was appointed by the Manchester Social Services Department in 1972 and many other social services departments now have welfare rights officers working as a separate team or as a specialist in teams supporting social workers (Simpson, 1978).

One development which has emerged as a result of the appointment of welfare rights officers is the local authority organized take-up campaigns. The first campaign was launched in Strathclyde in the last quarter of 1980. Ten thousand households were sent a postcard by the Regional Council which encouraged them to claim supplementary benefits and discretionary additions, by returning the card direct to the DHSS. The result of this was that local officers became overwhelmed with claims – 12,600 postcards and 10,000 *pro forma* leaflets (which had been issued at the same time) were returned and the DHSS estimated that only 340 people were identified who were entitled to some weekly benefit. However there was a very large increase in exceptional needs payments. Mrs Lynda Chalker, the Minister responsible, criticized the campaign for disrupting the normal work of offices fruitlessly (SSSC, 1981, p. 119). However a number of other local authorities have now adapted the Strathclyde idea and launched similar campaigns. Many of these campaigns have extended beyond DHSS benefits to encourage take-up of their own local authority benefits. They have also supported leafletting campaigns with advice services. The DHSS has begun to co-operate. 'We also aim to co-operate as fully as possible at local level with take-up campaigns organized by local authorities, to whom in turn we look for help to ensure that the impact of extra work fits in with all the other tasks which local offices have to perform' (*Hansard*, 429, 108 -- Lord Elton).

None of these campaigns has yet been systematically evaluated to assess their impact. Some of the local authorities have been disappointed that not more people have claimed as a result of their campaigns, but generally the view is that the cost of the campaign has been justified by the increase in take-up that resulted and the improvement in the knowledge and perception of the problem of non take-up by the voluntary workers and local government officers involved. In Cleveland a successful campaign in 1982 (County of Cleveland, 1982; *The Guardian* 10 January 1982) resulted in £600,000 being claimed in benefits at a cost of £47,000, and the authority have decided to establish a permanent welfare rights service.

The third development in advice-giving and one which is yet in its infancy is the use of the computer. A number of welfare rights software packages have been developed that enable either an advisor or a claimant to work out, at a terminal, what benefits they are entitled to. This type of computer package was first tested in an experiment in Inverclyde District Council (Adler, du Feu and Redpath, 1977), and a new generation is now being tried out in DHSS offices, CABx and social services departments. The DHSS in its *Operational Strategy* (1982) envisages a major role for computer-based advice-giving. It is envisaged that eventually terminals in the local offices will replace pen and paper as the working tool of benefit clerks and ensure that better information is provided for customers who could be treated as 'whole persons' instead of claimants having to move from one counter or office to another to claim different benefits.

## Simplification

The impact that these and other developments in advice-giving can make on non take-up may be substantial but they should not be exaggerated. Advice agencies do not exist in all parts of the country and many non-claimants never come into contact with formal sources of advice. It is therefore administrative devices which either aim to simplify the process of claiming or the benefits themselves to which one should look for perhaps the best hope of improvements in take-up. Changes are being and have been made to the administration of benefits. These are of four sorts.

1. *'Piggy-backing'*. This has already been discussed briefly in the context of advice-giving. The idea is that records can be used to locate and actually encourage those eligible to claim benefits. We have described how Harlow District Council located eligible non-claimants of FIS and SB using rent rebate records. The DHSS provide information about FIS in child benefit order books and SB in national insurance order books. From the beginning of 1982, all new claimants of unemployment benefit were issued with SB1 — the claim form for supplementary benefit. In these and other ways, claimants can be 'piggy-backed' from one benefit to another. One of the main aims of the Operational Strategy being introduced by DHSS over the next 10 years is to use the computer to store information centrally so that more 'piggy-backing' can take place.

2. *Combined assessment*. This is an extension of the 'piggy-back' principle from the provision of information to actual assessment of eligibility. The idea is that instead of having to apply for the different means-tested benefits to different departments on different application forms, either one department is responsible for assessing eligibility for all benefits using one form, or one form is used by a variety of departments.

This approach was in vogue in the mid-1970s. Following local government reorganization, a number of authorities followed the lead of Calderdale Metropolitan District Council in setting up a central assessment unit to carry out assessments of all the authority's means-tested benefits. Applicants for any benefit had to complete a simple application form ticking those out of a list of benefits that they required. They were then assessed for these and informed about any others which they were entitled to but failed to tick. The scheme simplified applications, reduced the assessment and verification work and increased take-up, particularly of education benefits.

At the same time DHSS established a series of local experiments in Salop (1975–6), Brighton (1977–8) and Down in Northern Ireland (1978–9), using a specially designed application form (M1) to replace most of the existing forms used to administer means-tested benefits by the DHSS and the local authorities in each area. An M1 form having been received by one department, it was then photocopied and sent to all other departments administering benefits. The three experiments were different in procedure and the benefits covered, but all resulted in only modest increases in successful claims. The conclusion was that for a single claim form to be used successfully on a universal basis some simplification of the benefits themselves would be needed so that they shared more common characteristics and had a uniform time-cycle (Peel, 1978; Graham and Brasier, 1979; Graham, 1980).

3. *Passporting*. Short of rationalizing the system, and yet a very successful means of increasing take-up, has been the use of passport benefits. Once eligibility for supplementary benefits or FIS had been established, claimants have an automatic entitlement to free school meals, free welfare milk, exemption from charges for prescriptions, dental treatment and spectacles, free legal aid and free hospital fares. Some local authorities also use these benefits as passports to eligibility for exemption from charges for services such as home helps, meals on wheels and educational benefits. The entitlement is automatic in the sense that it is not necessary to undergo a separate means test to obtain the passport benefits, although separate claims or declarations may still have to be made.

As we have seen, passporting resulted in a marked increase in the take-up of the passport benefits and there have been demands to extend passporting. The NCC (1976) urged local authorities to make greater use of passporting instead of running their own means tests. However, there are limits to the extent to which passporting can be further developed. SB cannot be used as a passport to housing benefit because they are alternatives. FIS is not a satisfactory passport to housing benefit (although housing benefit could be used as a passport to FIS) because eligibility for housing benefit extends further up the income scale than FIS. Apart from these problems, passporting increases the severity of the poverty trap: the one advantage of the variety and complexity of means tests is that because they use different income scales and other criteria, they are not all lost at the same time. However, with passporting, once eligibility for the key benefit is lost, so also the claimant loses entitlement to all the passport benefits. As we shall see in the next chapter, the cumulative loss of FIS and the associated passport benefits at the same point in the income scale already presents a very serious loss to claimants.

4. *Harmonization*. The final type of simplification proposed — that benefits should be harmonized — raises similar objections to the further extension of passporting. In fact there has already been a good deal of harmonization in benefits — in the unification of rent and rate rebates, in the principle of passporting, in the abolition of the school meals scale. Ideas for further harmonization have been discussed by the NCC (1976). They considered whether there was more room for benefits to have the same conditions: about evidence of earnings, disregards of earnings and other income; to be consistent in the use of net or gross income and the treatment of housing costs; and even to have a common income threshold. They concluded that there was little room for further harmonization, partly because simplification would undermine the fairness of benefits — for example the capacity of housing benefit to be sensitive to housing costs — and partly because harmonization would increase the chances of benefits being lost at the same point on the income scale.

*CONCLUSION*

There are those who believe that non take-up is a technical problem that can be overcome by breaking down barriers to access; that stigma to the extent that it exists is a throwback to a distant past and will wear out with sensitive and imaginative administration.

There are others who take the view that no amount of effort and adaptation can overcome the barriers to claiming. This was the view of the CPAG who concluded that 'no amount of tinkering with means-tested benefits will transform them into an effective means of eradicating poverty' (Lister, 1976, p. 7), and also the NCC (1976, pp. 79–82) who recommended 'a thorough-going reconstruction of the whole apparatus . . . means tests should go'.

We shall be discussing what form such a reconstruction might take in Chapter 9. But if it did prove possible to achieve the full take-up of means-tested benefits we would still be faced with the other major objection of means-tested benefits – the poverty trap – which we discuss in the next chapter.

*NOTES*

1. The 30 per cent of the FES sample who do not respond could be different from responders and therefore bias the estimate. There may be bias in reporting income. The FES provides information on income from capital, but not the level of the capital itself which might affect eligibility. Additional requirements payable on top of the basic scale rates are not taken into account. Allowance is made in the calculations of eligibility for those who would be better off on housing rebates but not for those on housing benefit who would be better off on SB. It is assumed that all those classified as 'unoccupied' in the survey are available for work and entitled. Finally there is sampling error to take account of.

2. This is likely to be due to the short-term sick not bothering to claim benefits, to those in receipt of non-contributory invalidity pension (NCIP) not claiming supplementary benefits to which they are likely to be entitled, or to disabled people who are living with others and dependent on them and hence not claiming their entitlement to either NCIP or SB.

3. The number of families eligible for FIS in the FES is very small indeed and thus the sampling error is substantial – in 1978 only 130 families in the FES had incomes at or below the FIS prescribed limit; there are also errors in reporting income particularly by the self-employed; there is bias in response rates – for example response is higher for larger families; data derived from the FES do not relate to a particular date because the survey is continuous and the eligible population is likely to vary at different times as the

FIS prescribed levels change or general earnings or unemployment rates vary; also the assessment of eligibility for FIS is based on five weeks' income prior to the claim — the FES income is assessed on the basis of normal or current income.

4. Assessment of take-up was based on recipients whose claim would have succeeded if delayed until interview as a percentage of recipients whose claim would have succeeded if delayed until interview plus non-recipients whose claim would have succeeded at the time of the interview.

# CHAPTER 8

# Poverty Trap

The last chapter considered the problem of the take-up of means-tested benefits. In this chapter we explore the nature of the other major defect of the modern means test – the poverty trap. We consider its impact and also discuss some of the ways in which the poverty trap might be mitigated, before going on in Chapter 9 to appraise some more thorough-going alternatives to means-tested benefits.

The term 'poverty trap' is often used very loosely. It is used here to describe the situation where a low-paid worker may lose a significant part of an increase in earnings because he has to pay more income tax and national insurance contributions and his means-tested benefits are reduced or withdrawn. It has been suggested (Bradshaw, 1980) that 'poverty plateau' is a more precise description of what actually occurs in practice, and we shall develop the distinction later in the discussion. The poverty trap is often confused with the unemployment trap. Indeed Ralph Howell MP has described both as the 'disincentive trap' (HC 331–ix, p. 407). Nevertheless, although both are concerned with incentives, there is a case for maintaining a distinction between them. The poverty trap is concerned with marginal tax rates and with differentials in the net incomes of people in work. The unemployment trap is concerned with differences between the incomes of those in work and those not in work. The poverty trap is created by means-tested benefits. While means-tested benefits play a part in the unemployment trap and could be used as a method of mitigating it, they do not cause it. The unemployment trap could exist without means-tested benefits and means-tested benefits could operate without creating the unemployment trap.

*THE ORIGINS OF THE POVERTY TRAP*

Until the 1970s the poverty trap was not a major issue. As we saw in Chapter 4, the problem of high marginal tax rates on low incomes was discussed in the selectivity/universality debate but it was Abel-Smith (1968b, pp. 696–7) who first noted that 'there are many people today who are already in a situation where an extra pound in earnings would lose them more than a pound in welfare benefits'. As we saw in Chapter 5, it was only in 1971 that the term 'poverty trap' was first used and only in the last decade has it been recognized as a major defect of means-tested benefits.

Three developments have led to its creation.

1. *Income tax*. Since the war there has been a steady decline in the tax threshold – the point where income is considered large enough to warrant income tax being paid. The reasons for this trend are complex and have varied from time to time. Part of the explanation is 'fiscal drag' – personal tax allowances which determine the tax threshold have not been increased in line with increases in earnings. Also the tax base – the proportion of income available to be taxed – has decreased. Thanks to generosity of tax reliefs only 47 per cent of personal income is now taxable (*Hansard*, 18, 159). As a result the Chancellor of the Exchequer has had to rely on taxing lower incomes to yield sufficient revenue. During the 1974–9 Labour government, the thresholds of families with children were also lowered by the phasing out of child tax allowances and their replacement by child benefits. More recently the Conservative government chose to reduce tax elsewhere and in its first budget in 1980 cut the standard rate of income tax and abolished higher rate bands above 60 per cent instead of raising personal allowances.

The net effect has been that more people on low incomes have found themselves paying income tax. Table 3 shows how tax break-even points have declined as a proportion of average earnings, particularly for families with children.

In 1982–3 the income tax threshold for a single person was £30.10 and for a couple it was £47.00. This compares

*Table 3 Changes in tax break-even points 1949 to 1982–3 as percentage of average male manual earnings*

| Tax year | Single person | Childless couple | Couple + 2 children | Couple + 4 children |
|---|---|---|---|---|
| 1949–50 | 39.4 | 62.8 | 122.7 | 185.6 |
| 1959–60 | 27.4 | 45.7 | 103.5 | 181.1 |
| 1969–70 | 25.4 | 37.3 | 68.0 | 109.8 |
| 1979–80 | 21.9 | 34.1 | 62.5 | 88.6 |
| 1982–3 | 21.7 | 33.9 | 60.1 | 86.4 |

*Source*: HC 331–ii, p. 82

with the ordinary scale rate of supplementary benefits from November 1982 of £25.70 for a single person and £41.70 for a couple. People are now liable to pay income tax at incomes which are little different from the official poverty line.

2. *National Insurance Contributions (NIC)*. The Beveridge national insurance scheme imposed contributions that did not vary with income. But by the late 1950s it was clear that, in order to pay adequate insurance benefits, the scheme would have to be funded by earnings related contributions. Such an element was first grafted on to the graduated pensions scheme in 1961 and extended in 1965 to other national insurance benefits. In 1975 the flat rate element was abandoned and contributions became wholly earnings related. Since then there has been a steady increase in the proportion of income taken in NIC from 5.5 per cent in 1975 to 9.0 per cent in 1983–4. This increase has occurred because of the need to fund a new pension scheme, because of changing demographic patterns, because of reductions in the Exchequer contribution to the National Insurance Fund (NIF), and, most recently, because of increased demands on the Fund from the unemployed.

3. *Means-tested benefits*. Before 1970 the poverty trap had

existed to the extent that income tax and NIC overlapped with free school meals and the loss of rate rebates. Even so, the then maximum theoretical marginal tax rate on an extra £1 earned was still only 51.75 per cent before 1970.[1] It was the new means-tested benefits introduced by the Conservative government between 1970 and 1974 that established the modern poverty trap (see Chapter 5).

First the family income supplement (FIS) added a marginal tax rate of 50 per cent on extra earnings from 1971. Next, the rent rebate scheme in 1972 added a marginal tax rate of 17 per cent or 25 per cent depending on income. A new rate rebate scheme was adopted to replace the old one in 1975 which added a marginal tax rate of 6 or 8 per cent depending on income. In addition to these new benefits, increases in charges for school meals, prescriptions and other health charges meant that exemptions from these charges became much more valuable.

## THE POVERTY TRAP NOW

The poverty trap in 1982–3 is made up of the following elements.

(1) *Income tax*. 30p is paid on each £1 above the tax threshold (£47.00 per week for a couple) up to the higher rate tax bands.
(2) *NIC*. If earnings exceed £29.50 then 8.75p is paid per £1 earned up to £220 per week.
(3) *FIS*. 50p is lost on each £1 of extra earnings below the prescribed limits.
(4) *Housing benefit*. 25p rent rebate and 8 per cent rate rebate is lost on each £1 below the needs allowance. 21p rent rebate and 7p rate rebate is lost for each £1 above the needs allowance.
(5) *School meals*. The value of free school meals is lost if income exceeds the FIS eligibility limits.
(6) *Exemption from health service charges*. The value of free prescriptions, free welfare milk and free dental or optical treatment is lost if income exceeds the FIS eligibility limits.

Thus families can have a theoretical marginal tax rate (excluding the loss of passport benefits) of

|  | *Income below needs allowance (%)* | *Income above needs allowance (%)* |
|---|---|---|
| Income tax | 30.00 | 30.00 |
| NIC | 8.75 | 8.75 |
| FIS | 50.00 | 50.00 |
| Housing benefit[2] | 16.50 | 14.00 |
| Total | 105.25 | 102.75 |

This is the formal or theoretical position, but for a number of reasons the full force of the poverty trap is not likely to be experienced to such an extent in practice. There are a number of interrelated reasons for this.

In practice, not all benefits are re-assessed as soon as income changes. FIS continues to be paid regardless of changes in circumstances for a year.[3] After a year the claimant's income may have increased but the FIS prescribed limit will also have been raised.[4] So, it is argued, the claimant would find on re-application that the limits would have at least kept pace with any normal increase in earnings. In fact the extent to which this has happened will depend on the size and timing of wage increases in relation to the timing of the renewal and increases in the prescribed limits (see HC 331—i, p. 11). In practice families may fall in and out of eligibility like a yo-yo. Nevertheless it is the case that extra earnings affect FIS and its passport benefits only at the point of renewal, not as soon as they are earned.

The position with regard to housing benefit is somewhat different. The benefit is assessed on the basis of five weeks' income for a six-month period, but householders are expected to report significant changes in circumstances. For the old rebate schemes, what constituted a significant change in circumstances was not defined by statute and there was a good deal of variation in local authority practice, with some authorities ignoring changes in income below a certain level

(Means and Hill, 1982). Under the housing benefit scheme, changes in income which alter rebates for rent by more than 20p and for rates by more than 10p will be taken into account, and if a tenant fails to report such changes the local authority can demand a refund.

So if we disregard the loss of FIS and its passport benefits, and just concentrate on the maximum that could be lost *pari passu* with a change in income then in 1982—3 it was

|  | Income below needs allowance (%) | Income above needs allowance (%) |
|---|---|---|
| Income tax | 30.00 | 30.00 |
| NIC | 8.75 | 8.75 |
| Housing benefit | 33.50 | 28.00 |
| Total | 71.75 | 66.75 |

These are still very large marginal tax rates and exceed, for example, the maximum rate of income tax of 60 per cent now charged on high incomes.

In order to cope with the complexity of the interaction between taxes and benefits, computer simulation models have been developed to illustrate the poverty trap. These models involve taking a family of a given size and type with children of certain ages, with certain housing costs and work expenses and simulating the effects of taxes and benefits on a range of incomes. These models have their advantages: they are probably the only means of reviewing the inter-action of taxes and benefits; they can be used to examine the effects of changes over time and also test the distributional consequences of reform. However, they have the disadvantage of obscuring the complexity of the real world. They typically ignore the administrative devices discusssed above. In addition they almost always assume that means-tested benefits are taken up which, as we have seen from the last chapter, is not the case. Townsend in particular has argued that the very variable take-up of means-tested benefits effectively mitigates the poverty trap in practice (HC 331-iii,

p. 170). However the Treasury and Civil Service Select Committee (hereafter called the Meacher Committee), which produced a report on taxes and benefits in 1983, decided 'it would be odd to argue that, because the system does not work very well, it does not create very great problems' (Meacher Committee, para. 4.8).

The simulation models also tend to give the impression that the 'model family' illustrated is typical. In fact, given the very large number of assumptions that have to be made, it is most unlikely that there is *any* family of the exact dimensions used in the simulation model. For example, the poverty trap may be described (as it is below) for a one-earner couple with three children aged 3, 8 and 11, paying average rent and rates. But in the majority of even three-child families the children will not be 3, 8 and 11, the wife will work, they may be owner-occupiers, or the housing costs will be higher or lower than average. For each variation in these characteristics, the poverty trap will be different in practice.[5]

### HOW SERIOUS IS THE POVERTY TRAP?

If for the reasons discussed above, an increase in earnings does not result in the increased taxes and loss of benefits to the extent that the formal or theoretical position might suggest, is it important? Does it matter? There are two arguments in reply to these questions.

First, although it may be unlikely for a family actually to suffer a fall in net disposable resources as a result of an increase in income, it is not at all unlikely for one family to have net disposable resources similar to another family despite the fact that their income is very different. Each year from 1975, *Social Trends* has contained a table based on the DHSS tax/benefit model which illustrates the poverty trap. This is shown in Figure 1 for 1982–3. It shows that a family earning £120 per week can be no better off than another family earning £70 per week. Effectively what the arrangement of taxes and benefit achieves is the flattening out of differentials in net income over a range of earnings. There

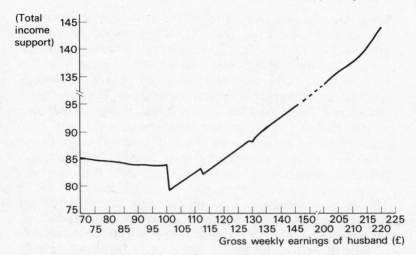

*Figure 1 The relationship between total income support and gross earnings of the husband for a married couple with three children aged 3, 8 and 11, with the wife not earning (as at November 1982)*

*Source*: DHSS, Tax/benefit model tables (1982)

can be no moral or economic justification for this distribution. If it was widely realized it would surely cause outrage. What in effect is happening is that over a wide range of below average incomes a family with a working wife, a father working overtime or receiving higher pay as a result of greater skill or qualifications is receiving little or no benefit from it. In evidence to the Meacher Committee, the Child Poverty Action Group suggested that there were three possible results of this situation.

(1) Workers and employers would 'negotiate' earnings to ensure continued receipt of benefit because it is in both their interests.
(2) Employees may be encouraged to press for 'outrageous' wage increases because 'reasonable' ones would not make any difference to their net incomes.
(3) Workers may experience general feelings of hopelessness because they cannot rise from the poverty plateau by their own efforts.

They are thought rich enough to pay tax and poor enough to receive FIS; sometimes they can get rebates, other times they cannot. Their lives are pervaded by repeated form filling and assessment by different agencies; the rationale and purpose of the system remains a mystery. The poverty plateau is thus not necessarily about work incentives, it is about the morality of governments' encouraging workers to work harder and to claim means-tested benefits even though the combined effect may simply trap them into poverty (HC 331–ii, p. 63).

The second argument is that although the very highest theoretical marginal tax rates are unlikely to occur in practice, nevertheless very high marginal tax rates are commonplace. It is very difficult to estimate the numbers of families caught in the poverty trap. Probably the best estimates are derived from the number of families receiving certain benefits.[6] The Family Expenditure Survey (FES) has also been used to estimate the number of families in the poverty trap. Estimates for 1975, 1977 and 1979 are that the number of families with theoretical marginal tax rates in excess of 50 per cent were 380,000, 360,000 and 270,000 (HC 331–ix, p. 406). The estimate for 1980 was that 700,000 tax units had marginal tax rates of over 50 per cent (Meacher Committee Table 2, p. xxii). An estimate for the tax year 1981–2 indicates that 120,000 families had marginal tax rates in excess of 80 per cent (HC 331–iv, p. 198).

There is also cause for concern because the poverty trap has been getting worse, both in terms of the numbers of people caught in it, and the amount that can be lost as a result of an increase in earnings (see also HC 331–iv, p. 199). The number of people subject to high marginal tax rates at low incomes has increased partly as a result of changes to taxes and benefits.[7] But it has also been increased by other measures. The legislation in 1980 which abolished the statutory free school meals scale and linked eligibility for school meals to receipt of FIS, together with increases in charges for meals, has meant that families above the margins of eligibility for FIS are likely to have considerably lower net disposable resources than those in receipt of FIS. Another measure which has increased the marginal tax rate in the poverty trap was the increase in the taper on incomes above the needs allowance in housing benefit compared with rent and rate rebate,[8] though this has also reduced the number eligible for benefit by an estimated 100,000.

## *SINGLE PARENTS AND THE POVERTY TRAP*

Single-parent families are a substantial group who are often ignored in discussions of the poverty trap. Yet because they are likely to have low earnings, they are particularly at risk of falling into the poverty trap range of incomes. Thus over half the recipients of FIS are single parents. The operation of the poverty trap is somewhat different for single-parent families because, unlike two-parent families, they are not required to register for work and have a choice between claiming supplementary benefit (SB) or, if they are working 24 hours or more, claiming FIS and housing benefit. If they claim SB, then earnings over £4 are affected by the tapered earnings disregard introduced in November 1980 as one of the package of measures following the supplementary bene-fits review.[9] For single parents there is a very complicated 'better off' calculation to be done, in order to decide whether to claim SB or FIS. The introduction of the tapered earnings disregard has effectively compressed the differential between single parents on FIS doing full-time work and those on SB doing part-time work. Between them, FIS and SB are now operating as a rather incoherent minimum income guarantee for single parents with its own unique form of poverty trap which affects not only those on FIS, but also those on SB (Weale, 1982).

## *INCENTIVES AND THE POVERTY TRAP*

One reason why there is concern at the poverty trap is that it is believed that it acts as a disincentive to work, to work more or, in a two-parent family, for the spouse to work.

There is in fact very little empirical evidence of the disincentive effects of the poverty trap (see HC 331–iv, p. 200). However some of the arguments produced in discussions of the labour supply consequences of high marginal income tax rates can be evinced in discussion of the poverty trap.

First, there is the theoretical argument that high marginal tax rates could just as well act as an incentive to work more as less. Losing income and benefits could actually encourage the earner to *increase* his earnings to maintain equivalent living standards. In the case of the poverty trap, there is the added incentive that there is a prospect of emerging from high marginal tax rates by earning enough to 'blast out' of the poverty trap.

Second, those who argue that means-tested benefits (or income tax) have a disincentive effect assume that the individual worker is in a position to increase his labour supply or earnings by moving to higher paid jobs, working overtime or by a spouse finding work. While there may be some flexibility in some jobs, it is likely to be very limited. Overtime is rarely a matter of individual choice – it is either worked by everyone in a plant or not worked. Overtime opportunities are diminishing anyway as are opportunities to change jobs or for a spouse to find work.

In a study (Weale, 1982) of single parents' response to the tapered earnings disregard, it was found that only 34 per cent of those earning thought they would be able to work longer hours in the present job if they wanted to, and only 31 per cent were able to shorten their hours if they wanted to. So even for these, mostly part-time, workers there is a limit to the flexibility of the hours that can be worked. Furthermore, in the case of single parents it is likely that the constraints of childcare are as important as employment opportunities and financial incentives in determining whether they work.

The most elaborate estimates of the effect of marginal tax rates on work effort have come from the negative income tax experiments in the US. These found that a 10 per cent increase in the 'benefits reduction rate' reduced hours worked per week by 30 minutes, and 1 hour 30 minutes for husbands and wives respectively, but *increased* hours worked by female single parents by 50 minutes. The latter result was thought to be an example of a group being induced to work more in order to make up for loss of income (Moffitt, 1981).

Third, there is the argument from complexity. Without a computer it is very difficult indeed to calculate the gains and losses that would result from an increase in labour supply because of the complex way the tax and benefit systems interact. Thus it is most unlikely that an individual will know what the full financial consequences of changing his work are. Nevertheless his behaviour may still be based on beliefs or myths. There is evidence (Brown, 1968, pp. 1–21) that a considerable amount of the antipathy to income taxation stems from a belief that it is higher than it is or that it takes a higher proportion of additional earnings than it does. In a study (Bradshaw, 1982) of single parents' response to the tapered earnings disregard, it was found that there was considerable ignorance of both the disregard and FIS: only nine parents out of a sample of 475 could accurately recall all the elements of the disregard and only four knew all elements of FIS. More significantly, over a third of those who said that losing SB was definitely a factor in deciding not to work longer knew nothing about the disregard of earnings, and over half of those who were not working and gave as a definite reason that if they did they would lose out on SB knew nothing about the disregard.

Finally there are the arguments that, for the reasons already explained, high marginal tax rates do not actually operate in practice — because FIS and the passport benefits associated with it are not lost immediately earnings increase and because many families are not claiming benefits they would not lose them if they worked more.

Taken together, these arguments suggest that the effect of the poverty trap on labour supply may not be as marked as is often suggested. Nevertheless high marginal tax rates must have some impact in encouraging effort (HC 331–i, p. 18). Certainly in the study of the tapered earnings disregard (Weale, 1982) there were single parents claiming that the disincentive of the earnings disregard was a definite factor in determining them not to work or work longer. It is also inconceivable that there are not many families who know and act on the knowledge that they may eventually be worse off if they earn more.

## SOLUTIONS TO THE POVERTY TRAP

We have identified two aspects of the poverty trap which are problematic. First, it may deter some families from working more or harder — it may literally trap them into poverty. Second, a poverty plateau has been created which has destroyed differentials in net incomes for families in the bottom half of the income distribution. The result is grossly inequitable.

What can be done about it? In the next chapter we shall consider some of the ways in which means-tested benefits might be replaced by major transformations of the tax and benefit system. In the rest of this chapter we concentrate on some reforms within the existing framework of taxes and benefits.

### Raise tax thresholds

By raising the personal allowance, or the married man's allowance (MMA) or by the reintroduction of child tax allowances, the threshold could be raised, so relieving some of the lowest paid from paying income tax. These families' marginal tax rates would be reduced by 30 per cent, their incomes would be raised and the incomes of those in work would be improved relative to those unemployed dependent on supplementary benefits.

We have shown that the tax threshold has fallen over the years — particularly for families with children. Between 1979 and 1980 a duty was imposed on the Chancellor to increase personal allowances in line with inflation by the 'Rooker/Wise' amendment. This was repealed in 1980 and since then personal allowances have not maintained their value. Thus it was estimated in 1980 that 100,000 recipients of FIS, 1 million recipients of rent rebates and allowances and 2.5 million recipients of rate rebates were also paying income tax (*Hansard*, 1000, 5–6).

The government, in evidence to the Meacher Committee, gave the lifting of tax thresholds as their preferred method of reducing the impact of the poverty trap (HC 331–ix, p. 410). However there are disadvantages to this method. Because the distribution of earnings is skewed, lifting the low paid out of tax is very expensive in tax revenue foregone. An increase of 10 per cent would cost £1,700 million (HC 331–iv, p. 200). It is because successive Chancellors have been so hard-pressed to balance revenue against expenditure that they have failed to maintain the real value of the tax threshold. Furthermore, lifting the tax threshold benefits all tax payers whether or not they are in the poverty trap, and benefits higher rate tax payers most. It also benefits all tax units whether or not they have dependent children – yet it is families with dependent children whose tax threshold has fallen most and who are most likely to be in the poverty trap.

Increasing the married man's allowance (MMA) and the additional personal allowance for single parents would target the increase better on families with children. Forty-seven per cent of recipients of MMA have children, compared with only 29 per cent of all tax payers (HC 331–x, p. 488). But there is the strongly held view that, far from being increased, the married man's tax allowance should be phased out and abolished on the grounds that it recognizes the dependence of a wife who is now most often not dependent and discriminates in favour of married men as against married women. These and other arguments were rehearsed in detail in the context of discussion on the Green Paper on the taxation of husband and wife (Cmnd. 8093). The majority of those responding to the Green Paper were in favour of phasing out the MMA in favour of improvements in child benefits or a home responsibility payment. As long as the MMA is increased, it becomes more expensive to replace and if it is considered anomalous it is not sensible policy to use it as a vehicle for raising tax thresholds.

Child tax allowances are no longer part of the armoury of Chancellors for raising tax thresholds, since they were phased out as child benefit was introduced. At the time there were very good reasons for doing this. Child tax allowances were

of no benefit to families with incomes below the tax threshold and they benefited most those families with highest
incomes. When they were replaced by child benefits, the
revenue was used to pay a child benefit for the first child
in the family and for the child interim benefit (now one-
parent benefit). However, the arguments against the child
tax allowance and in favour of child benefit are not as
powerful as they were because the tax threshold has fallen
so low that there are very few families with incomes from
work low enough not to pay income tax. Increasing child
benefit, for which there are strong arguments (see below)
does not lift families out of tax or relieve them of the marginal tax rate. The reinstatement of child tax allowance
would do both of these things – at less cost to the Exchequer
and be better targeted than improvements in personal allowances. However it is not likely that child tax allowances will
be reintroduced – not least because their abolition was a
major simplification of the task of the Inland Revenue,
saving 1,580 staff, and to reintroduce them would complicate
a tax system which successive governments are striving constantly to simplify.

The Low Pay Unit and Frank Field argued in evidence to
the Meacher Committee that in order for the tax threshold
to be raised, the tax base must be reconstituted. That is, the
battery of non-structural tax allowances – most important,
tax relief on mortgage interest and private pension contributions – should be restricted by setting cash ceilings on the
existing allowances so that they become 'vanishing exemptions' (HC 331–x, p. 474). If non-structural tax allowances
had been frozen in 1975–6, by 1980–1 the saving would
have been £3,825 million.

### Reduce the standard rate of tax

There are a variety of ways the standard rate of tax could be
reduced to mitigate the poverty trap. It could just be reduced
– and was in 1979 by the incoming Conservative government
from 33 to 30 per cent. A lower rate band could be introduced – such as existed up to 1970 and between 1978 and
1980. Alternatively, a more thoroughgoing system of progres-

sive tax rate bands could be introduced, probably starting below the present tax threshold at a lower rate of 5 to 10 per cent and rising with income to the existing higher rate band levels.

Each of these measures has similar but slightly different objections to it. Lowering the tax rate is feasible but it is expensive in revenue foregone — each 1 per cent reduction in the tax rate costs £950 million in lost revenue (HC 331–iv, p. 200). It is also a regressive way of cutting tax, benefiting all standard rate tax payers equally and higher rate tax payers most (assuming their rates are cut *pari passu*). It also benefits tax payers equally, regardless of family circumstance. Thus it is not a well targeted means of relieving the poverty trap which affects mainly families with children.

The lower rate tax band was abandoned because it was not considered that its benefits were worth the administrative cost and the revenue foregone (Morris and Warren, 1980). It effectively provided most relief for the taxpayers within the range of incomes covered by the reduced rate.[10] This is an advantage over a straight reduction in the standard rate, but to extend the band of incomes affected or reduce the rate further would be much more expensive in revenue foregone (HC 331–iv, p. 209).

The Inland Revenue are adamant that a more thoroughgoing reform of income tax — such as the introduction of progressive rates — is not feasible until after the end of the 1980s when the income tax system is computerized (HC 331–v, p. 255). They also pointed out in evidence to the Meacher Committee that at present 93 per cent of taxable income is covered by the basic rate band (HC 331–v, p. 258). The revenue required to cut taxes on low incomes could not be found other than by charging higher tax rates on higher incomes. The present government is not prepared to countenance such a move. As the Financial Secretary to the Treasury (Mr Leon Brittan MP) said:

Where we differ is about the desirability of robbing Peter to pay Paul . . . and I say that by reminding you constantly that Peter is not a man smoking a cigar and driving a Rolls Royce, but very often a man doing a

perfectly humdrum job whom nobody living nearby
would regard as living off the fat of the land (HC
331–ix, p. 418).

## National insurance contributions

NIC add a marginal tax rate of 9 per cent to the poverty
trap and we have seen that the contribution has tended to
increase over the years. Various proposals have been made to
reduce the impact of contributions on low incomes – including raising the point at which contributions become payable, charging contributions only on earnings above that
level, reducing the percentage contribution by lifting the
ceiling on contributions, reducing contributions by making a
larger payment from tax revenue into the National Insurance
Fund, or abolishing NIC altogether and paying for insurance
benefits out of tax revenue.

The point at which contributions become payable is effectively below the level of the lowest full-time wage. Therefore
to lift the threshold to relieve the low paid from contributions
would require a substantial increase in the threshold. If the
lower earnings limit was raised to the tax threshold and contributions charged only on incomes above the ceiling, £5
billion would be lost to the National Insurance Fund (HC
331–x, p. 463) or the rate would have to increase to 11.75
per cent. If contributions were charged as at present on all
income, there would be a sudden liability to pay a substantial
sum, creating a very high marginal tax rate similar to, but
worse than, that which already exists for part-time workers
(HC 331–i, p. 19). The measure would also be insensitive
to family circumstances, benefiting the single and childless
equally as much as families with children.

Abolishing the ceiling on the employer's national insurance
contributions would raise an extra £580 million in revenue
(*Hansard*, 14, 517). This would not actually relieve the
poverty trap unless the revenue was used specifically for that
purpose. To abolish the ceiling on NIC would be a move
away from the link between the level of contributions and
the level of benefit. However the Meacher Committee concluded that the fact that the combined marginal rate of tax

and NIC dropped by 8.75 per cent between £220 and £290 per week was 'an indefensible anomaly' (Meacher Committee para. 8.2).

The arguments for abolishing NIC altogether and paying for insurance benefits from general revenue have been developing in recent years. As the national insurance system is no longer funded but is a pay-as-you-go scheme, there is less justification for sustaining the link between contributions and benefits. Also the argument that contributions guarantee rights to benefit has been undermined by the abolition of earnings-related unemployment benefit, the abatement of short-term insurance benefits and the abolition of sickness benefit for the short-term sick. If these rights can be withdrawn by a government out to save public expenditure, what special inviolability do insurance contributions give to other rights? The concept of contributory rights has already been breached in the provision of non-contributory benefits to the disabled and arguably needs to be abandoned elsewhere to provide adequate cover for the long-term unemployed. The fact that very large numbers of contributors are actually having to supplement their insurance benefits with means-tested supplementary benefits is a further criticism. If the same revenue was raised from income taxation it would be more pregressive. In addition it would save 10,000 (one-seventh) of the staff employed in social security administration (HC 331–x, p. 462).

But ministers, civil servants and the TUC representatives appearing before the Meacher Committee argued that NI contributions still had value. As a hypothecated tax (one where the revenue is committed to a specific purpose) they were more acceptable to contributors and there was less resistance to paying NIC than income tax (see HC 331–x, p. 463; HC 331–ix, p. 413; HC 331–viii, p. 398; HC 331–vii, p. 350).

## Family income supplement

FIS alone contributes more than any other tax or benefit to the poverty plateau – although it is not as important in the actual operation of the poverty trap. The contribution of FIS could be mitigated by abolishing it, lifting people off it, or reducing the 50 per cent taper on extra earnings.

FIS has come to play an important part in supplementing the income of the low paid. It also makes a contribution to widening differentials between income in work and unemployment and it is most unlikely that any government would be prepared to forego these advantages. A more probable strategy is to try to diminish the role of FIS by lifting incomes above the prescribed limits either by raising child benefits or minimum earnings. These alternatives are discussed further below. The difficulty with this strategy is that it would be very expensive – the DHSS estimated that to lift everyone off FIS by increasing child benefits would cost £7.75 billion a year (HC 331–viii, p. 401). If child benefit were increased by £5 per child, at a cost of £2.75 billion, 60,000–70,000 families would be taken off FIS (Meacher Committee para. 11.21).

The alternative of reducing the taper from 50p to, say, 30p on extra incomes would reduce the marginal loss rate but it would result in FIS continuing to be paid to families with higher incomes. This would cost more unless there was a reduction in the proportion of the difference between income and the prescribed limits that is paid. Effectively this would mean redistributing resources from the poorest families to the not so poor.

*Free school meals* (similar arguments apply to the other passport benefits)

The loss of entitlement to free school meals, particularly for families with a number of children at school, can present a considerable extra financial burden. There are broadly three strategies for removing this element from the poverty trap: provide free school meals for all or at least reduce the charges substantially; abandon the school meals service or make everyone pay for their meals; reintroduce a separate means test for school meals.

The cost of providing free school meals for all would be £214 million in 1981–2 (*Hansard*, 1270, 50). It is not a policy that has been contemplated by any government since charges were introduced. The argument has always been that the money could be better spent on books or teachers or other educational facilities. If school meals were free, there would also have to be a substantial expansion in dining facilities, particularly in secondary schools, to cope with the added demand. The same arguments apply to a lesser extent in relation to a reduction in charges.

School meals could be abolished. There is no other country in the European Community that provides a school meals service (Bradshaw and Piachaud, 1980). Instead children go to school earlier or have a shorter working day and go home for a late lunch. But no government has been prepared to contemplate such a change in this country — apart from the objections of tradition and practice, female labour participation rates in the UK are higher than many other countries and to change the school day would be unpopular with working women. There is also the view that the school meal provides an important contribution to the diets of children, particularly poor children.

The old school meals means test had the advantage of providing eligibility beyond the limits of FIS (and SB), thus free school meals were not lost at the same point as FIS. It also had the advantage of tapering the withdrawal of free school meals within a family. Thus a family would not lose free meals for all their children at the same point. However, the statutory means test for free school meals added to the complexity of the system, and although many local authorities have retained their own means test, it is not likely to be reintroduced by any government purely to provide a marginal mitigation of the poverty trap.

### Housing benefit

Housing benefits contribute a maximum of 33 per cent to marginal tax rates on incomes below the needs allowance. This contribution could be reduced either by changing the structure of housing benefits or by larger scale reforms to housing finance and the rating system.

The room for manoeuvre within the housing benefit scheme is limited by the treatment of the housing costs of those on supplementary benefit. Under the housing benefit scheme, they are awarded nil rent and rate assessments. In order for equity to be maintained between those people in work or in receipt of insurance benefits and those on SB, the housing benefit means test must endeavour to ensure that those not in receipt of SB but with net incomes around the same level also have nil rent and rate assessments. Having established that base line, the housing benefit is then withdrawn as income increases. It is withdrawn at a faster rate up to the needs allowance and then at a rather slower rate. If those rates of withdrawal were to be reduced, then either housing benefit would continue to be payable further up the income scale at increased cost, or the capacity of the scheme to meet full housing costs at incomes about SB level would diminish. This dilemma was faced when the rent and rate rebate schemes were being adapted to housing benefit. In order to ensure that pensioners on housing benefit were no worse off than they would have been on SB, the scheme had to be adapted in order to provide more generous benefits at low incomes. This was achieved by more than doubling the taper below the needs allowance from 33 per cent to 70 per cent. To do this without incurring increases in public expenditure, the taper for non-pensioners with incomes above the needs allowance was increased from 23 per cent to 28 per cent and about 100,000 tenants lost entitlement to benefit. The poverty trap was effectively worsened to bring the scheme into line with SB and to avoid increases in public expenditure (see Lansley, 1982; Hemming and Hills, 1983).

Alternatives to means-tested rate rebates were considered by the Layfield Committee (Cmnd. 6453) and rejected by the Labour government (Cmnd. 6813). The Conservative government, which is still committed to the abolition of the rating system, has not yet formulated proposals for an alternative. Assessment of the merits of possible alternatives to rates must go beyond consideration of the poverty trap — involving questions of balance in the relationship between central and local government, the buoyancy of an alternative tax, and the administrative costs of collecting the tax, as well as the progressivity of the tax. It is not necessarily the case that an alternative such as a local income tax, perhaps the most radical alternative proposed for rates, would provide either more relief for low-income families or a lower marginal tax rate.

The system of housing finance was considered in the Housing Policy Review (Cmnd. 6851) during the 1974–9 Labour government, though the attention given in that review to ideas for relieving the housing costs of low-income households was disappointing. In general, the most often advocated alternative to housing benefit is some kind of universal housing benefit (UHB) payable regardless of tenure and without a means test. There are a variety of practical problems in delivering such a benefit. If it is to avoid many householders being worse off than they are with housing benefit or tax relief on mortgage interest payments, then it must vary with housing costs and cover the housing costs of the poorest tenants and owner-occupier in full. But if it is to be universal, then even if it was to vary with rent, it would be much more expensive than present arrangements. To be feasible it might need to involve a residual means-tested element. One of the principal justifications for UHB is to establish a greater degree of equity between subsidies paid to tenants and the revenue foregone in tax relief on mortgage interest, but no political party had yet been prepared to grasp the nettle of owner-occupiers' privilege. Without some transfer of tax expenditure from owner-occupiers to tenants, there is really little prospect of a UHB being a viable proposition in the present economic climate. It would also require a more progressive tax system to claw back the benefit from higher income earners (Goss and Lansley, 1982).

## Child benefits

Of all the measures that could be taken to reduce the impact of the poverty trap, improving child benefit has the most potential. This is a view that was shared by almost all those appearing before the Meacher Committee, whether inside or outside government. Increasing child benefits would lift families out of poverty and diminish the extent to which they would need to supplement income by claiming means-tested benefits. Child benefit increases are a better focused method of reducing the poverty trap because virtually only families with children are caught in it — the other measures would benefit other types of household as well as families with children. There are strong arguments for increasing child benefits quite apart from the poverty trap — child support has diminished over the years absolutely and relative to the childless, is inadequate to prevent low-wage earners living on poverty incomes and appears to be lower in comparison with other countries (Bradshaw and Piachaud, 1980). Child benefit increases are also a very effective method of widening the gap between the incomes of those in work and the unemployed. As Patrick Jenkin said 'increasing child benefit is one of the best ways of mitigating the "Why Work?" problem' (*Hansard*, 1000. 1020).

There are two major constraints on increasing child benefits — first the position of the family in national values and institutional arrangements, and second the cost of increasing child benefits.

We have already seen that the cost of increasing child benefits to the level necessary to replace FIS is £7.75 billion. Each 1p increase in child benefit costs an extra £5.5 million per year. Unlike other social security benefits, child benefits are not linked to an index, though there is an informal political commitment to increase them in line with prices subject to economic circumstances. In fact, every year a major campaign has to be mounted in Parliament and elsewhere to protect child benefits. The cost of increasing child benefits across the board has led to consideration of whether they could be made more selective without a means test. There seems little advantage in paying them at a higher rate for older children or larger families (Piachaud, 1982). There may in time be an advantage in taxing child benefits, but at present the tax threshold is so low that taxing child benefit would only claw back the benefit from the poorest families. However, there does appear to be some advantage in concentrating an increase in child benefit on single parents and families with a child under five, on the grounds that because of their home responsibilities the single parent or the spouse is much less likely to work and therefore more likely to be in poverty. The cost of a taxable child benefit premium for families containing a pre-school-age child would be roughly £108 million for each £1 (*Hansard*, 9 pt II, 505–6).

It is not really enough to explain the inadequate level of child support in Britain in terms of the cost of increasing it. Other countries find the resources. Why has the family in Britain done so badly in the last 20 years?

There is the view that the fault lies with Britain's national attitudes to children (Bradshaw, 1983). These 'national attitudes' have been reflected in the absence of a central concern with the family and children in successive government programmes. Also policy making for families is particularly incoherent. In the field of cash benefits this has most obviously been revealed in the disjunction between fiscal and benefit policy. The most recent example of this lack of integration in planning in Whitehall is the Green Paper (Cmnd. 8093) on the taxation of husband and wife which goes out of its way to draw a distinction between 'fiscal arguments' and 'social considerations'.

### Minimum wage

The final measure that could be taken to reduce the poverty trap is to raise low earnings by a statutory minimum wage. Means-tested benefits exist because the incomes of some wage earners are considered inadequate to meet their family commitments. Low pay is endemic in Britain and many families live in poverty because their breadwinner earns too little. But, although there may be a strong case for increasing the earnings of the low paid, there are more cost-effective ways of lifting families with children out of the poverty trap. A statutory minimum wage would be expensive in public expenditure, increase labour costs and thus increase unemployment among marginal workers and possibly cause wage-led inflation as the higher paid strove to reimpose differentials.

Historically, wage bargaining has been conducted using notions of the 'family wage' – enough for a man and a dependent wife and one or two children. Trade unions are now beginning to recognize that, because the majority of wives are not dependent and partly because wages are an expensive and relatively ineffective means of compensating for children and lifting families out of the poverty trap, they should press for family benefits rather than the narrow 'family wage' (Coussins and Coote, 1981).

## CONCLUSION

The poverty trap exists because of the interaction of taxes and benefits at low incomes. It has been getting worse in recent years. It creates disincentives for single parents and couples with children — though possibly not to the extent that might be supposed. More seriously it undermines differentials between wage-earning families over a wide range of incomes. It is possible to mitigate the poverty trap by reforms within the present system of taxes and benefits. An improvement in child benefits presents the best opportunity for lifting families out of the poverty trap, but this and all other measures discussed involve increasing public expenditure. To date the inequities presented by the poverty trap have not been considered important enough to justify that expenditure.

## NOTES

1. Free school meals were worth 37.5 per child per week in 1969. The means-tested rate rebate which had been introduced in 1966 benefited very few families with children but there was a marginal loss rate in the old scheme of 25 per cent. Income tax and NIC amounted to 36.75 per cent. Before 1970 the maximum theoretical marginal tax rate on an extra £1 earned was only 51.75 per cent.
2. Note that if a family are in receipt of FIS the loss of housing benefit may eventually be only half of the actual taper because half of the income increase would be lost in reduced FIS.
3. It was originally six months but was extended to a year in order to mitigate the poverty trap.
4. At least once a year since the scheme was introduced, and in recent years above the rate of inflation.
5. Atkinson and Sutherland (1983) have compared the characteristics of these families in the DHSS simulation model with those in the

Family Expenditure Survey. They found only 3.6 per cent of households consisted of a couple with one child aged 0–4 and one child aged 5–15.

6. In 1980, 530,000 non-pensioners were receiving a rent rebate or allowances and rate rebates (HC 331–viii, p. 400). Most of these would have been subject to at least the *minimum* marginal tax rate of 66.75 per cent. Many more would have experienced this tax rate if they had claimed rebates. In November 1982, 139,000 families were receiving FIS (HC 331–vii, p. 401), of which about 80 per cent were also paying tax and therefore subject to marginal tax rates in excess of 100 per cent.

7. An earnings disregard was introduced into housing rebates in 1979, partly in recognition of work-related expenses and partly to increase the gap between the income of those in work and those not in work. This change also had the effect of extending entitlement to housing rebate further up the income scale. The maximum FIS payable and the prescribed limits have been increased faster than earnings and FIS has been extended to single parents working 24 hours or more. These changes, altogether with increased short-time working and fewer opportunities for overtime consequent upon the recession have led to a substantial increase in the number of families receiving FIS from 80,000 in 1979–80 to 120,000 in 1982–3.

8. From 17p to 21p for rent rebates and 6p to 7p for rate rebate.

9. For each £1 earned over £4 a week up to a limit of £20 per week, only 50p is deducted from benefit.

10. In 1979–80 3–3.5 million tax payers at a cost of £900 million.

# CHAPTER 9

# Alternatives to the Means Test

Despite the expansion that has taken place in the modern means test in the last two decades, it is still not a popular vehicle for delivering social benefits. There are few if any voices prepared to espouse means tests — even the Institute of Economic Affairs (IEA) have recently published a pamphlet analysing the harmful effects of means-tested benefits (Parker, 1982). It was seen in Chapter 5 that even the 1970–4 Conservative government's affection for means-tested benefits was short lived. Political parties' attitudes to means-tested benefits tend to range from obloquy to mild regret and for all of them it is more or less of a priority to diminish the role of means-tested benefits.

There are broadly two strategies that can be adopted in pursuit of the abolition of the means test. These can be characterized as Back to Beveridge and the Clean Sweep.

## BACK TO BEVERIDGE

Back to Beveridge has been the implicit strategy adopted by successive governments since the war. Before the Thatcher government, perhaps only the Heath government rejected Back to Beveridge policies, first by making a serious attempt to develop the means test and then by striving for a clean sweep solution in the tax credit scheme. Most, if not all other governments have struggled to make incremental changes in the system and reduce the role of means-tested benefits. In all cases their achievements have fallen very far short of their aspirations, and they have rarely presented reforms as part of a coherent strategy. But the advocates of the strategy still argue 'that the solution to the problem of providing adequate income support lies not in the merger of the tax and social security systems but rather in their coordination and development . . . harmonization rather than unification' (Atkinson, 1973, p. 80; see also Atkinson, 1971).

There were two fundamental defects in the Beveridge scheme for social security and in the way the scheme was implemented. First, the level of benefits paid in return for contributions was too low — lower than those paid on the basis of a test of means. Second, Beveridge did not provide contributory benefits for single-parent families and the civilian disabled, and contributory unemployment benefit as it was implemented after 1951 failed to provide cover for the long-term unemployed (Deacon, 1981b).

### Raising the level of benefits

The first aim of a Back to Beveridge strategy is to raise the level of non means-tested benefits. For those not in work this would involve increases in the level of insurance benefits in order to float people off supplementary benefit. For those in work it would involve increases in child benefits, and a home responsibility benefit to float the low paid off family income supplement and the means-tested benefits paid in work. Since the war, attempts have been made to implement a floating-off strategy: the earnings-related short-term insurance benefits introduced in the 1960s and the pension scheme and child benefit introduced in the 1970s had this as at least one of their intentions. But these measures have not been particularly successful — as we have seen in Chapters 6 and 7, the numbers of people both in and out of work dependent on means-tested benefits have continued to grow.

A number of Back to Beveridge strategists have developed schemes including Atkinson (1971) and the Meade Committee (Meade, 1978: see also Judge, 1980). Perhaps the most consistent advocates of the Back to Beveridge strategy have been the Child Poverty Action Group (CPAG) (Lister, 1975). They would replace the existing structure with flat-rate benefits paid for by higher earnings-related contributions. There would be no distinction between short- and long-term insurance benefits and the level of benefit would be well above supplementary benefit. Because, until the introduction of housing benefits, housing costs were paid on top of SB, the CPAG proposal was for insurance benefits to be increased £3 above long-term SB rates — the extra £3 was to allow for an average rent payment (in 1975). Since the introduction of housing benefit the problem of rent is less, at least for tenants — their housing costs are covered by local authorities. Nevertheless increasing all national insurance benefits to the level of the long-term rates of supplementary benefits would prove very expensive. It would cost £503.5 million in 1982–3 (*Hansard*, 1274, 197–8). This is after savings in SB and assuming that insurance benefits would be taxable. Where would the money come from to pay for these increases? CPAG proposed that it should be found from the withdrawal of tax concessions on occupational pension schemes and other tax allowances, the abolition of the ceiling on national insurance (NIC) and a greater contribution from the Exchequer to the National Insurance Fund — paid for out of a more progressive income tax system.

Despite the general anxiety at the level of means testing in British social security systems, no government has been prepared to countenance dealing with it with this degree of redistribution. Indeed the Thatcher government has been moving in the opposite direction by reducing the level of short-term insurance benefits and abandoning earnings-related supplement to unemployment benefit. These measures were motivated more by concern to reduce public expenditure and increase work incentives than an explicit decision to rely more on means-tested benefits, but that is what they have achieved.

### New benefits

A Back to Beveridge strategy for reducing the role of means-tested benefits could not rely just on increasing existing insurance benefits. Single parents other than widows were not covered by Beveridge, and with rising rates of separation and divorce they have become one of the largest groups dependent on means-tested benefits — whether in or out of work. Beveridge also did not cater for the civilian disabled.

Those injured in war or at work were covered, but the congenitally disabled and those who were never able to build up a contribution record were left dependent on means-tested benefits. Beveridge's proposals for unemployment benefit were never fully adopted — unemployment benefit ends after one year and with rapidly increasing long-term unemployment, more and more of the unemployed have become dependent for their income on means-tested SB. So, in order to reduce dependence on means-tested benefits for these groups, new benefits are required.

For one-parent families there have been few improvements in non means-tested benefits since the war. In 1974 the Finer Committee (Cmnd. 5629) recommended a major new benefit — a 'guaranteed maintenance allowance' (GMA) — to reduce dependence on supplementary benefit. The GMA was to have two elements, an allowance for the parent and an allowance for each child. The children's allowance would be paid to all lone parents irrespective of their level or source of income. However, the allowance for the parent was to be means-tested — the first £4 would be disregarded, but after that 50 per cent of net earnings would be deducted from the allowance up to a cut-off level set at about average earnings. The Labour government rejected the Finer scheme on the grounds, it claimed, that it was means-tested, but they failed to come forward with a non means-tested alternative. The alternative now advocated is for a non-contributory, non means-tested, taxable benefit paid irrespective of whether the lone parent is in full-time employment (Lister, 1975).

There are two major difficulties with such a scheme. First, the cost; and second, the problem of equity with married people. For example, there are fears that a benefit paid to single parents and not available to two-parent families would encourage the break-up of marriages. Also, what would happen to the benefit on remarriage — if it is withdrawn this would be a disincentive to remarriage; if it continued to be payable does it then again discriminate against the married? These problems of cost and equity have effectively blocked any substantial development of non means-tested benefits for single parents. In advance of the introduction of child benefits, the Labour government introduced child interim benefit (CHIB) for the first child in a single-parent family in 1976. This subsequently became one-parent benefit (OPB). The level of OPB is not high enough to lift many one-parent families off SB and it has had no impact on the numbers dependent on FIS because it is disregarded. The Green Paper (Cmnd. 8093) on the taxation of husband and wife considered increasing the level of OPB by utilizing the resources foregone in the additional personal tax allowance payable to one-parent families. But the cost of paying increases in OPB to all at a level sufficient to ensure that none of those who lack the additional personal allowance are worse off — £40 million in 1982–3 (*Hansard*, 1273, 420–1) — appears to have deterred the government from making this change.

Meanwhile the number of one-parent families dependent on means tests has continued to grow: between 1971 and 1981 the number on SB increased from 246,000 to 392,000 (DHSS, 1982b, Table 34.32) and the number on FIS increased from 15,000 to 63,000 (Table 32.10).

In contrast some progress has been made in extending non means-tested benefits to the civilian disabled and reducing the number on SB (Baldwin *et al*, 1981). Invalidity benefit and an invalidity allowance replaced long-term sickness benefit in 1971, non-contributory invalidity pension was introduced in 1975 and extended to married women in 1977, and an invalid care allowance was introduced in 1976 to provide a non means-tested benefit for those who gave up work to care for disabled relatives. Between them these benefits have filled the gaps left by Beveridge in income replacement for the disabled. They fall a long way short of the package of benefits called for by the disability lobby — but if they were paid above SB level they could provide a non means-tested income for those of working age who cannot earn because of their disablement. Of course, their defect is that they are not paid at that level. Indeed, on the grounds that they are non-contributory and to save money, they were introduced at a rate of 60 per cent of other long-term insurance benefits and as a result the majority of the disabled receiving these benefits are also dependent on supplementary benefit.

The Disability Alliance (1975) have also called for a non means-tested non-contributory benefit paid to the disabled, whether or not they work, assessed according to the degree of incapacity. Such a scheme would help to reduce dependence on means tests by those disabled people in work whose earning capacity is reduced, because of their incapacity, to a level where they presently have to apply for means-tested benefits payable to those with low earnings.

The unemployed are the third group for whom entitlement to non means-tested benefits must be extended if they are to be lifted off means-tested benefits. Unemployment benefit lasts for only one year. There is no justification for this arbitrary time limit on the payment of unemployment benefit. It could be scrapped and unemployment benefit paid as long as unemployment lasts. The net cost of extending eligibility for unemployment benefit is relatively modest — £450 million — because most of those affected are already receiving supplementary benefit.[1] The main objection to improvements in the scope and coverage of unemployment benefit comes from anxiety that work incentives would be undermined. In fact, lifting unemployment benefit up to SB level will not have any impact on the replacement ratios of those already dependent on supplementary benefit.

The main distinction between Back to Beveridge strategies and Clean Sweep strategies for diminishing the role of means tests is that the latter aim to integrate social security and taxation. This is not to say that Back to Beveridge strategists ignore the tax system. As we have seen, improvements in non means-tested benefits call for substantial increases in transfer payments, and Back to Beveridge strategists have typically identified two means of raising this revenue: first, increases in the ceiling on national insurance contributions and the introduction of a more progressive income tax system; second, the reconstitution of the tax base by the abolition or phasing out of income tax allowances, the raising of tax thresholds and the taxation of non means-tested benefits (HC 331–x, pp. 474–82; see also Meacher Committee Report).

## CLEAN SWEEP SOLUTIONS

While the Back to Beveridge strategy seeks reform by the manipulation of taxes and benefits separately, the essence of the Clean Sweep strategy is that taxes and benefits are merged, the separate systems of social security benefits and income tax allowances are swept away, to be replaced by a single system. Clean Sweep solutions have inherently more appeal than incremental reforms to the variety of benefits and tax systems implied in the Back to Beveridge strategy. The cause of the present confusion in the tax/benefit system can be traced to the incremental unplanned development of social security and taxation; it is difficult to justify why families are receiving means-tested benefits at the same time as paying taxes, especially why poor families should receive benefits to relieve their poverty and at the same time pay as much back to the Exchequer in income tax. As the Meacher Committee put it, 'we are now taxing the poor to help the poor' (para. 1.4).[2] As taxation and social security have been entangled, why not integrate them totally in a single, simple coherent system of benefits?

These then are the arguments put up in support of Clean Sweep solutions. How might such a scheme operate? There are two types of scheme discussed in the literature — social dividend and negative income tax.

### Social dividend

The principle of social dividend is that everyone in society receives a dividend or payment by virtue of citizenship. The payment may vary by family composition, age or status. This payment is tax free, but all other income is taxable. All benefits, both means-tested and non means-tested, would be abandoned in favour of the dividend which might be set at about the level of current benefits. All tax allowances and reliefs would also be scrapped and all income above the dividend would be taxed. The purpose of the social dividend is to abandon the distinction between taxes and benefits, abolish the problems of means-tested benefits and do away with the unemployment trap. By doing away with the distinction between work income and unemployment benefit, everyone would receive the dividend whether they worked or not.

Figure 2 illustrates how a social dividend scheme might operate in this case, assuming a 45 per cent tax rate above the dividend.

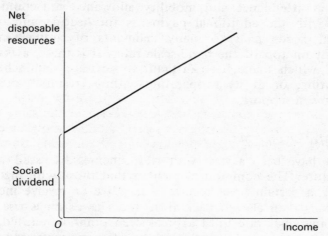

*Figure 2 Operation of a social dividend scheme*

There are a number of difficulties with a social dividend scheme. If the dividend is to maintain the incomes of the population at reasonable cost, then it has to vary with family composition, the number of children and possibly also housing costs. As soon as the dividend is adjusted in these ways it begins to become complicated. Furthermore, to pay SB level dividends to all, regardless of whether they work, will require higher tax rates than exist at present. The Meade Committee estimated that a marginal tax rate of 55 per cent would be required to finance a dividend at about 40 per cent of average income (Meade, 1978). The disincentive effects of that marginal tax rate could be mitigated by higher tax rates on either initial earnings or higher earnings or both, but only at the cost of further complicating the scheme. It is also unlikely that a social dividend scheme could replace all means-tested benefits without leaving some people worse off. For example, it is unlikely that those families with no income from work would have a dividend high enough to absorb free school meals, exemptions from health service charges and their full housing costs. Also, a social dividend paid at SB level could not easily be adapted to cope with the varieties of need which exist in the real world. Certainly it could not incorporate the special benefits for the disabled, such as attendance and mobility allowance and could not cope with the additional payments for heating and other special needs paid to many claimants of supplementary benefit on top of the basic scale rates. It is these 'awkward cases' which make it so difficult to envisage such schemes operating, or at least operating without residual separate systems in support.

## Negative income tax

There have been a variety of NIT schemes discussed in the literature. The common element is that those with incomes below a certain level receive a negative or reverse income which is then clawed back from them as earnings rise at a high marginal rate until a break-even point is reached. Because payments of negative income tax are restricted only to those below the threshold, it is a much cheaper scheme than social dividend. It also involves higher marginal tax rates at low-income levels. Most of the redistribution in the scheme is concentrated in the lowest proportion of the income distribution, and NIT schemes have generally been advocated by economists committed to a residual role for the state in market transactions and a minimal view of poverty. Figure 3 depicts one conception of NIT.

In this example, the negative tax is withdrawn £ for £ on the first *tranche* of income until the negative tax is 'repaid' and then tax is charged at the normal rate.

The main difficulty with negative income tax schemes is that either the reverse income tax has to be very low, or the withdrawal rate very high to ensure that the reverse income and the high marginal tax rates do not extend too far up the income distribution. An IEA scheme which was designed to replace social security benefits had a tax rate of 70 per

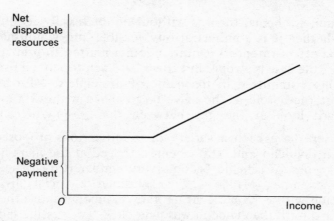

*Figure 3 Operation of a negative income tax scheme*

cent up to the 'break-even point' (where tax payable matches negative income) and even with a tax rate at that level the break-even point was above the existing tax thresholds. The IEA concluded that the problem for incentives implied by these tax rates '. . . is the unavoidable price for helping people in need, but the cost in lost effort would only be a fraction of the incomes of the small minority whose earnings from full-time work leave them in poverty'. (Christopher *et al*, 1970, p. 76)

There are also formidable practical problems. It would be impossible to collect all the information needed to assess entitlement to the reverse income tax on a standard form and so separate procedures would be necessary. A way would also have to be found of collating the earnings of husbands and wives. Moreover, the Inland Revenue is used to carrying out annual assessments, whereas the scheme would require weekly assessments in some cases. Otherwise, urgent needs could not be met and the existing supplementary benefits scheme would have to be retained (Christopher *et al*, 1970, pp. 84–6).

The twin problems of administrative feasibility and incentives raise serious doubts about the viability of the NIT proposal. Even its advocates have been cautious. Lees (1967, pp. 14–15), for example, concluded:

Such a scheme, then, is without doubt fiscally feasible. Whether it is administratively feasible and would have the effect intended is quite another matter. In principle ... the case is strong. But there has been too much fiscal folly committed in the name of principle ... for any but the heroic or the naive to go ahead without a long hard look at the gap between theory and delivery.

There have been a variety of modifications proposed for social dividend and NIT schemes. Indeed at the margins the two types of scheme become very similar (Collard, 1980). For example, Meade (1978) outlined a social dividend scheme with a 78 per cent tax rate on income above the dividend – until the dividend was paid back. They estimated that this would enable marginal tax rates on income above the amount needed to pay back the dividend to be reduced to 45 per cent. Far from removing the problem of the poverty trap, this type of scheme would institutionalize it.

Another modification discussed by Meade was for different dividends to be paid to families of different labour market status. A lower dividend would be paid to those in the labour market. The advantage of this would be that the tax rate above the dividend could be reduced to about 42 per cent. The disadvantages are that it would complicate the scheme and undermine the incentives to take work. As Collard (1980, p. 197) concludes: 'Once one has abandoned the grand simplicity of the pure social dividend the various schemes run into the sands of reality'.

## Tax credits

One of the difficulties about appraising Clean Sweep proposals for the tax/benefit system is that few of them have been subjected to detailed scrutiny. The Meade Committee attempted to cost some social dividend schemes, but was not able to carry out a full appraisal of their administrative viability and redistributive consequences. The only one of the many possible schemes that has been systematically pre-evaluated, and also the only scheme to get anywhere near the statue book, was the tax credit scheme devised by the 1970–4 Conservative government.

Their proposals were first announced in the budget speech in March 1972 and the details were published in October 1972 in a Green Paper (Cmnd. 5116). These proposals were referred to a Select Committee of the House of Commons which considered them in detail, producing a report in July 1973 (HC 341–i). It was envisaged that the scheme would be phased in by 1977, but progress towards this goal was halted when Mr Heath went to the country in February 1974 and lost the election.

The proposals were presented jointly by the Chancellor of the Exchequer and the Secretary of State for Social Services. They had been devised by the Chancellor's special adviser on taxation, Lord Cockfield, and were subsequently seen through the Select Committee by a working party of officials from both departments working under his direction. The scheme had three aims (Cmnd. 5116, iii):

(1) 'to provide better support for those who . . . are hard pressed';
(2) 'to create a new and simpler system which . . . will bring together what people pay and what they receive';
(3) 'Fewer people will be means-tested and others means-tested less often . . .'

This scheme does not do everything, but it would be the most far-reaching change in our systems of personal taxation and social security for a quarter of a century, *and it would achieve much that is obviously desirable including greatly reduced dependence on means-tested benefits*' (Authors' emphasis).

These quotations are taken from the introduction to the Green Paper by Barber and Joseph and they indicate that, as well as administrative simplification, diminishing the role of means-tested benefits was an important motive for the scheme. It would replace the existing system of personal tax allowances, family allowances and FIS with tax credits. 'For illustrative purposes' (Cmnd. 5116, para. 9) the credits would be £4 for a single person, £6 for a couple and £2 for each child. Income tax payable at 30 per cent would be set against the credits and if the tax payable exceeded the credit, the balance would be payable in tax. If income tax payable was less than the credit, the family would receive the balance from their employer or from the social security office. Two examples — for a man, wife and three children — are shown below.

| | | |
|---|---|---|
| 1.  Income  =  £20 per week | Tax credits  = | £12 |
| Tax payable at 30 per cent | = | £6 |
| | Credit received | £6 |

*Total net income  =  £26*

| | | |
|---|---|---|
| 2.  Income  =  £40 | Tax credits  = | £12 |
| Tax payable at 30 per cent | = | £12 |
| | Balance | nil |

*Total net income  =  £40*

Debate about the advantages and disadvantages of the scheme covered a variety of questions (Sandford, 1980). Initially there was a good deal of heat generated by the issue of to whom child credits should be paid. 'The question whether child credits should be paid to the father or the mother is however, a matter which the Government regard as entirely open . . .' (Cmnd. 5116, para. 82). However, after a vigorous campaign by women's organizations they were soon persuaded to close the matter in favour of mothers.

The debate over tax credits was also much preoccupied with gainers and losers. It was difficult to pin down the government on this issue because they insisted that the level and balance of the credits was purely illustrative and the actual level of the credits would be determined in the light of economic circumstances at the time the scheme was introduced. However the Green Paper (para. 118) did acknowledge that 'it will only be possible to introduce the scheme at substantial cost'. The net cost of the scheme at the illustrative credits was estimated at £1,300 million. With this input of resources, almost everyone appeared to gain from the scheme. But Atkinson (1973) pointed out that, in assessing gains and losses, the government had ignored the fact that an extra £1,300 million would have to be raised and redistributed by direct or indirect taxes. He estimated that credits would have to be lower than proposed by 17.5 per cent, or value added tax increased from 10 to 17.5 per cent, or the rate of income tax raised from 30 to 33.5 per cent. When this redistribution was taken into account, there were rather more losers and rather fewer gainers from the scheme. Indeed, if account was taken of the financing of the scheme, then not even FIS could be phased out without there being some losers.

The effect on means-tested benefits was also much less than the aspirations of the Green Paper. The scheme hoped to replace FIS and, by raising the incomes of insurance beneficiaries, lift about a million people off supplementary benefit, but for another two million households SB would remain operating alongside tax credits. In addition, free school meals, rent and rate rebates and health service charge exemptions would continue to operate. Indeed, out of 44 means-tested benefits, the Tax Credit Study Group admitted that 43 would remain, Many families would lose FIS and with it the associated passport benefits. If tax credits were taken into account in assessing eligibility for means-tested benefits, a number of families would be lifted off these benefits and the numbers subject to high marginal tax rates would be reduced, but an analysis by Nevitt and Bradshaw (1973) indicated that the problem of the poverty trap would remain.

The reason why the scheme had relatively little impact on recipients of means-tested benefits was that most of the extra cost of the scheme was not going to help low-income groups: Atkinson (1973) estimated that 58 per cent of the extra cost would go to those with above average earnings. The only way the tax credit scheme could acheive a more substantial reduction in th numbers dependent on means-tested benefits would be to pay higher credits. But higher credits would have to be paid for by a higher rate of tax: the Tax Credit Study Group estimated that, if credits were raised to the level necessary to replace supplementary benefits, tax rates would have to be raised to at least 45 per cent. It is inevitable in the tax credit scheme, or any other social dividend scheme that pays a credit to all regardless of income, that the cost of boosting the level of the credit is very high because everyone receives it. Or, to put it another way, there is a very direct trade-off between the level of credit and the basic rate of tax. The only way to lower the cost of increasing credits is to claw back the value of credits by taxing higher incomes more than lower incomes. But this was impossible in this tax credit scheme with its single basic rate of tax. To introduce progressive rates of tax would have required the retention of a cumulative system of taxation at the cost of the staff economies in the scheme. 'The conflict between administrative considerations and distributional policy would be intensified by the introduction of the tax credit' (Atkinson, 1973, p. 70).

It was this inflexibility in the scheme which became the critical objection and led the Labour government in 1974 to turn its back on the proposals. However they rescued the concept of child credits and, renamed 'child benefit', these were phased in from April 1977, despite an attempt to ditch them (Field, 1982). The Conservatives' commitment to tax credits waned during their opposition years, and when they returned to power in 1979, no proposals were brought forward for Clean Sweep reform. For a government committed to cutting taxes, a viable scheme would be too expensive. The cost of introducing the full scheme in 1982 was estimated to be £8.1 billion. A more limited scheme that would lift 100,000 pensioners off SB would cost £600 million (HC 331–v, pp. 302–3).

Despite the experience of tax credits, others have not been deterred from devising other schemes.

## The Liberal tax credit proposals

The Liberals are the only political party that continues to be committed to tax credits. Their scheme is a much more elaborate version of the Barber/Joseph scheme (Vince, n.d.). There would be four basic credits: a personal credit payable at one rate to everyone over 18 and another rate for children, a long-term credit for those dependent on social security for over six months, a short-term credit for short-term social security claimants, and a housing credit which would replace mortgage tax relief and rent rebates. There would also be a variety of other credits to people in special circumstances.

Overall, as presented, most people would benefit from the proposals, with families with dependent children and one earner gaining most. However, the cost of the scheme is very high. In 1977 terms, after a 40 per cent tax rate, £14,100 million would need to be found. It is proposed that this could be raised by a new payroll tax, which would increase prices by 5 per cent, and changes in VAT and excise duties. The proposals for housing credits have not been fully worked out; while all housing subsidies have been taken as revenue to finance the scheme, it is not at all clear that housing credits could match 100 per cent rent rebates or the benefit being obtained by those paying a large amount of interest on a mortgage. It is also not clear that the proposals would enable FIS and free school meals to be replaced, and it is admitted that supplementary benefits would remain, if only in a residual role. There is also no doubt that the scheme will present administrative difficulties in linking all the different individual credits to the same family unit.

## The Social Democratic Party scheme

The SDP (1982) policy for social security and personal taxation proposes to replace existing schemes with a new means-tested benefit that they claim will eliminate poverty, reduce the poverty trap, simplify the system and eventually eliminate claiming altogether. They turn their backs on universalism because they think it is too costly. They propose a basic benefit which will be calculated according to the number of children and housing costs. This will replace FIS, housing rebates, free school meals and SB. 'Those families with a low income will receive all of their entitlement as a Basic Benefit to supplement that income. Families with slightly higher income will receive some of their entitlement as a Basic Benefit; those with comfortable incomes will neither need nor receive any Benefit' (p. 4). Child benefit would remain unchanged by the scheme. Insurance benefits would continue but be increased.

Basic benefit would be withdrawn at the rate of 30 per

cent for single people and 45 per cent for families with children — this is on top of the normal rate of income tax and national insurance contributions. The credits proposed are:

(1) a personal credit of £19 per single person and £32 per married couple;
(2) a credit of £22.50 for the first child (necessary in order to phase out FIS);
(3) a credit of £8.50 per child;
(4) a credit for housing costs that would amount to 60 per cent of rent and rates and 30 per cent of mortgage interest.

There are a number of commendable aspects of the SDP scheme: in particular it would improve the incomes of poor families and at the same time replace the variety of means-tested benefits. However, there are also difficulties, three of which will be discussed.

First, it is not proposed to improve child benefits. Poor families will be helped by child credits in basic benefits, but families on average incomes will not benefit. The redistribution in the scheme is almost all vertical rather than horizontal. In effect, average families will be paying for higher benefits for low-income families.

Second, the preamble to the proposals is much taken up with the inequity of the poverty trap and the need to lower marginal tax rates for people caught in it. Although the proposals would do away with the *theoretical* marginal rates in excess of 100 per cent by replacing FIS, these will be replaced with *actual* marginal tax rates of 83.95 per cent and many more people will be subjected to it. It is doubtful whether this is necessarily an improvement.

Third, they seriously understate the problems of successfully operating a means-tested benefit on this scale. There is little consideration given to how local authorities (who will be responsible for administering the scheme) will be able to cope with assessing and re-assessing the basic benefit as circumstances change, nor is there any discussion of who the benefit will be paid to, nor of who will be paid the benefit if the head of the household is not employed. Furthermore, there is no discussion of the likely take-up problem;

it is just assumed that everyone will go along and claim. But there is little to suggest that this means-tested benefit will be any more successful than others in achieving complete take-up. True, there will be only one benefit to claim and it will be more valuable than the variety it replaces, but at the margin of eligibility it will not be easy for the individual to establish eligibility.

The long-term aim of the SDP, when the computerization of the income tax system allows, is to replace the requirement to claim the basic benefit with automatic assessment on a weekly basis with end-of-year final corrections being made for overpayment or underpayment. A great deal more work needs to be done to test whether that is a viable aspiration.

## The basic income guarantee scheme (BIG)

An ambitious social dividend scheme has been developed by Hermione Parker which was put to the Meacher Committee by Sir Brandon Rhys Williams (HC 331–ix, pp. 420–54). Under this scheme, all benefits, tax allowances and tax reliefs would be replaced by a number of personal basic incomes for adults, householders, children, expectant mothers, lone parents, old people, home care, invalidity and disability. There would be no earnings rule. The cost of the full scheme would be £84.8 billion, which would be met by a tax on all incomes of 50 per cent, and from the abolition of existing benefits and tax allowances. The scheme is particularly designed to avoid the unemployment trap and the black economy by paying the basic income, whether or not the person is in employment. The scheme would involve significant redistribution from 'rich to poor and from people without dependents to people with dependents' (p. 425). 'Inevitably in a redistribution programme of this sort there must be losers. The existing system is so full of anomalies that some people are bound to be worse off' (p. 426). Among those who will lose are non-householders, two-wage couples, mortgagees and pensioners with substantial non-pension income.

The Meacher Committee considered the scheme. 'We

cannot claim to have formed a final judgement on the accuracy of the costings and the redistributional effects or to have been able to assess the administrative problems involved in carrying out such a massive reform . . .' (para. 13.30), and later 'we recommend that the Government should put such work in hand' [para. 13.35]. 'It is hard to believe that the replacement of the whole complex system of social security benefits by relatively simple categories of basic incomes . . . would not result . . . in losers as well as gainers . . .' (para. 13.29).

The scheme allows for residual means-tested housing benefits and supplementary benefits for exceptional cases and the Meacher Committee pointed out that the poverty trap would remain if there were a substantial number of people receiving these means-tested benefits with their own withdrawal rate on top of the scheme's marginal rates of 50 per cent.

## CONCLUSION

There is no doubt that the Clean Sweep alternatives to the existing systems of taxes and benefits have, in principle, many advantages. In particular their simplicity contrasts favourably with the complexities of the present morass. But whether this simplicity can be preserved in a fully worked out arrangement is not so clear.

As we have seen, many of the schemes proposed have to be supported by residual schemes of means-tested benefits if they are to leave no-one worse off and yet be implemented at reasonable cost. At present it is difficult to judge whether the upheaval of the existing systems can be justified by the benefits that would be obtained. As the Meacher Committee concluded: 'It is clear to us that a good deal more work needs to be done on such schemes before it can be said with confidence that they are feasible' (para. 13.35).

Meanwhile there is little prospect that the kind of incremental reforms that are feasible in the present political and economic climates will achieve much of a diminution in the scope of means-tested benefits.

*NOTES*

1. (HC 123, 1983, p. xxii.) The Social Security Advisory Committee (1982, para. 3.17), however, decided that:

   [although they] do not believe that means-tested benefits should be seen as the normal way of meeting the needs of unemployed people . . . increases in the level and duration of contributory benefits . . . would be costly and would not increase the incomes of those who are already getting supplementary benefit . . . We therefore feel the priority must be the extension of the long-term supplementary benefit rate to help those most in need. Only when this has been achieved might options for improving contributory unemployment benefit be worth pursuing.

2. Though a spokesman for the Inland Revenue made the opposite point:

   I do not think it is necessarily wrong that the Government is on the one hand paying out social security benefits and on the other hand collecting taxes . . . It can well . . . be easier to have large gross flows moving around than to try to cut them off at a particular point (HC 331–v, p. 263).

# CHAPTER 10

# Conclusion

There is no doubt that means tests have their attractions to policy makers. They can be employed to mitigate social problems whilst avoiding the political and economic consequences of higher public spending and increased taxation. In support of means tests it can be argued that it is more sensible to channel resources directly to those who need them than to distribute them indiscriminately to rich and poor alike; and that non means-tested benefits are not only wasteful but also unjust, since to make equal provision for everyone merely upholds and reinforces the inequalities which already exist.

We have seen, however, that the growing use of means tests has resulted in a system without coherence or unity of purpose, and which involves large numbers of people in repeated declarations of their financial circumstances and sometimes obtrusive investigations of their personal lives. We have seen also that it is a system which fails to deliver benefits to many of the people who need them and have a right to them. Moreover, the interaction between means tests and taxes has given rise to gross distortions in the distribution of income amongst poorer families, while the neglect of insurance benefits and the increasing reliance upon means-tested supplementary benefits means that many beneficiaries receive little in return for the contributions they have paid.

A further disadvantage of means tests which we have not yet discussed is that they are expensive to administer. By their nature they require that information on the income and circumstances of literally millions of people be collected and assessed at regular intervals, whilst a continual effort has to be made to publicize the existence of the benefits and encourage those eligible to apply for them. In 1982 the DHSS (HC 306–i) estimated that the cost of administering national insurance benefits represented 4.6 per cent of total expenditure on benefits, compared with 10.9 per cent for supplementary benefits.[1] The Meade Committee also investigated the administrative costs of different types of benefits. They found that the administration of insurance benefits cost 3.8 per cent of the benefits paid out, compared with 13.4 per cent for supplementary benefits, 15.4 per cent for rate rebates and 8.3 per cent for FIS (1978, pp. 303–7). Why then, have means tests continued to grow and flourish? It cannot be argued that governments have been unaware of these problems. True, they may have been confused by exaggerated estimates of the take-up of benefits and the last Labour government was certainly misled by the Layfield Committee and the Housing Policy Review as to the effectiveness of housing rebates. Since the mid-1970s, however, governments have pressed on with the use of means tests despite a certain knowledge of their defects. Why? Is it just that their advantages outweigh their disadvantages, or do means tests serve a more subtle or fundamental purpose in society than just being one way of helping the poor?

Peter Townsend (1979, p. 880) has argued that means tests should be seen as a form of social control, and that in every means-tested service there is 'an uneasy and fitful compromise' between its 'poverty alleviation' function and its 'implicit social control function'. Means-tested benefits are essentially 'devices which ration and control', and the regulations which determine access to them 'reflect values approved by society of residential stability, probity of marriage and the family, regular work, prompt payment of debt and conformity in general with the social order'. It is not surprising, therefore, if people who do not conform to those values 'tend to be deprived of the benefits of means test services', nor does this necessarily mean that the services are not achieving their aim.

There is no doubt that some means-tested benefits have been governed 'less by unconditional motives of generosity towards the poor than by unbending concern ... to control ... and shepherd them into unquestioning conformity with economic and social values' (p. 881). An obvious example discussed in this book is the administration of unemployment assistance in the 1930s, and the fact that the unemployed still receive less on supplementary benefit than do pensioners and the long-term sick, reflects a continuing preoccupation with work incentives. We have also shown that it was primarily the unemployed and single parents who suffered from the 'mucking around' of applicants practised by some NAB officers in the 1950s and early 1960s. The fact remains, however, that there are similar elements of social control in personal income tax and non means-tested benefits. It is not only means-tested benefits which may penalize people 'who live rough, disrespect marriage . . . are particular about the kind of employment they accept . . . [or] . . . are in arrears with their rent' (Townsend, 1979, p. 880). The 'undeserving' claimant is as likely to meet indifference and hostility at the Job Centre as at the supplementary benefit office.

The other objection to explanations of the growth of means testing in terms of social control is that they do not take account of the pragmatic and often muddled way in which that growth has occurred. The confused interaction of different benefit rates in the 1940s, the unwilling introduction of prescription charges and the 'temporary expedient' of rate rebates in the 1960s, even the managerial innovations and preoccupation with public spending of the 1970s and 1980s do not point to an explicit motive of social control. Means tests do operate as mechanisms of social control, indeed they could hardly do otherwise. However, the fact that they have this function is not the sole or even the most important reason for the expansion of means-tested benefits in recent years.

The growth of means testing must be seen in the context of the enormous increase in spending on the social services which has occurred since the 1960s. Between 1961 and 1975 social expenditure rose from 18 per cent of Gross National Product to 29 per cent, (Gough, 1979, p. 76) and by the early 1980s it represented well over half of all public expenditure (Walker, 1982). This increase has stemmed from a combination of demographic change — chiefly the rise in the proportion of the population who were over pension age —

rising standards, and the tendency for the cost of the labour-intensive social services to increase faster than the general price level. The relative importance of these factors has been discussed elsewhere (Gough, 1979; Walker, 1982). What matters here is the response of successive governments to this increase and its implications for taxation.

The levels of public expenditure and taxation are issues which have traditionally divided the parties, although the differences have been more marked in their aspirations and rhetoric than in their performance in office. The Conservatives have always emphasized the danger that high personal taxation will reduce incentives to work and save, especially for high earners. Thus, Leon Brittan told the Meacher Committee that, whilst the poverty trap was a serious and genuine problem it could not be 'an overriding determinant of policy ... I think it would be a pity if to tackle the poverty trap ... we were to reduce incentives for other people' (HC 331–ix, p. 441; HC 331–x, p. 464). A constant theme in Conservative writing on social policy since *One Nation* has been the need to ensure that the rise in social expenditure does not outstrip the growth in national income. The poor performance of the British economy, together with the pressures for higher spending mentioned earlier, meant that this was always an argument for restraining the rate of increase in spending. In recent years it has become an argument for reducing its overall level.

The Labour Party has long believed that higher social expenditure is essential for the alleviation of poverty and the reduction of inequality. In office, however, it has felt constrained both by popular resistance to increases in taxation and by an apparent decline in public support for the welfare state. We saw in Chapter 4 that it sought to resolve this dilemma by arguing that higher expenditure could be financed by a faster rate of economic growth. In office, however, the failure to achieve the anticipated growth led to real fears of a backlash against welfare spending amongst working-class voters. This happened in both the late 1960s and the mid-1970s and on both occasions the resentment aroused by higher taxation was exacerbated by allegations of laxity in the administration of benefits and of widespread scrounging and abuse (Deacon, 1978; Golding and Middleton, 1982). We have seen that there is some evidence that attitudes to the poor are more hostile in Britain than elsewhere in Europe (CEC, 1977), whilst the lack of priority given to family policy and the needs of children was noted in Chapter 8.

The attraction of means tests is thus that they produce a mechanism through which governments can provide for the needs of low-income households without the need for additional taxation. Moreover, there is a 'rachet' effect in that, once a means-tested benefit is established, it quickly becomes very expensive to withdraw it without making some people worse off. The classic example is FIS, and it was seen in Chapter 8 that it would now cost £7.75 billion to provide the same level of support to poor families through child benefits.

It must be emphasized, however, that this 'rachet' effect arises not only from the cost of withdrawing means-tested benefits without losers, but from the socially divisive nature of means testing itself. As Donnison (1982, p. 12) has argued, 'services specially designed for poor people always tend to be poor services. They provoke resentment amongst the poor and against the poor. They divide society, creating second class citizens who get second class treatment.' These divisions within public provision have been reinforced by the rapid development of occupational and fiscal welfare, and Adrian Sinfield (1978) has shown that the social division of welfare has become increasingly important since it was first analysed by Richard Titmuss (p. 62 above). We saw in Chapter 8 that only 47 per cent of personal income is currently subject to tax, and that higher rate tax is levied on only 7 per cent of that. Thus, any serious attempt to reduce the role of the means test must involve, not only an increase in the taxation of wealth, but also the curtailment of the tax concessions now granted in respect of mortgages, and occupational benefits such as pensions or company cars. These concessions, however, are now enjoyed by a large proportion of the electorate, whilst a growing number of manual workers have become owner-occupiers or beneficiaries of occupational welfare. The latter may not see any identity of interest between themselves and the poor, and some writers have argued that the growth of means testing and of occupational benefits, together with the unequal distribution of unemployment, has reopened the historic divide between the 'respectable' working class and the residuum. Donnison, for example, has pointed to the gulf between those forced to rely on supplementary benefits and those who are in secure jobs and are entitled to sick pay and a pension from their employer. It is the latter whose interests are represented by the TUC, not 'the low paid, the unskilled, the unemployed, the one-parent families, the disabled and the handicapped' (1982, p. 88). Similarly, MacGregor (1981, pp. 174–9) has questioned whether or not it is 'naively optimistic' to expect the 'organised labour movement' to 'promote the interests of the poor', who could be seen as constituting an 'underclass'.

The extent to which the long-term unemployed, one-parent families or other groups dependent upon means-tested benefits for long periods should be seen as an 'underclass' is beyond the scope of this book. The important point here is that the growth of means testing has had social consequences which both increase the pressure upon subsequent governments to introduce further means tests, and make it easier for them to do so. This does not mean that the trend towards means tests is inevitable. It could be reversed by a government which was prepared to raise and redistribute the necessary revenue or to cut back on other areas of public spending. There seems little prospect, however, of such a strategy securing widespread popular support in the forseeable future.

We have seen, however, that the position was very different immediately after the war, and the subsequent change in public attitudes towards the welfare state has been interpreted from a range of political perspectives. Economic Liberals such as Harris and Seldon (1979, p. 10) have argued that a decline in support for universalist social policies was inevitable since they rested upon too rosy a view of human nature:

> Universal selflessness is devoutly to be wished; the error is to suppose it has arrived, or can be created by the state. The reality is almost the opposite. The increasing realisation that everyone is paying taxes for welfare

benefits induces everyone to take not as little as he must, but as much as he can. It encourages everyone to draw as much in benefits as he can and contribute in taxes as little as he cannot evade.

Others, however, see the change as the result of the way in which the social services have been portrayed in the mass media, the unfairness of the tax system and the failure of the Labour movement to campaign and work for radical change (Golding and Middleton, 1982). The extent to which more resources could be made available without increasing the burden upon working-class tax payers has long been debated within the Labour Party, and the important exchanges between Peter Townsend and Richard Crossman were discussed in Chapter 4. The significance of that debate, however, is questioned by Marxist writers such as Ralph Miliband (1969) and David Coates (1980). They see the decline of the welfare state as only one manifestation of the failure of successive Labour governments to secure a fundamental redistribution of income and wealth. That failure stems in turn from an acceptance of the central feature of capitalist society, namely the concentration of economic power in private hands. Miliband (1969, p. 270), for example, has written that whilst it would be 'trivial to depict the men in whose hands state power lies as indifferent to poverty, slums, unemployment', they are the 'prisoners, and usually the willing prisoners, of an economic and social framework which necessarily turns their reforming proclamations, however sincerely meant, into verbiage'.

It is not the purpose of this book to assess the validity of the different analyses which have been made of the role of social policy within contemporary society, and such ideological debates have had a limited impact upon policy making. We saw in Chapter 4, for example, that the prevailing view in Whitehall was profoundly sceptical of the viability of a return to the private market and, as Pinker (1971, p. 108) has pointed out, the universality *versus* selectivity debate 'was largely the invention of an intellectual minority'. Similarly, there is little evidence of clear public support for the wholesale withdrawal of the state from such fields as health or education,[2] and even less evidence of support for the socio-economic changes advocated by Professor Miliband. The fact remains, however, that popular support for the existing social services does appear to have diminished, and this has been a crucial factor in the decision of successive governments to countenance or encourage the growth of means testing.

All of this would suggest that the means test will continue to play a major role within British social policy. A government which attempts to return to the universality of the 1940s is likely to find it extremely difficult to secure the electorate's support for the requisite redistribution. Indeed, the evidence contained in this book confirms the accuracy of the comment with which Beveridge concluded his *Report* (Cmd. 6404, p. 172):

> The prevention of want and the diminution and relief of disease . . . are in fact a common interest of all citizens. It may be possible to secure a keener realisation of that fact in war than it is in peace, because war breeds national unity. It may be possible, through sense of national unity . . . to bring about changes, which when they are made, will be accepted on all hands as advances, but which might be difficult to make at other times.

A further Conservative government may not positively advocate means tests but will continue to expand them as a residuum of other economic and social policies. Increased reliance on private provision, higher charges for health and personal social services, increased rents and any attempt to reduce social security expenditure will lead to more means tests. They will be constrained, however, by the public support which still exists for some services, by their aspirations to limit the growth of civil service manpower, by an anxiety about the poverty trap and by a fear that the machinery of government — already tottering under the strain of administering means tests to a quarter of the population — will finally collapse.

If it is unrealistic to expect a major reduction in means

testing within the foreseeable future, it is important to recognize what this means, not only for claimants, but for the cohesion of our society. There is a great danger that familiarity with the means test will breed complacency, and that evidence of low take-up or of the poverty trap will attract less attention. There is no reason to expect that these problems will diminish in the future, nor that the means test will become less socially divisive. History suggests otherwise. The paradox of the means test is that it has a discredited past and an expanding future.

*NOTES*

1. There is also considerable variation in the costs of administering supplementary benefit to different types of claimant. In 1976, the average annual administrative cost per claimant was £120 in the case of the unemployed, £134 in the case of one-parent families but only £36 in the case of pensioners (Cmnd. 6910, p. 23).
2. The IEA claims to have found evidence of such support in its periodic surveys of public opinion, the most recent of which is reported in Harris and Seldon (1979). Judge and his colleagues, however, have re-analysed the data from this survey and conclude that 'the pattern of support for public and private welfare is much more complex than Harris and Seldon would lead us to believe' (1983, p. 6).

# Bibliography

Abel-Smith, B. (1963) 'Beveridge: another viewpoint', *New Society*, 28 February.

Abel-Smith, B. (1964a) *The Hospitals 1800–1948*, London, Heinemann.

Abel-Smith, B. (1964b) *Freedom in the Welfare State*, London, Fabian Society.

Abel-Smith, B. (1968a) 'The need for social planning', in *Social Services for All? Part Four*, London, Fabian Society.

Abel-Smith, B. (1968b) 'Paradoxes of the welfare state' *The Listener*, 79:2044, 30 May 1968, pp. 696–7.

Abel-Smith, B. and Townsend, P. (1965) *The Poor and the Poorest*, London, Bell and Sons.

Addison, P. (1977) *The Road to 1945*, London, Quartet Books (first published 1975).

Adler, M., du Feu, D. and Redpath, A. (1977) *Welfare Benefits Project Working Papers 1957–77*, University of Edinburgh Department of Social Administration.

Allison, F.M. (1982) 'The non take-up of welfare benefits – the would-be claimants' obstacle course', MSc thesis, University of Bath.

Aronovitch, B. (1974) *Give It Time*, London, André Deutsch.

Atkinson, A.B. (1969) *Poverty in Britain and the Reform of Social Security*, Cambridge, Cambridge University Press.

Atkinson, A.B. (1971) 'Policies for poverty', *Lloyds Bank Review*, 100.

Atkinson, A.B. (1973) *The Tax Credit Scheme and the Redistribution of Income*, London, Institute for Fiscal Studies.

Atkinson, A.B., Maynard, A.K. Trinder, C.G. (1981) 'National Assistance and Low Incomes in 1950' *Social Policy and Administration*, 15.

Atkinson, A.B. and Sutherland, H. (1983) 'Hypothetical families in the DHSS tax/benefit model and families in the FES 1980', Research Note 1 (unpublished).

Bakke, E.W. (1935) *Insurance or Dole*, New Haven, Yale University Press.

Baldwin, S., Bradshaw, J., Cooke, K. and Glendinning, C. (1981) 'The disabled person and cash benefits', in D. Guthrie (ed.) *Disability*, London, Macmillan.

Banting, K. (1979) *Poverty, Politics and Policy*, London, Macmillan.

Barker, D. (1971) 'Negative income tax' in D. Bull (ed.) *Family Poverty*, London, Duckworth.

Bennett, T. (1981) *Making People Better Off*, Harlow Community Services Department.

Bissett, L. and Coussins, J. (1982) *Badge of Poverty*, London, Child Poverty Action Group.

Bowley, M. (1945) *Housing and the State 1919–1945*, London, Allen & Unwin.

Bradshaw, J. (1972) 'Social security under the Tories' in K. Jones (ed.) *The Yearbook of Social Policy in Britain 1971*, London, Routledge & Kegan Paul.

Bradshaw, J. (1973) *Rate Rebates in England and Wales 1971–72*, London, Child Poverty Action Group.

Bradshaw, J. (1980) *Equity and Family Incomes*, London, Study Commission on the Family.

Bradshaw, J. (1982) 'Knowledge of the tapered earnings disregard', University of York Social Policy Research Unit. Mimeo.

Bradshaw, J. (1983) 'Tax and benefit policy for the family' in Franklin A. White (ed.) *Family Matters*, Oxford, Pergamon.

Bradshaw, J. and Piachaud, D. (1980) *Child Support in the European Community*, London, Bedford Square Press.

Bradshaw, J., Taylor-Gooby, P. and Lees, R. (1976) *The Batley Welfare Benefits Project*, Papers in Community Studies No. 5, University of York.

Bradshaw, J. and Wicks, M. (1970) *Where Have All the Rate Rebates Gone?*, London, Child Poverty Action Group.

Briggs, E. and Deacon, A. (1973) 'The creation of the Unemployment Assistance Board', *Policy and Politics* 2:1.

Brockway, A.F. (1932) *Hungry England*, London, Gollancz.

Brown, C.V. (1968) 'Misconception about income tax and incentives', *Scottish Journal of Political Economy*, 15:1, pp. 1–21.

Brundage, A. (1978) *The Making of the New Poor Law 1832–39*, London, Hutchinson.

Bull, D. (1971) 'The rediscovery of family poverty' in D. Bull (ed.) *Family Poverty*, London, Duckworth.

Bull, D. (1978) 'Open government and the review of supplementary benefits' in S. Baldwin and M. Brown (eds) *The Yearbook of Social Policy in Britain 1977*, London, Routledge & Kegan Paul.

Burgess, K. (1980) *The Challenge of Labour*, London, Croom Helm.

Burgess, P. (1974) 'Rate rebates – their right or our duty', *Municipal and Public Services Journal*, 3 May 1974, p. 535.

Butler, R.A. (1971) *The Art of the Possible*, London, Hamish Hamilton.

CEC (Commission of the European Communities) (1977) *The Perception of Poverty in Europe*, Brussels, Commission of the European Communities.

Central Statistical Office (1982) *Economic Trends*, No. 339.

Christopher, A., Polanyi, G., Seldon, A. and Shenfield, B. (1970) *Policy for Poverty*, London, Institute of Economic Affairs.

Cmd. 3273 (1929) *Local Government Bill 1928: Explanatory Memorandum on the Provisions of the Bill*, London, HMSO.

Cmd. 3307 (1929) *Education in 1928: Report of the Board of Education and the Statistics for Public Education in England and Wales*, London, HMSO.

Cmd. 3920 (1931) *Report of Committee on National Expenditure* (May), London, HMSO.

Cmd. 4044 (1932) *Report of Ministry of Labour for 1931*, London, HMSO.

Cmd. 4184 (1932) *Final Report of the Royal Commission on Unemployment Insurance* (Gregory), London, HMSO.

Cmd. 4200 (1932) *Report of Committee on Local Expenditure* (Ray), London, HMSO.

Cmd. 4281 (1933) *Report of Ministry of Labour for 1932*, London, HMSO.

Cmd. 4364 (1933) *Education in 1932: The Report of the Board of Education and the Statistics for Public Education in England and Wales*, London, HMSO.

Cmd. 4861 (1935) *Report of Ministry of Labour for 1934*, London, HMSO.

Cmd. 4968 (1935) *Education in 1934: The Report of the Board of Education and the Statistics for Public Education in England and Wales*, London, HMSO.

Cmd. 5177 (1936) *Report of Unemployment Assistance Board for 1935*, London, HMSO.

Cmd. 5526 (1937) *Report of Unemployment Assistance Board for 1936*, London, HMSO.

Cmd. 5752 (1938) *Report of Unemployment Assistance Board for 1937*, London, HMSO.

Cmd. 6013 (1939) *Education in 1938: Report of the Board of Education and the Statistics for Public Education for England and Wales*, London, HMSO.

Cmd. 6021 (1939) *Report of Unemployment Assistance Board for 1938*, London, HMSO.

Cmd. 6338 (1942) *Report by the Assistance Board on the Administration of the Determination of Need Regulations*, London, HMSO.

Cmd. 6404 (1942) *Social Insurance and Allied Services* (Beveridge Report), London, HMSO.

Cmd. 6550 (1944) *Social Insurance*, London, HMSO.

Cmd. 6700 (1945) *Report of the Assistance Board for 1944*, London, HMSO.

Cmd. 6883 (1946) *Report of the Assistance Board for 1945*, London, HMSO.

Cmd. 7184 (1947) *Report of the Assistance Board for 1946*, London, HMSO.

Cmd. 7426 (1947) *Education in 1946: The Report of the Ministry of Education*, London, HMSO.

Cmd. 7502 (1948) *Report of the Assistance Board for 1947*, London, HMSO.

Cmd. 7767 (1949) *Report of the National Assistance Board for 1948*, London, HMSO.

Cmd. 8900 (1953) *Report of the National Assistance Board for 1952*, London, HMSO.

Cmd. 9333 (1954) *Report of the Committee on the Economic and Financial Problems of the Provision for Old Age* (Phillips), London, HMSO.

Cmnd. 2582 (1965) *Report of the Committee of Inquiry into the Impact of Rates on Households* (Allen), London, HMSO.

Cmnd. 2764 (1965) *The National Plan*, London, HMSO.

Cmnd. 2923 (1966) *Local Government Finance*, London, HMSO.

Cmnd. 3042 (1966) *Report of the National Assistance Board for 1965*, London, HMSO.

Cmnd. 3338 (1967) *Ministry of Social Security Annual Report 1966*, London, HMSO.

Cmnd. 4515 (1970) *New Policies for Public Spending*, London, HMSO.

Cmnd. 4728 (1971) *Fair Deal for Housing*, London, HMSO.

Cmnd. 4741 (1971) *The Future Shape of Local Government Finance*, London, HMSO.

Cmnd. 5116 (1972) *Proposals for a Tax-Credit System*, London, HMSO.

Cmnd. 5629 (1974) *Report of the Committee on One Parent Families* (Finer), London, HMSO.

Cmnd. 6453 (1976) *Report of the Committee of Inquiry into Local Government Finance* (Layfield), London, HMSO.

Cmnd. 6615 (1976) *SBC Annual Report 1975*, London, HMSO.

Cmnd. 6813 (1977) *Local Government Finance*, London, HMSO.

Cmnd. 6851 (1977) *Housing Policy: A Consultative Document*, London, HMSO.

Cmnd. 6910 (1977) *SBC Annual Report 1976*, London, HMSO.

Cmnd. 7175 (1978) *Report No. 6 of the Royal Commission on the Distribution of Income and Wealth: Lower Incomes*, London, HMSO.

Cmnd. 7392 (1978) *SBC Annual Report 1977*, London, HMSO.

Cmnd. 7725 (1979) *SBC Annual Report 1978*, London, HMSO.

Cmnd. 7773 (1979) *Reform of the Supplementary Benefits Scheme*, London, HMSO.

Cmnd. 8033 (1980) *SBC Annual Report 1979*, London, HMSO.

Cmnd. 8093 (1981) *The Taxation of Husband and Wife*, London, HMSO.

Cmnd. 8789 (1983) *The Government's Expenditure Plans 1983–4 to 1985–6*, London, HMSO.

Coates, D. (1980) *Labour in Power?*, London, Longmans.

Cole, D. and Utting, J. (1962) *The Economic Circumstances of Old People*, Codicote Press.

Collard, D. (1980) 'Social dividends and negative income tax' in Sandford, Pond and Walker (eds).

Collins, C.D.E. (1965) 'The introduction of old age pensions in Great Britain', *Historical Journal* 8.

Conservative Central Office (1974) *The Campaign Guide 1974*, London.

Corden, A. (1983) *Taking Up a Means Tested Benefit: The Process of Claiming FIS*, DHSS London, HMSO.

Cosgrave, P. (1978) *Margaret Thatcher: A Tory and Her Party*, London, Hutchinson.

County of Cleveland (1982) *The Welfare Benefits Campaign*, County of Cleveland.

Coussins, J. and Coote, A. (1981) *Families in the Firing Line*, London, Child Poverty Action Group.

CP (Conservative Party) (1967) *National Union Annual Conference Report 1966*, 84, London.

Craig, F.W.S. (1970) *British General Election Manifestos 1918–1966*, Chichester, Political Reference Publications.

Craig, F.W.S. (1975) *British General Election Manifestos 1918–1970*, Chichester, Political Reference Publications.

Croham, Lord (1981) 'The IEA as seen from the civil service' in A. Seldon (ed.) *The Emerging Consensus,* London, Institute of Economic Affairs.

Crossman, R.H.S. (1967) *Socialism and Planning*, London, Fabian Society.

Davison, R.C. (1938) *British Unemployment Policy*, London, Longmans Green.

Deacon, A. (1976) *In Search of the Scrounger: The Administration of*

*Unemployment Insurance in Britain 1920–1931*, London, Bell and Sons.

Deacon, A. (1977) 'Concession and coercion: the politics of unemployment insurance', in A. Briggs and J. Saville (eds) *Essays in Labour History 1918–1939*, London, Croom Helm.

Deacon, A. (1978) 'The scrounging controversy', *Social and Economic Administration*, 12:2.

Deacon, A. (1980) 'Unemployment and politics in Britain since 1945', in A. Sinfield and B. Showler (eds) *The Workless State*, Oxford, Martin Robertson.

Deacon, A. (1981a) 'Thank you God for the means test man', *New Society*, 25 June, 1981.

Deacon, A. (1981b) 'The duration of unemployment benefit under the National Insurance Act 1946', in L. Burghes and R. Lister (eds) *Unemployment: Who Pays the Price?*, London, Child Poverty Action Group.

Deacon, A. (1982) 'An end to the means test? Social Security and the Attlee government', *Journal of Social Policy*, 11:3.

Deacon, A. and Briggs, E. (1974) 'Local democracy and central policy: the issue of pauper votes in the 1920's', *Policy and Politics*, 2:4.

DES (Department of Education and Science) (1981) *School Meals Census*, London, HMSO.

DHSS (Department of Health and Social Security) (1978a) *Take-up Supplementary Benefits: A Report on a Survey of Claimants*, London, HMSO.

DHSS (1978b) *Social Security Statistics 1976*, London, HMSO.

DHSS (1978c) *Social Assistance: A Review of the Supplementary Benefits Scheme in Great Britain*, London, HMSO.

DHSS (1981) 'The take-up of FIS: note on the estimate derived from the Family Finances Survey', Statistics Branch (SR3), 6 July (unpublished).

DHSS (1982a) *Social Security Operational Strategy: A Framework for the Future*, London, HMSO.

DHSS (1982b) *Social Security Statistics 1982*, London, HMSO.

Disability Alliance (1975) *Poverty and Disability*, London, Disability Alliance.

DoE (Department of the Environment) (1982) *Housing and Construction Statistics: Annual Report 1982*, London, HMSO.

Donnison, D. (1982) *The Politics of Poverty*, Oxford Martin Robertson.

Dow, J.C.R. (1970) *The Management of the British Economy 1945–1970*, Cambridge, Cambridge University Press.

Elton, D.H. (1974) 'Estimating entitlement to FIS', *Statistical News*, 24 February 1974, p. 24.9.

Evason, E. (1980) *Ends that Won't Meet*, London, Child Poverty Action Group.

Field, F. (1971a) *Poor People and the Conservative Government*, London, Child Poverty Action Group.
Field, F. (1971b) *Poverty 1972 Style*, London, Child Poverty Action Group.
Field, F. (1973) *An Incomes Policy for Poor Families*, London, Child Poverty Action Group.
Field, F. (1975) 'The lost benefit', *New Society*, 27 March 1975, pp. 790–1.
Field, F. (1982) *Poverty and Politics*, London, Heinemann.
Field, F. and Piachaud, D. (1971) 'The poverty trap', *New Statesman*, 3 December 1971, pp. 772–3.
Foot, M. (1973) *Aneurin Bevan 1945–1960*, London, Davis Poynter.
Ford, P. (1939) *Incomes, Means Tests and Personal Responsibility*, London, King.
Fraser, D. (1973) *The Evolution of the British Welfare State*, London, Macmillan.
Fry, G.K. (1975) 'Economic policy-making and planning 1945–70. A survey', *Public Administration Bulletin*, 18/19.
Fry, G.K. (1982) *The Administrative Revolution in Whitehall*, London, Croom Helm.

Gamble, A. (1974) *The Conservative Nation*, London, Routledge & Kegan Paul.
Gibson, G. (1964) 'The income guarantee', *New Society*, 26 November 1964.
Gilbert, B.B. (1966) *The Evolution of National Insurance in Great Britain*, London, Michael Joseph.
Gilbert, B.B. (1970) *British Social Policy 1914–1939*, London, Batsford.
Golding, P. and Middleton, S. (1982) *Images of Welfare*, Oxford, Martin Robertson.
Goldman, P. (ed.) (1958) *The Future of the Welfare State*, London, Conservative Political Centre.
Gosden, P.J. (1973) *Self-Help*, London, Batsford.
Gosden, P.J. (1976) *Education in the Second World War*, London, Methuen.
Goss, S. and Lansley, S. (1982) *What Price Housing?* (2nd edn), London, SHAC.
Gough, I. (1979) *The Political Economy of the Welfare State*, London, Macmillan.
Graham, J. (1980) *Multi-purpose Claim Form Trial in N. Ireland*, Stormont, Department of Finance.

Graham, S. and Brasier, F. (1979) *The Multi-purpose Claim Form Trial in Brighton*, DHSS London, HMSO.

Hagenbuch, W. (1953) 'The rationale of the social services', *Lloyds Bank Review*, 29

Hammerton, H.J. (1952) *Turbulent Priest*, London, Cuttworth Press.

Hancock, K. (1962) 'The reduction of unemployment as a problem of public policy 1920–29', *Economic History Review*, 15.

Harris, J.F. (1977) *William Beveridge: A Biography*, Oxford, Clarendon.

Harris, J.F. (1981) 'Some aspects of social policy in Britain during the Second World War', in W.J. Mommsen (ed.) *The Emergence of the Welfare State in Britain and Germany*, London, Croom Helm.

Harris, J.F. (n.d.) 'Workers and social welfare: G.D.H. Cole's survey of consumer opinion' (unpublished).

Harris, R. and Seldon, A. (1979) *Over-ruled on Welfare*, London, Institute of Economic Affairs.

Hay, J.R. (1975) *The Origin of the Liberal Welfare Reforms 1906–14*, London, Macmillan.

HC 123, *First Report of the Social Services Committee 1983*, London, HMSO.

HC 306–i, *Second Report of the Social Services Committee 1982*, London, HMSO.

HC 331–i, ii, iii, iv, v, vii, viii, ix, x, Treasury and Civil Service Committee Sub-Committee: *The Structure of Personal Income Taxation and Income Support: Minutes of Evidence 1982*, London, HMSO.

HC 341–i, *Report of the Select Committee on Tax-Credit 1973*, London, HMSO.

HC 535, *Eleventh Report from the Expenditure Committee General Sub-Committee, The Civil Service. 1976–7*, Vol. II, London, HMSO.

Heclo, H. (1974) *Modern Social Politics in Britain and Sweden*, New Haven, Yale University Press.

Hemming, R. and Hills, J. (1983) 'The reform of housing benefits', *Fiscal Studies*, March 1983.

Hill, M. (1969) 'The exercise of discretion in the National Assistance Board', *Public Administration*, 47.

Hill, M. (1972) 'Selectivity for the poor', in Townsend and Bosanquet (eds).

Hoffman, J.D. (1964) *The Conservative Party in Opposition*, London, MacGibbon and Kee.

Houghton, D. (1968) *Paying for the Social Services*, London, Institute of Economic Affairs.

Howe, G. (1961) 'Reform of the social services' in L. Beaton *et al. Principles in Practice*, London, Conservative Political Centre.

IMTA (Institute of Municipal Treasurers and Accountants) (1972) *Housing Statistics 1970–71*, Part 2.

Jewkes, J. *et al.* (1964) *Monopoly or Choice in Health Services?*, London, Institute of Economic Affairs.
Judge, K. (1980) 'Beveridge: past, present and future' in Sandford, Pond and Walker (eds).
Judge, K., Smith, J. and Taylor-Gooby, P. (1983) *New Directions in Social Policy? Public Opinion and the Privatisation of Welfare*, Canterbury, University of Kent Personal Social Services Research Unit.

Keegan, W. and Pennant-Rea, R. (1979) *Who Runs the Economy?*, London, Temple Smith.
Kerr, Scott A. (1982a) 'Deciding about supplementary pensions: a provisional model', *Journal of Social Policy*, II:4, pp. 505–17.
Kerr, Scott A. (1982b) 'Differential take-up of supplementary pensions', (unpublished).
Klein, R. (1975) 'Priorities in the age of inflation', in R. Klein (ed.) *Inflation and Priorities*, London, Centre for Studies in Social Policy.
Knight, I.B. (1976) *Two Parent Families Receiving FIS in 1972: A Follow Up Survey a Year Later*, DHSS Statistics and Research Report No. 13.
Kopsch, H. (1970) 'The approach of the Conservative Party to social policy during World War Two', PhD thesis, University of London.

Labour Party (1934) *Up with the Houses! Down with the Slums!*, London.
Lansley, S. (1982) *Alternatives to Housing Benefit*, London, Child Poverty Action Group.
Lapping, B. (1970) *The Labour Government 1964–70*, Harmondsworth, Penguin.
Lees, D. (1961) *Health through Choice*, London, Institute of Economic Affairs.
Lees, D. (1967) 'Poor families and fiscal reform', *Lloyds Bank Review*, 86
Lister, R. (1974) *Take Up of Means Tested Benefits*, London, Child Poverty Action Group.
Lister, R. (1975) *Social Security: The Case for Reform,* London, Child Poverty Action Group.
Lister, R. (1976) *Take-up: Same Old Story*, London, Child Poverty Action Group.
Lynes, T. (1963) *Pension Rights and Wrongs*, Tract 348, London, Fabian Society.
Lynes, T. (1969) *Welfare Rights*, Tract 395, London, Fabian Society.

Lynes, T. (1982) 'Benefit print-out', *New Society*, 9 December 1982.
Lynes, T. (n.d.) 'Benefit levels in public assistance', (unpublished).

McDonagh, T. (n.d.) *Final Report of the Haringay Rent Allowance Study*, London, DoE.
MacGregor, S. (1981) *The Politics of Poverty*, London, Longman.
McKibbon, R. (1975) 'The economic policy of the second Labour government', *Past and Present*, 68.
MacLeod, I. and Powell, E. (1952) *The Social Services: Needs and Means* (1st edn), London, Conservative Political Centre.
MacLeod, I. and Powell, E. (1954) *The Social Services: Needs and Means* (2nd edn), London, Conservative Political Centre.
MacNicol, J. (1978) 'Family allowances and less eligibility' in P. Thane (ed.) *The Origins of British Social Policy*, London, Croom Helm.
Marplan (1973) *Second Report on an Evaluative Study of the Fair Rent Laws Campaign*, Vol. 1, London, Marplan.
Marquand, D. (1977) *Ramsay MacDonald*, London, Jonathan Cape.
Marsh, D. (1950) *National Insurance and Assistance in Great Britain*, London, Pitmans.
Marshall, H.W. (1943) 'Public assistance' in W.A. Robson (ed.) *Social Security*, London, Fabian Society.
Martin, J.P. and Williams, S. (1959) 'The effects of imposing prescription charges', *The Lancet*, 3 January 1959.
Marwick, A. (1982) *British Society since 1945*, Harmondsworth, Penguin.
Mass Observation (1943) 'Social Security and Parliament' *Political Quarterly*, 14.
Maynard, A. (1980) 'Medical care and the price mechanism', in K. Judge (ed.) *Pricing the Social Services*, London, Macmillan.
Meacher Committee (1983) HC 386 Treasury and Civil Service Committee. *The Structure of Personal Income Taxation and Income Support: Report*, London, HMSO.
Meacher, M. (1972a) *Rent Rebates: A Study of the Effectiveness of Means Tests*, London, Child Poverty Action Group.
Meacher, M. (1972b) 'Wealth: Labour's Achilles Heel', in Townsend and Bosanquet (eds).
Meacher, M. (1972c) 'Means tests' (unpublished, quoted in Lister, 1974, p. 6).
Meade, J.E. (1978) *The Structure and Reform of Direct Taxation*, London, Allen & Unwin and Institute for Fiscal Studies.
Means, R. and Hill, M. (1982) 'The administration of rent rebates', *Journal of Social Welfare Law*, July 1982, pp. 193–208.
Miliband, R. (1969) *The State in Capitalist Society*, London, Weidenfeld & Nicolson.
Millar, J. (1982) 'DHSS cohort study of the unemployed. The take-up of means tested benefits while in work' (unpublished).

Miller, F. (1974) 'National insurance or unemployment assistance: The British Cabinet and relief policy, 1932–33', *Journal of Contemporary History*, 9.

Miller, F. (1979) 'The British unemployment assistance crisis of 1935', *Journal of Contemporary History*, 14.

Millet, J.D. (1940) *The Unemployment Assistance Board*, London, Allen & Unwin.

Ministry of Housing and Local Government (1967) *Rent Rebate Schemes*, Circular 46/47, London, HMSO.

Minkin, L. (1981) 'Radicalism and Reconstruction: The British Experience', *Proceedings of the 4th International Colloquim of the Intercenter for European Studies, Montreal*.

MPNI (Ministry of Pensions and National Insurance) (1966) *Financial and Other Circumstances of Retirement Pensioners*, London, HMSO.

ML (Ministry of Labour) (1932) *Minutes of Evidence to Royal Commission on Unemployment Insurance*, London, HMSO.

Moffit, R.L. (1981) 'The negative income tax: would it discourage work', *Monthly Labour Review*, April 1981, pp. 23–7.

Moore, P. (1980) 'Counter-culture in a social security office', *New Society*, 10 July 1980.

Morris, C.N. and Warren, N.A. (1980) 'The reduced rate band', *Fiscal Studies*, July 1980, pp. 34–43.

NCC (National Consumer Council) (1976) *Means Tested Benefits: A Discussion Paper*, London, National Consumer Council.

Nevitt, D. and Bradshaw, J. (1973) 'Proposals for a tax credit system', in *Evidence to the Select Committee on Tax-Credit*, HC 341–iii, London, HMSO, pp. 149–71.

Nixon, J.M. (1979) *Fatherless Families on FIS*, DHSS Research Report No. 4, London, HMSO.

ONG (One Nation Group) (1950) *One Nation*, London, Conservative Political Centre.

ONG (1959) *The Responsible Society*, London, Conservative Political Centre.

Owen, D. (1968) 'Selectivity and the health service', in *Social Services for All? Part Four*, London, Fabian Society.

Page, D. and Weinberger, B. (1975) *The Take-up of Rent Rebates and Allowances in Birmingham*, Birmingham, Centre for Urban and Regional Studies.

Parker, H. (1982) *The Moral Hazard of Social Benefits*, London, Institute of Economic Affairs.

Parker, R.A. (1967) *The Rents of Council Houses*, London, Bell and Sons.

Peacock, A. and Wiseman, J. (1964) *Education for Democrats*, London, Institute of Economic Affairs.

Peel, L. (1978) *The Multipurpose Claim Form Trial in Salop*, DHSS London, HMSO.

PEP (Political and Economic Planning) (1937a) *The British Social Services*, London, Political and Economic Planning.

PEP (1937b) *Report on the British Health Service*, London, Political and Economic Planning.

Piachaud, D. (1971) 'Poverty and taxation', *Political Quarterly*, 42, pp. 31–44.

Piachaud, D. (1979) *The Cost of a Child*, London, Child Poverty Action Group.

Piachaud, D. (1982) *The Distribution and Redistribution of Incomes*, London, Bedford Square Press.

Pinker, R. (1971) *Social Theory and Social Policy*, London, Heinemann Educational Books.

Powell, E. (1952) 'Social sevices: theory and practice', *The Listener*, 17 April 1952.

Poynter, J.R. (1969) *Society and Pauperism*, London, Routledge & Kegan Paul.

PRO (Public Records Office) (1931) Report of General Inspector's Conference, 18.12.31, MH 57/14.

PRO (1932a) CAB 24/227, CP8 (32) 11.1.32.

PRO (1932b) CAB 24/228, CP 84 (32) 26.2.32.

PRO (1932c) CAB 24/230, CP 186 (32) 16.6.32.

PRO (1932d) CAB 27/50, Proceedings of 20.11.32.

PRO (1933) CAB 27/501, U.I. (32)10, 17.1.33.

PRO (1935a) Minute from Divisional Officer, Liverpool to Regional Office, 9.11.34, A51 M/154.

PRO (1935b) CAB 27/576, UAR4, 26.2.35.

PRO (1935c) CAB 27/576, UAR5, 19.3.35.

PRO (1937) AST 12/9, Memo 194, 5.3.37.

PRO (1938) Letter Fieldhouse (UAB) to Divisional Offices, AST 7/154,21.10.38.

PRO (1940a) CAB 67/4, WP(G) (40) 5, 12.1.40.

PRO (1940b) CAB 67/8, WP(G) (40) 259, 10.10.40.

PRO (1940c) CAB 71/1, LP(40) 36, 16.10.40.

PRO (1941a) AST 12/13, Memo 362, 9.9.41.

PRO (1941b) AST 12/13, Memo 365, 15.10.41.

PRO (1942) AST 12/13, Memo 382, 20.11.42.

PRO (1943a) CAB 71/14, LP(43) 231, 15.10.43.

PRO (1943b) Report of Official Committee on Beveridge Report (n.d.) PIN 8/115.

PRO (1944) AST 12/52, Memo 404, 6.10.44.

Purnell, C. (1973) *The Prospects for Rent Allowances*, Wandsworth People's Rights.

Ravetz, A. (1974) *Model Estate*, London, Croom Helm.

Reddin, M. (1968) 'Local authority means tested services', in *Social Services for All?*, London, Fabian Society.

Rhodes James, R. (1972) *Ambitions and Realities: British Politics 1964–1970*, London, Weidenfeld & Nicolson.

Richardson, A. (1978) *The Take-up of Supplementary Benefits*, London DHSS.

Ritchie, J. and Matthews, A, (1982) *The Take-up of Rent Allowances: An In Depth Study*, London, Social and Community Planning Research.

Rose, R. (1974) *The Problem of Party Government*, London, Macmillan.

Rowntree, S. and Lavers, G.S. (1951) *Poverty and the Welfare State*, London, Longmans.

Sandford, C. (1980) 'The tax credit system', in Sandford, Pond and Walker (eds).

Sandford, C., Pond, C. and Walker, R. (eds) (1980) *Taxation and Social Policy*, London, Heinemann.

SBC (Supplementary Benefits Commission) (1979) *Response of the Supplementary Benefits Commission to Social Assistance: A Review of the Supplementary Benefits Scheme in Great Britain*, London, HMSO.

Schiffres, S. (1975) 'Tenants struggles in the 1930's', MA thesis, University of Warwick.

Schlackman Research Organisation (1978) *Report on Research on Public Attitudes towards the SB System*, London, Schlackman Research Organisation.

SDP (Social Democratic Party) (1982) *A New Deal for Britain: Attacking Poverty*, London, Social Democratic Party.

Seldon, Anthony (1981) *Churchill's Indian Summer: The Conservative Government 1951–55*, London, Hodder and Stoughton.

Seldon, Arthur (1960) *Pensions for Prosperity*, London, Institute of Economic Affairs.

Simon, B. (1965) *Education and the Labour Movement*, London, Lawrence and Wishart.

Simon, B. (1974) *The Politics of Education Reform*, London, Lawrence and Wishart.

Simpson, T. (1978) *Advocacy and Social Change: A Study of Welfare Rights Workers*, London, National Institute for Social Work.

Sinfield, A. (1978) 'Analyses in the social division of welfare', *Journal of Social policy*, 7:2.

Sinfield, A. (1982) 'Discriminating Against the Long Term Unemployed in the Social Security System' *Unemployment Unit Bulletin*, 4.

Skidelsky, R. (1970) *Politicians and the Slump* Harmondsworth, Penguin.

SSAC (Social Security Advisory Committee) (1982) *First Report of the Social Security Advisory Committee 1981*, London, HMSO.

SSSC (Social Services Select Committee) (1981) *Third Report Session 1980/81*, Vol. II, London, HMSO.

SSSC (1982) *Second Report: 1982 White Paper: Public Expenditure on the Social Services*, London, HMSO.

Stanton, D. (1977) 'The take-up debate on the UK family income supplement', *Policy and Politics* 5.

Stevenson, J. and Cook, C. (1977) *The Slump: Society and Politics during the Depression*, London, Jonathan Cape.

Stewart, M. (1977) *The Jekyll and Hyde Years: Politics and Economic Policy since 1964*, London, Dent.

Syson, L. and Young, M. (1975) 'The Camden survey', in M. Young (ed.) *Poverty Report 1975*, London, Temple Smith.


Taylor-Gooby, P. (1974) 'Means testing and social policy', MPhil thesis, University of York.

Taylor-Gooby, P. (1976) 'Rent benefits and tenants' attitudes. The Batley rent rebate and allowance study', *Journal of Social Policy*, 5:1.

Titmuss, R.M. (1950) *Problems of Social Policy*, London, HMSO and Longmans.

Titmuss, R.M. (1952) 'Crisis in the social services', *The Listener*, 14 February 1952.

Titmuss, R.M. (1958a) 'The social division of welfare', in R.M. Titmuss *Essays on 'The Welfare State'*, London, Allen & Unwin.

Titmuss, R.M. (1958b) 'Pension systems and population change', in R.M. Titmuss, *Essays on 'The Welfare State'*, London, Allen & Unwin.

Titmuss, R.M. (1968) *Commitment to Welfare*, London, Allen & Unwin.

Titmuss, R.M. (1971) 'Welfare rights law and discretion', *Political Quarterly*, 42.

Townsend, P. (1952) 'Poverty: Ten Years After Beveridge' *Planning*, 344.

Townsend, P. (1954) 'Measuring poverty', *British Journal of Sociology*, 5:2.

Townsend, P. (1962) 'The meaning of poverty', *British Journal of Sociology*, 13:3.

Townsend, P. (1967) *Poverty, Socialism and Labour in Power*, Tract 371, London, Fabian Society.

Townsend, P. (1968) 'Does selectivity mean a nation divided', in *Social Services for All? Part One*, London, Fabian Society.

Townsend, P. (1973) *The Social Minority*, London, Allen Lane.

Townsend, P. (1979) *Poverty in the United Kingdom*, London, Allen Lane.

Townsend, P. and Bosanquet, N. (eds) (1972) *Labour and Inequality*, London, Fabian Society.

Vernon, T. (1980) *Gobbledegook*, London, National Consumer Council.

Vince, P. (n.d.) *To Each According . . .*, London, Liberal Information Department.

Walker, C. (1982) 'Social assistance: The reality of open government', *Policy and Politics*, 10:1.

Walker, C. (forthcoming) 'The reform of the supplementary benefits scheme: For whose benefit?', in C. Jones and J. Stevenson (eds) *The Yearbook of Social Policy in Britain 1982*, London, Routledge & Kegan Paul.

Walker, R.L. (n.D.) *Canvassing Rent Allowances in Bristol and Westminster*, London, DoE.

Warburton, E. and Butler, C. (1935) *Disallowed: The Tragedy of the Means Test*, London, Wishart.

Watkin, B. (1978) *The National Health Service: The First Phase*, London, Allen & Unwin.

Weale, A. (1982) 'The tax benefit trap for female headed single parent households', Working Paper 123, University of York Social Policy Research Unit.

Webb, A. (1975) 'The abolition of national assistance' in P. Hall *et al. Change, Choice and Conflict in Social Policy*, London, Heinemann.

Williams, P. (1979) *Hugh Gaitskell*, London, Jonathan Cape.

Wilson, G. (1939) *Rent Rebates*, London, Fabian Society.

Wilson, P. (1981) *Free School Meals*, Occasional Paper 23, OPCS Social Survey Division.

Winch, D. (1969) *Economics and Policy*, London, Hodder and Stoughton.

# Index

Abel-Smith, B.   61, 63–4,
        70–1, 74, 151
Addison, P.   34–6, 46
Allen Committee   89
Allison, F.   134
Assheton, R.   42
Assistance Board   36, 38, 41,
        114
    increase in scale rates 1944
        40–1
    popularity of   39
    use of discretion   38–9
Atkinson, A.   103, 107, 174n,
        177, 188–9

Banting, K.   61, 63
Barber, A.   78–9, 96, 187
basic income guarantee scheme
        193
better-off problem   85, 88
Betterton, N.   20
Bevan, A.   47, 53
Beveridge Report   1
    Conservatives and   42–3
    official response   43–4
    popular response   42
Beveridge strategies, back to
        176–81
Beveridge, W.   98, 152, 203
Bevin, E.   39–40
Bow Group   76–7
Bowers, Ministry of Labour
        22
Boyd Carpenter, J.   69
Braddock, Bessie   48
Bradshaw, J.   90, see also
        Nevitt, D.

Brittan, L.   169, 199
Buchanan, G.   37
Burgess, P.   85
Butler, R.A.   45, 52, 55

Calderdale Metropolitan District
        Council   145
Callaghan, J.   69
Carr, R.   52
Central Office of Information
        141
Central Statistical Office   97n
Chalker, L.   143
Chamberlain, N.   22
charges
    chiropody   4n
    convalescent homes   4n
    day nurseries   4n
    dental treatment   2, 53, 93
    education   93
    exemption from, advertising
        94
    health   49n, 93
    meals   4n
    opthalmic treatment   2,
        4n, 93
    residential accommodation
        4n
    see also poverty trap, take-up
child benefits   82, 151, 163–4,
        190
    cost of   172–3
    premium for pre-school
        children   173
    taxation of   172
    see also poverty trap
child interim benefit   180

Child Poverty Action Group
68, 71, 78, 80, 94,
143, 148, 157, 177—8
national welfare benefits
handbook   143
child tax allowances   68, 82,
151, 163—4
claw back   78, 80
*see also* income tax
Churchill, Sir W.   34
Coates, D.   202
Cockfield, Lord   187
Collard, D.   186
Conservative government 1970—
74   chapter 5 *passim*
Conservative Party
Advisory Committee on
Policy   76
Central Office   82
Conference, 1966   77
manifesto, 1970   78
computer advice-giving   144
Inverclyde District Council
144
*see also* DHSS operational
strategy
Corden, A.   138, 139—40,
141—2
Cost of Living Index, official
49n, 50n
London and Cambridge
Economic Service   49n
Cripps, Sir S.   52
Croham, Lord   72
Crosland, A.   87
Crossman, R.   67, 69, 70—1,
89, 202

dental charges   *see* charges
Department of the Environment
86, 88, 128—9
Department of Health and Social
Security   123, 126, 141
operational strategy   144—5
Determination of Needs Act,
1941   39
deviancy theory   134—5
Disability Alliance   181

disability benefits   180—1,
*see also* Beveridge
strategies, back to
Donnison, D.   112—13, 117,
200—1

Eady, W.   17
earnings-related supplement
125, 178
Education Act, 1944   30
Education Act, 1980   127
educational maintenance
allowances   4n, *see
also* charges
Ennals, D.   112
European Community   3
Evason, E.   138
exceptional circumstances
additions   110, 121n,
*see also* supplementary
benefits
exceptional needs payments
110—15, 118, *see also*
supplementary benefits

fair rents   86—7
family allowances   35, 44,
68, 79, 82, 96n, *see
also* child benefit,
child tax allowances
family budgeting patterns   136
family expenditure survey   87,
97n, 123, 126, 148—9,
158, 175n
family finances survey   126—7
family income supplement   2,
69, 79—83, 93—6, 200
abolition of   168
prescribed limits   127
and school meals   169
*see also* poverty trap
*see also* take-up
family wage   172—4
Field, F.   71, 81, 85—6, 130,
164
Finer Committee   82, 179
Fraser, D.   31

Gaitskell, H. 53
Gamble, A. 55, 77
general election, 1945 34
general election, 1974 95
genuinely-seeking-work test 8
Gibson, G. 105
Goldman, P. 76
graduated pension scheme 102, 152
Gray, M. 16
Greenwood, A. 37
Griffiths, J. 45
guaranteed maintenance allowance 179

Hannington, W. 20
Harlow District Council 141, 145
Harris, J. 48
Harris, R. 59, 201, 204n
Hagenbuch, W. 55
Healey, D. 67
Heath, E. 52, 76—8, 95
Herbison, M. 80
higher education awards 4n
Hill, M. 108
Houghton, D. 68, 74n
household means test
    abolition of 39—40, 47—8
    administration of 16—17, 27—8
    numbers affected 17—18, 21, 26, 29n
    popular opposition to 19
housing benefit 2, 87—8, 117, 125
    and supplementary benefits 170
    tapers 175n
    *see also* poverty trap, rate rebates, rent allowances, rent rebates, take-up
housing, fair deal for, white paper on 84
Housing Finance Act, 1972 86—7
housing policy review 88, 171, 197

housing rebates *see* housing benefit, rate rebates, rent allowances, rent rebates
Housing Rents and Subsidies Act, 1975 87
housing revenue account 86
Howe, G. 76—7
Howell, R. 150

incentives to work 150, 157—62, 178, 186
income guarantee scheme 66, 105—6
income tax 150—1, 153—5
    additional personal allowance 180
    break-even points 152
    computerization of 165
    local 91
    lower rate bands 165
    married man's tax allowance 162—3
    opposition to 67, 199
    personal allowances 151, 162, 181, *see also* poverty trap
    reliefs 164, 171
    standard rate, reductions in 164—5
    threshold 151—2, 162—5, 181—2
    *see also* child tax allowances
Inland Revenue 164—5, 185, 195n
Institute of Economic Affairs 56—61, 64—66, 76, 176, 184—5

Jenkin, P. 172
Jenkins, R. 69
Jenkinson, Rev. C. 14
Joseph, Sir K. 77—8, 187
Judge, K. 204

Keegan, W. 9
Kerr, S. 139—40
Klein, R. 134

Knight, I.   136
Kopsch, H.   42

Labour government
    1964–70   66–73
    manifesto promises, 1959
        74n
    manifesto promises, 1964
        66
Labour Party, manifesto, 1970
    78
Layfield Committee   91–3,
        170, 197
Layfield, F.   91
Lees, D.   59, 185
Liberal Party, measures, 1906–14
    6
    tax credit proposals   190–1
local government finance, green
        paper on   89, 90, 92
Low Pay Unit   164
Lynes, T.   110

McDonagh, T.   133
MacDonald, R.   15
MacGregor, S.   201
MacLeod, I.   52–3, 55, 62,
        78–9, 101
MacNicol, J.   35
Macmillan, H.   53
marginal tax rates   153, 157–9,
        164, *see also* poverty
        trap
Markham, V.   38
Marplan   86
Marsh, D.   47
Mathews, A.   *see* Ritchie, J.
May Committee   10, 16, 26
Meacher Committee   83, 156–7,
        163, 166–7, 171, 177,
        182–3, 186, 193–4, 199
Meacher, Michael   94
Meacher, Molly   90, 133, 137
means tests in the 1930s   chapter
        2 *passim*
means-tested benefits
    administrative costs   196–7
    definition of   2

and social control   197–8
and social divisions   200
Millar, J.   136, 138
Miliband, R.   202
minimum wage, and poverty
        trap   172–4
Ministry of Housing and Local
        Government   83
Minkin, L.   35
municipal hospitals, charges for
        8–9

national assistance
    numbers in receipt of   1, 4n,
        46, 49n, 98, 100
    one-parent families in receipt
        of   102n
    scale rates   100
    take-up of   102–3
National Assistance Act, 1948
        45–6
National Assistance Board   1,
        3n, 31, 98, 102–9
    use of discretion   104
    Labour Party and   104
National Consumer Council
        129–30, 141, 146–8
National Economy Act, 1931   15
national health service   30
national insurance   6
    benefits   100, 152, 167, 178
    contributions   152–5,
        166–7, 178, 181
        abolition of   167
    earnings-related supplement
        115
    fund   101, 152, 166, 178
    *see also* poverty trap
National Insurance and
        Supplementary Benefits
        Act, 1973   121
National Plan   66, 70
national superannuation   105
National Superannuation and
        Social Insurance Bill,
        1969   78
National Unemployed Workers
        Movement   20

negative income tax   59–60,
        64, 72, 160–1, 184–6
Nevitt, D.   189
non-contributory pension   1, 7,
        28n, 49n
Nixon, J.   138


One Nation Group   54, 56, 58
one-parent benefit   179–80
one-parent families   107, 109,
        180, *see also* Beveridge
        strategies, back to
opthalmic charges   *see* charges
Owen, D.   68


Page, D.   129
Parker, H.   193
passport benefits   127, 146–7,
        155, 161
Peacock, A.   59
Peake, O.   100
Pennant-Rea, R.   96
Phillips Committee
    on Beveridge Report   43–4
    on pensions   102, 120n
Phillips, T.   42
Piachaud, D.   81
Pike, M.   77
Pinker, R.   200
poor law   5, 6
    Boards of Guardians   8
    liability of relatives   28n
    Speenhamland system   81
    status of pauper   6
poverty, family   68
    rediscovery of   60–1
poverty plateau   150
poverty trap   chapter 8 *passim*
    and child benefits   153,
        171–3
    computer simulation models
        155–6
    and exemptions from charges
        153
    and family income supplement
        153–5, 158–9, 161,
        167–8, 174n

and housing benefit   153–5,
        159, 169–71, 174n
    and incentives   159–62
    and income tax   151–2,
        172n, 174n
    and minimum wage   172–4
    and national insurance
        contributions   153,
        167, 174n
    numbers in   158, 175n
    origins of   151–2
    and school meals   153,
        158, 168–9, 174n
    and single parents   159–61
    solutions to   162–74
    and supplementary benefits
        159
    and take-up   155–6
Powell, E.   52–3, 55, 62, 102
prescription charges   2, 4n,
        54, 93
Prevention and Relief of Distress
        scheme   36
Prices and Incomes Board   70
private affluence, growth of   60
private medical insurance in the
        1930s   9
public assistance committees   8
public expenditure, white paper
        on, 1970   78
public expenditure on social
        services   198
Purnell, C.   130


rate rebates   1, 4n, 75, 89–93,
        128, 170–1
    cost of   91
    numbers in receipt of   91
    scheme, 1966   89
    taper   90–1, 97n
    *see also* take-up
rate support grant   91
rates
    alternatives to   90
    impact of   89–92, 97n
Ray Committee   12
Reddin, M.   83

rent allowances 75, 83—9,
        95, 128, *see also* housing
        benefit, rent rebate,
        take-up
rent rebates 69, 74n, 75, 83—9,
        90—3, 95, 128
    advertising campaign 86—7
    in Birmingham 14
    in Leeds 13—14
    in the 1930s 11—14
    local authority schemes 83
    needs allowance 84
    statutory particulars 97n
    tapers 85
    *see also* housing benefit,
        take-up
reference group theory 135
Reid, G. 40
reverse income tax *see* negative
        income tax
Rhys Williams, B. 193
Richardson, A. 138
Ritchie, J. 136, 140—1
Rowntree, S. 47, 50n, 60
Royal Commission on Local
        Government 89

Schlackman Research
        Organisation 135
school meals 1, 2, 4n, 33, 93
    free 94
    in Europe 169
    and family income supplement
        168—9
    *see also* poverty trap, take-up
school uniform grants 4n
scroungerphobia 108, 200
Second World War
    coalition government 34
    evacuation scheme 32
    hostels for victims of bombing
        33
    public attitudes during 30—6
secondary education
    free places 9—11
    special places 10—11
selectivity chapter 4 *passim*
Seldon, A. 56, 76, 201, 204n

Shore, P. 88
Simon, Sir J. 37
Sinfield, A. 200
Smith, A. 57
Snowdon, P. 10
social assistance chapter 6
        *passim*
Social Assistance, Report
        113—15
Social Democratic Party, scheme
        for social security and
        personal taxation
        191—3
social dividend 182—4
social division of welfare 62,
        200
social insurance, white paper
        on 44
Social Security Act, 1966 120n
Social Security Act, 1980 112
    effects of 116—18
Social Security Advisory
        Committee 118,
        121n, 195n
Social Security (No. 2) Act,
        1980 115
*Social Trends* 156
Stanley, O. 23
stigma
    Assistance Board 105
    National Assistance Board
        104—5
    *see also* take-up, factors
        affecting
supplementary benefits 85,
        92—3, 97n, 178, 195n
    administrative costs 204n
    appeal tribunals 116, 121n
    fraud and abuse 108
    industrial action 99, 117
    numbers in receipt of 1,
        98—9, 107, 116
    one-parent families 107,
        116
    Penguin guide to 143
    reductions in staffing 111
    scale rates 117—19
    single payments 118

staff attitudes 109
unemployed 107—8, 116,
119, 120n, 121n
*see also* take-up
Supplementary Benefits
Commission 88,
105—6, 108, 114—15,
130, 136, 141
abolition of 115, 121n
handbook 143
use of discretion 109—12
supplementary benefits review
88, 112—15, 125, 135
supplementary pensions
administration of 38—9
during Second World War
36—9, 41
numbers applying 37
Sutherland, H. *see* Atkinson, A.
Syson, L. 131

take-up chapter 7 *passim*
amount unclaimed 130—1
of exemption from charges
94, 130
factors affecting 131—40
complexity 132, 136
ignorance 132—3
incentive 136
stigma 132—6, 147
of family income supplement
80—1, 125—7, 130—1,
148n
of free school meals 127—8,
130—1
methods for improving
140—8
advertising 141
advice 142—4
combined assessment
145—6
harmonization 147
information 140—2
local experiments 146
passporting 146
simplification 145—7
simplification of forms
146

models of 139—40
of national assistance 102—4
of rate rebates 90—2,
128—31, 148n
of rent allowances 128—31,
148n
of rent rebates 87, 128—31,
148n
of supplementary benefits
106, 123—5, 130—1
by sick and disabled 148n
take-up campaigns
Cleveland 144
Strathclyde 143
tapered earnings disregard 159,
161, 175n
taxation of husband and wife,
green paper on 163,
173, 180
tax-credits scheme 82, 95,
186—90
and means-tested benefits
189
child credits 188, 190
costs of 188—90
green paper on 187—8
select committee on 187
study group 189
Taylor-Gooby, P. 129, 133,
134, 135, 137
Titmuss, R. 32, 33, 34, 36,
61, 63, 64, 65, 72,
110, 200
Townsend, P. 30, 61, 63,
65, 70, 71, 72, 74,
155, 197, 202
Tory Reform Committee 44
Trades Union Congress 207
transitional payments 14—22
administration of 16
numbers in receipt of 16
local authorities and 20—1

unemployed 107, 109, 116,
127
unemployment assistance
numbers in receipt of 25—6,
49n

restrictions on short-term
   claims   50n
Unemployment Assistance Board
   22—6
   accusations of laxity   25
   creation of   22—3
   opposition to   23
   standstill   23—4
   use of discretion   24—5
unemployment insurance benefit
   7, 15, 181, 183, 195n
   anomalies in regulations
   18
unemployment review officers
   142
unemployment trap   150, 183
universal benefits in the 1940s
   chapter 3 *passim*

wage stop   81, 96n
Walker, C.   113, 117
Walker, R.   133, 138
Webb, A.   98
Weinberger, B.   *see* Page, D.
welfare milk   93
welfare rights campaigns
   109—10
welfare rights courses   142
welfare rights handbooks   142
welfare rights officers   142—3
Wicks, M.   90
Wilson, P.   133
Wiseman, J.   59

Young, M.   *see* Syson, L.